MW01485496

Finding God in the Unexpected

A Recovering Atheist's Journey to Faith Through Science and Logic

S. M. CARLSON

Finding God in the Unexpected: An Atheist's Journey to Faith.

First Edition

ISBN: 978-1-7336755-5-0 (paperback)
ISBN: 978-1-7336755-6-7 (hardcover)

This book is lovingly dedicated to my parents, who nurtured my spirit with morals and integrity. Your unwavering faith and love have shaped my journey and brought light into the darkest paths. To my stepfather, your willingness to step into the male role model position after my father's passing has been a beacon of hope and strength. Your guidance and love have been unyielding, and I am forever grateful.

I extend my heartfelt gratitude to Elders Landon Clayton, Colton Rochlitz, Gabriel Moon, and Justin Perry of the Church of Jesus Christ of Latter-day Saints. Your insight and support have been instrumental in deepening my understanding of Christianity, LDS, the Bible, and the Book of Mormon. Your wisdom and kindness illuminated my path, helping me to navigate the complexities of faith and spirituality. Without your invaluable help, this book would never have seen completion.

May this work stand as a testament to the combined efforts, love, and guidance of each one of you. Your influence reaches beyond these pages, touching the hearts and minds of all who walk a similar path.

– Steven

By the same author

Second Edition: Updated to include Trump re-election, Biden, 2022 War in Ukraine, Green New Deal, & more!

Delve into *America Hijacked,* a critical and expansive exploration spanning the past eighty years of US political history. This compelling narrative embarks on a journey from the conflicts of Vietnam and Korea, traversing through the tumultuous wars in the Middle East, unearthing the layers of deception and criminal corruption interwoven within the legacies of the Bush and Clinton families.

America Hijacked illuminates the insidious destruction of the American Dream as it outlines the substantial gains and profiteering of political dynasties amid national despair and global conflict. The text is composed in a clear, concise style, making it an accessible and engaging read for all, shedding light on the obscured truths of political maneuvers and the profound impact on the American narrative.

Make a foray into this significant exploration and unravel the intricate web that has ensnared the American political landscape. *America Hijacked* is available in paperback, hardcover, e-book, and Audible audio formats. It offers a seamless reading experience for all who seek to understand the depths of political corruption and its enduring implications for the United States.

www.SMCarlson.com

By the same author

Special Note:

In this book, I endeavor to present an unbiased and balanced examination of the essential elements of various faiths. While I acknowledge my inherent biases, I have strived to minimize them to the utmost extent.

No religious organization officially endorses the contents of this book, and the views and opinions expressed within these pages are exclusively my own.

That being said, as a member of the Church of Jesus Christ of Latter-day Saints, the testimony shared in this book is a heartfelt reflection of my spiritual journey from atheist to believer.

Request a Bible:

If you would like a FREE copy of the Holy Bible (King James Version), the Book of Mormon, or both, the Church of Jesus Christ of Latter-day Saints is happy to personally deliver one to your doorstep, absolutely free and with no obligations.

https://www.ChurchofJesusChrist.org/comeuntochrist/requests/free-holy-bible

Table of Contents

Prologue 12

Introduction 20

Part 1 – A Science-Based Approach 22

Science and Religion: Dichotomy or Dialogue? 23

Chapter 1: In the Beginning 25

The Creation – Genesis 1:1–3 25

The First Day – Genesis 1:4–5 29

The Second Day – Genesis 1:6–8 31

The Third Day – Genesis 1:9–13 35

The Fourth Day – Genesis 1:14–19 38

The Fifth Day – Genesis 1:20–23 41

The Sixth Day (Creation of Man) – Genesis 1:24–31 48

The Sixth Day (The Giving of Food) – Genesis 1:29–31 54

Chapter 2: Adam and Eve vs. Evolution. 60

Genesis 2:21–25: The Creation of Eve.................................... 60

The Dilemma of Literalism vs. Science 62

Embryonic Development and the Intricacies of Sex Determination 64

Diverse Christian Perspectives.. 66

Chapter 3: The Great Flood and Noah's Ark............................. 72

The Pervasiveness of Deluge Myths....................................... 73

Did a Global Flood Actually Occur? 75

Two of Every Species—Is that Possible?................................ 78

Historical Large-Scale Floods: Nature's Testament 79

Native American Flood Myths and Parallels with Noah's Ark 81

The Latter-Day Saints' View of the Great Flood 83

Chapter 4: The Age of the Planet 85

Deciphering Earth's Age through Radiometric Dating 86

Tracing Earth's Age Through Plate Tectonics 88

Deciphering Earth's Timeline through Fossils 89

Dinosaurs and Doctrine: Wrestling with Biblical Interpretation 91

Christian Views on Earth's Age.. 93

Science and Faith Juxtaposed 95

Chapter 5: Bringing it All Together 98

Part 2 – Venturing Deeper into Religious Understanding 103

Chapter 5: Defining the Divine: What are Miracles? 104

Miracles Across the Ages.. 105

Philosophical Perspectives: Beyond the Observable............................ 107

Miracles in World Religions... 109

The LDS Perspective on Miracles.. 112

Miracles and Science: Can They Coexist? 114

Stories of Modern-Day Miracles... 118

Chapter 6: Why Does God Allow Evil to Happen?............................. 124

The Age-Old Question of Theodicy 126

Biblical Insights on Suffering and Evil... 128

Free Will: Humanity's Blessing and Curse... 130

Religious and Philosophical Responses to Theodicy............................ 132

Modern Theological Views and Critiques... 135

Personal Faith Amid Suffering 137

Conclusion: The Journey of Faith Amid Shadows 139

Chapter 7: Prayer, Song, and Connecting with God 142

The Essence and Evolution of Prayer 144

Fasting: Physical Sacrifice for Spiritual Gain 147

Sacred Rituals and Ordinance 151

Nature and the Divine.. 155

Sacred Music and Worship 157

Scripture Study: Conversing with God Through Holy Texts............... 164

Personal Revelation: God's Guidance in Daily Life............................. 167

Conclusion: How Prayer Changed Me 170

Chapter 8: Understanding the Sacred Texts... 172

The Origin and Importance of Scriptures 174

The Bible – A Beacon of Christianity 176

The Book of Mormon – Another Testament of Jesus Christ 177

Other LDS Scriptures – Doctrine and Covenants, Pearl of Great Price 185

A Respectful Glimpse into Other Faiths' Sacred Texts 189

Scriptures and Modern-Day Revelation 194

Conclusion: In Praise of the Divine Word and Our Shared Spiritual

Journey 197

Chapter 9: Atonement and Salvation: Concepts of Redemption in

Christianity 200

Historical Understanding of Atonement in Christian Theology 201

Salvation: A Broad Overview 208

Nuances of Salvation in Various Christian Denominations 211

Salvation in LDS Theology 219

The Central Role of Jesus Christ in Salvation Across Denominations .. 223

Conclusion: The Unifying Theme of Redemption in Christianity 227

Chapter 10: Temples and Sacred Spaces: The Role of Physical Places 230

The LDS Temple: A House of God 232

Churches in Christian Denominations: More Than Just Buildings 235

Sacred Spaces in Various Religious Traditions 240

The Broader Concept of "Sacred Space" 252

Challenges and Controversies Surrounding Sacred Spaces 258

Conclusion: Why Temples Resonate Across Cultures 265

Chapter 11: Life Beyond Death: Heaven, Hell, and the Afterlife 268

Historical Overview of Mainstream Christian Beliefs 270

LDS Perspective on the Afterlife 273

The Soul: Its Origin, Journey, and Destiny 285

Resurrection and Eternal Life 289

Challenging Questions and Contemporary Views 292

Conclusion 296

Chapter 12: Faith Under Fire 298

Doubt: The Unexpected Stepping Stone of Faith 300

The "Woke" Era and Its Impact on Religious Views 303

Spotlight on Current Events: Religion in the Crosshairs 306

American Society in Flux: A Closer Look at Structural Changes 310

Religion's Role in Social Cohesion 315

Challenges and Opportunities: Faith in the Modern Age 319

Faith's Resilience – Charting the Course Amidst Societal Flux 321

Final Thoughts and Conclusion 324

Prologue

The following text recounts a fifteen-minute oral testimony I delivered at a local meetinghouse of the Church of Jesus Christ of Latter-day Saints during Sunday services. To paint the picture, this marked my inaugural visit to an LDS church, a day filled with anticipation and nervousness. In a room full of strangers, yet united by faith, I stood at the pulpit to introduce myself to the ward. It was an experience that served not only as my introduction but also as the beginning of a profound spiritual journey that would take me from skepticism to belief, from the periphery of faith to the heart of a community. In the following pages, I will share the words I spoke that day and the reflections that led me there.

> If I may have just a few minutes of your time so I may introduce myself to everyone here and explain the journey I have embarked upon. I am new to your faith and ask for your patience and understanding if I misspeak or misinterpret any aspect of your doctrine. Just know I come to you in humility, bearing no intent to offend. I am here today in a sincere quest for truth.
>
> My name is Steven Carlson. I own a tech company in Virginia. I am also a certified paramedic, and I fly a helicopter around the country with my crew, filming it for my YouTube channels. I have a unique set of interests, to say the least.
>
> I grew up in the Tampa Bay Area, about an hour south of here in Pinellas County, and was raised as the only child of two amazing and loving parents. We were a middle-class family. My mother worked as a bank teller, and my father was a deputy sheriff. They both taught me the differences between right and wrong.
>
> One thing that was never taught or really even discussed was religion. Looking back, I know my father grew up with a solid

Christian background and went to private school as a youngster, and he took his religious studies very seriously. That was until he served multiple tours in Vietnam. Seeing the atrocities of what man can do to another man, you can forgive him for losing his faith.

I presume that is why we never had any religion in our family. In elementary school, I joined the Cub Scouts and, eventually, the Boy Scouts, sponsored by a local Presbyterian Church. We used their building for our meetings, and I even volunteered at the church with my dad to help with the food bank, but we never attended services. Looking back, I am not really sure why; it is just how I grew up.

Growing up without religious guidance, I adopted an atheistic view. To me, the entire notion of God was a fanciful myth, a superstition unworthy of serious consideration. My life was already pretty good, and I never felt the need for faith. It wasn't until my father passed away from pancreatic cancer during my senior year in high school that I experienced my first real existential crisis. But even then I buried the pain and kept pushing forward.

Shortly after graduating high school, I, like many in my generation, was shocked by the tragedy of 9/11, and I decided it was time to fight for my country. Just like my father, I enlisted in the world's greatest Navy as a corpsman (Navy medic).

The Navy took this Florida boy and shipped him off to Recruit Training Command, Naval Training Center, Great Lakes, IL, and for the first time in my life, I saw snow—a beautiful spectacle that swiftly lost its charm when I was tasked with shoveling it.

I stayed in the Navy for just under a year and was medically discharged for a cardiac condition. Thankfully, it was something I was able to recover from, but that is another much longer story, and I promised to take only fifteen minutes of your time.

When I returned to civilian life, my mother had since remarried and was living in North Carolina, so I moved in with her and my stepfather and went to school. I became a certified EMT and began working on an ambulance crew as I attended paramedic school. But I wasn't happy with my life. I missed my friends back home, so I packed everything I owned into my car and drove back to Florida.

I spent the next couple of years buying, fixing, and selling foreclosures. After the real estate crash in 2008, I moved to Virginia to start a computer business with a longtime friend.

The Shenandoah Valley, located in the northwestern corner of Virginia, is picturesque in its beauty, but it is also a very economically disadvantaged area. At the time the county couldn't afford full-time EMTs and paramedics and relied upon volunteers to staff the ambulances and fire trucks.

As a volunteer EMT/paramedic for over nine years, I bore witness to humanity's best and worst. Shootings, stabbings, drug overdoses, drunken fights, you name it, and I saw it. But I also had some of the most amazing experiences where I know I positively impacted someone's life.

I could tell you hundreds of stories about people and how, in hindsight, there may have been some divine intervention. But if you would indulge me for one quick moment. I want to share a little story about a patient I had, and I promise it will all tie together with my story.

It was a cold fall night, probably about 2:00 a.m. Like most normal, sane people, I was sound asleep in my bed when the pager went off for an unknown medical emergency. I listened as the dispatcher gave the information on the radio: "Rescue 3, person down, corner of Broad and Main Street, law enforcement en route, Rescue 3, this is your second call." This last part was critical; it told me that the county ambulance crew was already on another call, so no one was available to respond to this emergency.

I remember begrudgingly wiping the sleep out of my eyes and yawning as I said to myself, "Aghh, it's probably another drunk passed out. I'll just let law enforcement handle it and go back to sleep." But something told me to get up; I don't know why, but I did.

So, I pulled on a pair of jeans, put on my shoes and socks, ran down the stairs, and jumped into my car. I sped down the road with my red strobe light flashing on my dashboard. On the way, I stopped at the station, grabbed the department's Ford Expedition, and responded to the call with lights flashing and siren blaring.

I pulled up on the scene to see a man in his mid-thirties slumped over. Still figuring it was a drunk person, I walked up cautiously, as law enforcement was also busy on other calls, so I was alone on the side of the road in a completely unknown situation.

Despite my assumptions, this was not a case of simple overindulgence. No, it was a man on the brink of death. With just one glimpse of him, I knew he was very sick. I placed the cardiac monitor on him, and his pulse rate was 170; he was sweating, short of breath, and in severe pain. This man was in supraventricular tachycardia, a life-threatening cardiac medical emergency where the heart beats at an unsustainably high rate until eventually it gives out, stops beating altogether, and the patient suffers a massive cardiac arrest.

An ambulance was responding to help me, but they were coming from the other end of the county and wouldn't be there for another twenty minutes. This man did not have twenty minutes; he would be dead in the next five minutes if I didn't act fast.

Together with another off-duty medic who showed up to help, we performed the necessary medical intervention of cardioversion. Once he was stable, we transported him to the hospital. Typically, once we drop a patient off at the hospital, that is the end of the story for us, as we rarely ever see the same person again. But not this time.

Several years later, I had some contractors working at my house, redoing my basement and laying concrete. One of the men approached me and said, "You probably don't remember me, but you saved my life a few years ago." He went on to describe the call, and I instantly remembered him. He broke down in tears, saying how scared he was that his little girl would lose her daddy that night. This was a big, strong man, and he was bawling his eyes out.

What compelled me to get out of bed? Was it God? Was it a message from the Holy Ghost? I don't know; all I know is if I had ignored that voice inside of me, that man would have died.

I tell you this not to seek praise for myself or for you to applaud me. No, I say this to share a message of not jumping to judge people. When the pager first went off, I passed judgment without knowing the facts. It was 2:00 a.m., and some random person was passed out in the middle of town on the side of the street. I had been to similar calls at least a hundred times, and it was always a drunk passed out, covered in urine and feces. And I can tell you, it is difficult to motivate yourself to get out of bed and volunteer your time to help someone in such a situation.

I told you this whole long story as an introduction to why I am here today, but I promise I am almost finished taking up your time, as I am sure you have much better things to tend to than to have an outsider, one who grew up as an atheist nonetheless, blab on and on about his past.

I was watching a YouTuber that I highly respect, Dave Sparks. You may know him better as HeavyD from the Diesel Brothers Show on Discovery Channel. He and his lifelong best friend, Dave Kiley, run a very popular YouTube channel. I was studying their videos to see why they are so successful and trying to learn to improve my videos as well. Somewhere in the back of my mind, I knew they were both members of the LDS Church, but it was one of those facts that goes in one ear, bounces around for a second, and leaves without any real thought about it.

The video I watched was more of a behind-the-scenes interview where HeavyD showed a bit more of his personality and dove into his faith. At first, I was like, "Whoa, what? Those people in Utah with silly underwear? How in the heck could he believe in that nonsense?" He kept his conversation light and didn't go super in depth, but I could see his passion and how he earnestly believed what he was saying.

I paused for a minute. Was I projecting and judging again without knowing any facts? At that time, all I knew about

Mormons was what I saw on *South Park* or in comedy sketches. I didn't have any actual knowledge or facts to base my opinion on. Heck, I didn't even know the proper name of your Church. I, like many outsiders, mistakenly thought you were called Mormons.

Like any logical individual, I started my exploration with a healthy dose of skepticism, searching Google for articles that were critical of your faith.

While I won't bore you with all the disorganized, schizophrenic, and mindless dribble I read, none of the articles could come up with a single, valid, concrete argument against your faith.

Point after point, I found myself, a self-proclaimed atheist, agreeing with what I read about the LDS Church. I needed to take a moment and pause. Maybe you aren't crazy, and perhaps you have some knowledge that I lack.

I closed the tabs in my browser and started a new Google search, this time for your official church website. I cannot tell you why or how or who or what or anything tangible, but as I read the text on the screen, I began to cry. Now, I am a person who is almost always fully in control of my feelings, and I have never had a rush of uncontrollable emotions as I felt at that time.

This led me to contact your church and invite the missionaries into my home. Two amazing, kind, and caring young men showed up to share their beliefs with me. I have started a journey to study your doctrine as I pray and ponder.

I found this quote from your scripture, 2 Nephi 31:20, that resonated with my journey: "Wherefore, ye must press forward with a steadfastness in Christ, having a perfect brightness of hope, and a love of God and of all men. Wherefore, if ye shall press forward, feasting upon the word of Christ, and endure to the end, behold, thus saith the Father: Ye shall have eternal life."

So, here I stand before you, admitting there is so much I still don't know. I am not sure what I believe, but I am humbled by the journey and grateful to be welcomed among you. Thank you for your time.

– Steven

Introduction

My journey from fervent atheism to becoming a member of the church known officially as the Church of Jesus Christ of Latter-day Saints—not the Mormons, as many outsiders call it[1]—was a winding and surprising trek. My path was marked by reflection, exploration, and a willingness to question my deeply held beliefs and assumptions. My transition was not merely a change of religious labels but a transformation that reached deep into the core of my identity and my worldview.

In my early years, atheism provided a framework through which I engaged the world. My reliance on atheism worked for most of my adult life. I viewed various situations, experiences that believers would refer to as miracles, as simply a random happenstance born out of simple statistical probabilities. But as time passed, questions began to emerge that science and reason alone could not answer. The surprising nature of my eventual conversion lay in the profound shift in perspective that unfolded as the idea of faith, which I had once dismissed, took on a new significance.

This book chronicles my exploration of these questions and the path that led me to Christ. It is a journey filled with challenges and surprises, doubts and revelations. I delve into the apparent conflicts between science and religion, the nuances of belief and unbelief, and the discovery of a far more complex and beautiful spiritual landscape than I had ever imagined.

My intention is not to present a one-size-fits-all answer but to share my personal experience and reflections, inviting readers to consider their perspectives and beliefs. I explore the harmonious relationship between scientific understanding and religious faith, providing insights into how they can complement each other rather than conflict with one another.

---

[1] Russell M. Nelson, "The Correct Name of the Church," Church of Jesus Christ of Latter-day Saints, Oct. 2018. https://www.churchofjesuschrist.org/study/general-conference/2018/10/the-correct-name-of-the-church.

Ultimately, my story is one of growth, transformation, and the realization that pursuing truth does not have to be confined to a single domain. Science and faith, reason and revelation, and skepticism and belief are not mutually exclusive realms but different facets of the rich tapestry of human existence. They are threads that can weave together to form a more complete and satisfying understanding of life and our place in the universe.

Join me as we embark on this fascinating exploration, a journey that traverses the boundaries of science and spirituality, challenging assumptions and opening new horizons. Whether you are a believer, an atheist, or somewhere in between, I hope this book will provide food for thought, inspiration, and a fresh perspective on some of humanity's most profound and enduring questions.

Part 1 – A Science-Based Approach

Science and Religion: Dichotomy or Dialogue?

In the annals of human intellectual pursuits, the relationship between science and religion is among the most intricate and fiercely debated. These two domains, each holding its distinct methodology and worldview, have been protagonists in the grand narrative of our collective consciousness, often perceived as standing at opposing corners of the intellectual arena. Science, with its rigorous methodologies, seeks to unravel the mysteries of the universe through evidence and reason. It celebrates the tangible, the quantifiable, and the replicable. On the other hand, religion delves into the intangible realms of the spirit, providing a moral compass, answering profound existential questions, and often offering solace in times of uncertainty.

Beneath the surface-level dichotomies lies a more nuanced tapestry of interaction. As we journey through the pages of history and contemporary thought, we're beckoned to explore not just the stark contrasts but also the harmonies, the intersections where empirical inquiry meets spiritual introspection. Is the perceived rift between science and religion real, or is it merely a construct of a limited perspective? As we embark on this expedition, I hope readers will see that the relationship between science and religion is not just a battleground of divergence but also a fertile ground for collaboration and mutual enrichment.

Navigating this intricate interplay between science and religion, one can't help but grapple with personal biases, preconceived notions, and experiences that shape our perspectives. Many people approach this topic with numerous questions and uncertainties. How can one mesh the rigidity of scientific proofs with the fluidity of faith?

Taking a step back to survey the landscape of various religions often leads to a perspective where many religious practices and beliefs appear arbitrary or even nonsensical. Growing up with skepticism, I viewed these rituals and doctrines with a critical eye, unable to reconcile them with logic or empirical evidence. These customs, sacred to many, seemed shrouded in mystery, defying reason and existing outside the boundaries of rational understanding. It was a world that seemed closed off to me, wrapped in symbolism and tradition, yet this complexity and depth eventually beckoned me to explore further.

While the subjects addressed in these chapters could each warrant entire books or even a series of volumes to explore their complexities and nuances fully, it is essential to provide a foundational understanding of some of the issues I had when approaching faith. In the following chapters, we will review some of the critical aspects that I've found intriguing and challenging. This overview will offer insights into scientific and religious perspectives as a starting point for those who wish to delve deeper into these multifaceted topics.

Belief in Adam and Eve, the Great Flood and Noah's Ark, the age of the planet, and other fundamental religious narratives initially posed a significant intellectual challenge for me. These concepts did not readily reconcile with a scientific approach, at least not in the way I had come to understand the world through the lens of empirical evidence and rational thought. Or perhaps more accurately, they did not neatly fit within the confines of how I believed they needed to be explained.

These narratives, steeped in tradition and faith, seemed to defy the laws of nature and the principles of science that I held as immutable. The juxtaposition of faith-based understanding with scientific inquiry created a tension that I found both perplexing and unsettling. I felt like I was caught between two worlds, one governed by logic and proof and the other by belief and spiritual understanding. Little did I realize how inaccurate such a description of the relationship between faith and science would turn out to be.

Chapter 1: In the Beginning . . .

The Book of Genesis is a monumental cornerstone in the foundation of Judeo-Christian thought, anchoring countless generations in their understanding of the world's beginnings. Imbued with poetic grandeur and profound philosophical insights, this ancient text has beguiled theologians, philosophers, and everyday seekers for millennia. Across its verses it weaves a tapestry of creation, beginning with the vast expanses of the universe and culminating in the intricacies of human existence. As we embark on this exploratory journey, there's no better point of departure than the evocative verses of Genesis 1. Through its words, we'll endeavor to unravel the layers of meaning and context, providing a deep dive into a narrative that has shaped civilizations, sparked debates, and nurtured faiths for centuries.

The Creation – Genesis 1:1–3

Genesis 1:1 sets the stage succinctly as we journey through the narrative. A structured progression emerges: light, sky, land, flora, celestial bodies, fauna, and finally, humankind.

> In the beginning, God created the heaven and the earth.
>
> And the earth was without form, and void; and darkness was upon the face of the deep. And the Spirit of God moved upon the face of the waters.
>
> And God said, Let there be light: and there was light.

These verses relay not just the act of creation but also the ethos behind it—an intent, a consciousness, and a masterful orchestrator. The depiction of Earth as "without form, and void" and enshrouded in darkness conjures images of potential waiting for a guiding hand, suggesting a chaotic primordial state. The subsequent infusion of light signifies the literal dispelling of darkness and symbolizes wisdom, understanding, and God's unifying presence.

Such imagery, while succinct, distills an immensely complex narrative into a foundational story, laying the groundwork for all of human history by narrating the creation of everything. A revered biblical scholar, Walter Brueggemann, observes that this Genesis narrative showcases a God who transforms chaos and orders the formless void into a structured cosmos.[2]

While the author's words resonate with poetic beauty, they also compress a monumental narrative into a deceptively concise prologue. Given the gravity of chronicling something as vast as the creation of the universe, the four short sentences may seem lacking in the details and depth one might anticipate. This brevity suggests that the primary objective of Genesis might not have been to point to every facet of creation. Instead, it seems to underscore the overarching message: before God's intervention, there was nothing. His divine will brought everything into existence, and the particulars of the process or its duration are not the author's central concern.

A description more attuned to empirical data would have appealed to me and gone a long way toward alleviating my initial skepticism. However, it's vital to recall that these scriptures were crafted by humans, framed in the language and worldview of their time, striving to make vast cosmic truths comprehensible to their contemporaries. In the late Middle Ages, concepts of other planets in distinct solar systems orbiting their stars, akin to our relationship with the sun, came into human contemplation and the realization of the myriad of solar systems and galaxies populating our observable universe.[3]

Building on this notion of contextual understanding, the Church of Jesus Christ of Latter-day Saints introduces a profound belief that offers clarity and guidance in our advanced age. As humanity's knowledge and comprehension have evolved, so has God's communication with us. The LDS faith posits that modern prophets continue to receive divine revelation

---

[2] Walter Brueggemann, *Genesis: A Commentary* (Westminster: John Knox Press, 1982).
[3] Thomas Kuhn, the *Copernican Revolution: Planetary Astronomy in the Development of Western Thought* (Boston: Harvard University Press, 1957).

tailored to our advanced cognition and more intricate worldviews.[4] This ongoing guidance ensures that God's teachings remain relevant and understandable, adapting to the ever-expanding horizons of human understanding while emphasizing the constancy of God's presence throughout time.[5] As we delve deeper into LDS doctrines, we find their scriptures complement and augment the biblical narrative, providing layers of insight that harmonize ancient teachings with contemporary revelation.

The Pearl of Great Price, published in 1851, offers a distinctive perspective on creation in Moses 2:1–3, echoing and providing variations from the familiar Genesis account.[6]

> And it came to pass that the Lord spake unto Moses, saying: Behold, I reveal unto you concerning this heaven, and this earth; write the words which I speak. I am the Beginning and the End, the Almighty God; by mine Only Begotten I created these things; yea, in the beginning I created the heaven, and the earth upon which thou standest.

> And the earth was without form, and void; and I caused darkness to come up upon the face of the deep; and my Spirit moved upon the face of the water; for I am God.

> And I, God, said: Let there be light; and there was light.

The LDS perspective understands creation as more of an organization rather than an ex nihilo (creation from nothing) event. This organizing

[4] Joseph Smith, Doctrine and Covenants (Salt Lake City: Church of Jesus Christ of Latter-day Saints, 2013), 1:38.

[5] Encyclopedia of Mormonism: The History, Scripture, Doctrine, and Procedure of the Church of Jesus Christ of Latter-day Saints, ed. Daniel H. Ludlow (London: Macmillan, 1992).

[6] Franklin D. Richards, The Pearl of Great Price: Being a Choice Selection from the Revelations, Translations, and Narrations of Joseph Smith (Salt Lake City: Church of Jesus Christ of Latter-day Saints, 2013).

perspective emphasizes a divine plan where God shapes and structures the universe from pre-existing matter.[7][8][9]

> Now, the word create came from the [Hebrew] word baurau, which does not mean to create out of nothing; it means to organize; the same as a man would organize materials and build a ship. Hence, we infer that God had materials to organize the world out of chaos—chaotic matter, which is element.. . . Element had an existence from the time [God] had. The pure principles of element are principles which can never be destroyed; they may be organized and re-organized, but not destroyed.[10]

> In these respects we differ from the Christian world, for our religion will not clash with or contradict the facts of science in any particular . . . whether the Lord found the earth empty and void, whether he made it out of nothing or out of the rude elements; or whether he made it in six days or in as many millions of years, is and will remain a matter of speculation in the minds of men unless he give revelation on the subject.[11]

> God created the earth as an organized sphere; but He certainly did not create, in the sense of bringing into primal existence, the ultimate elements of the materials of which the earth consists, for 'the elements are eternal' (Doctrine & Covenants 93:33).[12]

Stepping away from the theological arena, science offers its narrative of the universe's inception. The Big Bang Theory, a cornerstone of modern astrophysics, describes the universe's birth as a rapid expansion from a

[7] James E. Talmage, *Articles of Faith* (Salt Lake City: Deseret Book Co., 1984).
[8] Smith, Doctrine and Covenants, 93:29.
[9] Richards, Pearl of Great Price, Abraham 3:24.
[10] Joseph Smith, "The King Follett Sermon," *Ensign*, April 1971.
[11] Brigham Young, *Journal of Discourses* vol. 14 (Salt Lake City: Deseret Book Co., 1873), 116.
[12] John A. Widtsoe, "Is God a Scientist?", *Improvement Era* 55, no. 1 (1952): 22.

singular point, a colossal surge of energy that, intriguingly, could align with the divine command, "Let there be light."[13] Dr. Francis Collins, a renowned geneticist and devout Christian, further bridges the gap between science and faith, suggesting: "The Big Bang cries out for a divine explanation.... Only a supernatural force that is outside of space and time could have done that."[14]

Intriguingly, LDS scriptures and conceptual interpretations were put forth nearly a century before the Big Bang Theory was first proposed by Georges Lemaître in 1927.[15]

The First Day – Genesis 1:4–5

> And God saw the light, that it was good: and God divided the light from the darkness.
>
> And God called the light Day, and the darkness he called Night. And the evening and the morning were the first day.

These verses have inspired a myriad of interpretations and discussions regarding the nature of "day" and "night" and the duration of creation days.

Renowned biblical scholar Walter Brueggemann observes that these verses reflect a God who brings order from chaos: "In Genesis, God's utterance and the subsequent creation of light presents a God who is able to create order in the midst of primeval chaos."[16]

---

[13] Stephen Hawking, *A Brief History of Time* (New York: Bantam Books, 1988). This book provides a detailed yet accessible explanation of the Big Bang Theory, among other cosmological concepts.

[14] Francis S. Collins, *The Language of God: A Scientist Presents Evidence for Belief* (Glencoe, IL: Free Press, 1996).

[15] Georges Lemaître, "The Beginning of the World from the Point of View of Quantum Theory," *Nature* 127 (1931): 706.

[16] Walter Brueggemann, *Genesis: Interpretation: A Bible Commentary for Teaching and Preaching* (Westminster: John Knox Press, 1982).

"How long is a day in Genesis?" is a topic of vigorous debate among theologians and believers. Proponents of a young Earth, including Dr. Jason Lisle, emphasize a literal interpretation: "The text defines a day in the context of an earth's rotation—a single evening and morning, suggesting a 24–hour period."[17] The problem with this interpretation is that countless scientific discoveries regarding the time frame of Earth's existence refute this as a possibility.

Conversely, old Earth creationists like Dr. Hugh Ross offer a different viewpoint: "The Hebrew term 'yôm,' translated 'day,' can be understood as a long epoch, accommodating the vast timescales of cosmic history."[18]

The LDS interpretation provides further nuance. Although they recognize the scriptural use of "day" in creation, their teachings suggest a less fixed, more organizational approach. The Doctrine and Covenants, another LDS scripture, reads: "And it was in the night time when the Lord spoke these words unto me: 'Behold, I will prepare you against the time of day."[19] This seems to hint at a flexible understanding of "day."

Furthermore, Abraham 4:5 in the Pearl of Great Price echoes Genesis but offers some differentiation: "And the Gods called the light Day, and the darkness they called Night. And it came to pass that from the evening until morning they called night; and from the morning until the evening they called day; and this was the first, or the beginning, of that which they called day and night."[20] This passage mirrors the Genesis account but includes the idea of collective "Gods" in the act of creation, a topic we will cover later in this book.

---

[17] Jason Lisle, *Understanding Genesis: How to Analyze, Interpret, and Defend Scripture* (Green Forest, AR: Master Books, 2015).
[18] Hugh Ross, *A Matter of Days: Resolving a Creation Controversy* (Covina, CA: RTB Press, 2015).
[19] Smith, Doctrine and Covenants, 106:4.
[20] Richards, Pearl of Great Price, Abraham 4:5.

From a scientific perspective, the concept of "dividing" light from darkness is fascinating. Dr. Alan Guth, a cosmologist, describes the initial moments after the Big Bang: "As the universe cooled, photons became decoupled from matter, resulting in the first 'light' or cosmic microwave background radiation we can detect today."[21] This "birth of light" can be seen as a metaphorical parallel to the biblical "let there be light."

Planetary formation also supports the concept of division between day and night. Astrophysicist Sara Seager notes: "The rotation of planets on their axes is what gives us our familiar cycle of day and night. This regular pattern is a result of the initial conditions during planetary formation and subsequent cosmic events."[22]

Therefore, the division between day and night in Genesis might be seen not merely as an arbitrary separation but as a representation of fundamental cosmic principles—the periodicity and order that govern our universe.

In conclusion, Genesis 1:4–5, despite its brevity, encapsulates profound truths about the nature of our universe, further nuanced by LDS scriptures. While grounded in empirical observation, scientific perspectives unexpectedly echo these ancient texts. Together, they paint a picture of a universe governed by divine intent and natural laws.

The Second Day – Genesis 1:6–8

The verses of Genesis 1:6–8 introduce the concept of the "firmament," an entity that divides "waters from the waters." The term has been a subject of theological and scientific debate for centuries.

> And God said, Let there be a firmament in the midst of the waters, and let it divide the waters from the waters.

[21] Alan Guth, *The Inflationary Universe: The Quest for a New Theory of Cosmic Origins* (New York: Basic Books: 1997).

[22] Sara Seager, *Exoplanet Atmospheres: Physical Processes* (Princeton: Princeton University Press, 2010).

And God made the firmament, and divided the waters which were under the firmament from the waters which were above the firmament: and it was so.

And God called the firmament Heaven. And the evening and the morning were the second day.

In biblical Hebrew, the word for "firmament" is *raqia*, which can be interpreted as "expanse," "vault," or "dome."[23] The ancient Israelites visualized the universe as a snow globe: a flat Earth with a solid dome on top that separated the terrestrial waters below from the celestial waters above.

Before exploring further, addressing a widespread misconception regarding ancient civilizations' cosmological beliefs is pertinent. The idea of a flat Earth is commonly attributed to ancient civilizations, including the Israelites. However, the Bible does not categorically state that Earth is flat. This misconception likely arose from specific scriptural phrases and the overarching cosmological understanding of the time. For instance, the Bible mentions "the ends of the Earth" in various passages, such as Psalm 104:5: "Who laid the foundations of the earth, that it should not be removed for ever." Likewise, Isaiah 11:12 reads, "And he shall set up an ensign for the nations, and shall assemble the outcasts of Israel, and gather together the dispersed of Judah from the four corners of the earth."

Such expressions, although metaphorical, might have been interpreted literally by some and contributed to the flat Earth perspective.

However, it's crucial to understand these texts in their historical and cultural context. Many ancient civilizations had geocentric models of the universe, given their limited observational capabilities and understanding of celestial mechanics. This isn't to say that the Bible endorses a flat Earth but that it speaks in terms familiar to its original audience. Earth's sphere-

---

[23] John H. Walton, *The Lost World of Genesis One: Ancient Cosmology and the Origins Debate* Westmont, IL: InterVarsity Press: 2009).

like shape was recognized by ancient Greek philosophers such as Pythagoras[24] and Aristotle[25] centuries before the Common Era. The idea of a flat Earth seems more a result of human interpretation and the period's prevailing worldview rather than an explicit biblical doctrine.

Within LDS teachings, the firmament is often contextualized as the atmosphere or the sky. This interpretation aligns with the broader Christian viewpoint, where the firmament represents another step in God's creation, further bringing order from chaos. From the LDS perspective, the firmament's establishment is not just a physical act; it also signifies God's intent to distinguish between realms and set boundaries for his creations. The Book of Abraham in the Pearl of Great Price aligns with the Genesis account: "And the Gods also said: Let there be an expanse in the midst of the waters, and it shall divide the waters from the waters."[26]

Beyond theological interpretations, the concept of the firmament finds intriguing parallels in scientific understanding. Contemporary science identifies the "firmament" with our atmosphere, a multi-layered blanket of gasses enveloping our planet. Astrophysicist Jane Luu notes, "The Earth's atmosphere plays a crucial role in sustaining life, regulating temperatures, and protecting us from harmful cosmic radiation." [27]

This protective layer absorbs most of the sun's harmful ultraviolet (UV) radiation, shielding life on Earth from its damaging effects.

Furthering the scientific perspective, the "waters above" the firmament can be understood as referring to the water vapor and clouds present in the atmosphere. In his seminal work on planetary atmospheres, Dr. James Kasting suggests, "Clouds and water vapor play pivotal roles in moderating Earth's climate, reflecting sunlight, and contributing to the greenhouse

---

[24] W. K. C. Guthrie, *A History of Greek Philosophy: The Presocratic tradition from Parmenides to Democritus* Vol. 2 (Cambridge: Cambridge University Press, 1962).
[25] Aristotle, *De Caelo (On the Heavens)*, 350 BCE.
[26] Richards, Pearl of Great Price, Abraham 4:6.
[27] Jane Luu and David Jewitt, *Kuiper Belt Objects* (Boston: MIT Press, 2014).

effect."[28] This interpretation contrasts with the ancient worldview but coherently integrates the biblical narrative with contemporary knowledge.

On the other hand, the "waters below" the firmament can be seen as the vast oceans, lakes, rivers, and underground reservoirs on Earth. Dr. Sylvia Earle, a leading marine biologist, states, "Oceans cover more than 70% of our planet, acting as the planet's thermostat and influencing climatic patterns globally."[29] Thus, as described in Genesis, the separation of waters can be viewed as God's way of establishing distinct domains, each with its unique purpose and function.

The interplay between the "waters above" and the "waters below" is also crucial in understanding Earth's hydrological cycle. In his exploration of Earth's climate system, Dr. Raymond Pierrehumbert elaborates: "The constant exchange between atmospheric moisture and terrestrial waters, through evaporation and precipitation processes, maintains Earth's water balance and supports life."[30]

Reflecting on the LDS viewpoint, the division between these waters represents more than just a physical separation. It underscores the divine intention behind creation, emphasizing the universe's need for order, balance, and purpose. The Doctrine and Covenants, another foundational LDS text, alludes to God's hand in organizing the elements: "Yea, verily I say unto you, in the beginning, the Lord created the heaven, and the earth upon which thou standest."[31]

Genesis 1:6–8 provides a profound insight into the ancient understanding of the world's structure, layered with profound theological implications. The LDS teachings add further dimensions, aligning ancient scriptures with

---

[28] James Kasting, *How to Find a Habitable Planet* (Princeton: Princeton University Press, 2010).
[29] Sylvia Earle, *The World Is Blue: How Our Fate and the Oceans Are One* (Washington, DC: National Geographic Books, 2009).
[30] Raymond Pierrehumbert, *Principles of Planetary Climate* (Cambridge: Cambridge University Press, 2010).
[31] Smith, Doctrine and Covenants, 77:1.

modern revelations. Simultaneously, scientific perspectives offer a complementary lens, bridging ancient beliefs with modern discoveries. Through these multi-faceted lenses, the biblical narrative of the firmament unfolds as a tapestry of divine intention, cosmic organization, and the intricate balance that sustains life on Earth.

The Third Day – Genesis 1:9–13

> And God said, Let the waters under the heaven be gathered together unto one place, and let the dry land appear: and it was so.
>
> And God called the dry land Earth; and the gathering together of the waters called He Seas: and God saw that it was good.
>
> And God said, Let the earth bring forth grass, the herb yielding seed, and the fruit tree yielding fruit after his kind, whose seed is in itself, upon the earth: and it was so.
>
> And the earth brought forth grass, and herb yielding seed after his kind, and the tree yielding fruit, whose seed was in itself, after his kind: and God saw that it was good.
>
> And the evening and the morning were the third day.

The third day of creation holds a special significance in Christian theology. On this day, God creates both land and vegetation, thereby bringing stability and life to what had previously been a formless void.

The act of gathering waters to reveal the dry land can be perceived as establishing order, much like previous acts of separating light from darkness and waters from waters. For many Christians the act of naming by God ("Earth" for dry land and "seas" for the gathered waters) emphasizes the importance of language in ordering the cosmos. Naming becomes an act of dominion and, in many theological interpretations, reflects God's sovereignty over creation.[32]

The introduction of vegetation marks the beginning of life on Earth, with each plant having its seed, indicating a system of reproduction and continuity. It underscores the importance of sustenance, growth, and regeneration in God's divine plan.[33]

Within the LDS perspective, as previously stated, the act of creation is often viewed through the lens of organization rather than ex-nihilo creation.[34] Regarding the third day's events, this implies that the materials and elements were present. Still, God organized them into landmasses and introduced a life system through vegetation.

LDS scripture, particularly the Pearl of Great Price, offers additional insight into creation. Moses 2:9–13 essentially mirrors the Genesis account but with a notable addition: the phrase "I, God, commanded" or "I, God, said." This phrasing emphasizes God's direct role and intent in the process, underscoring his personal involvement in each creative act.[35]

The emergence of vegetation and its reproduction system aligns with the LDS view of eternal progression. Just as plants have seeds that enable continuity and growth, so does every soul have the potential for eternal growth and progression within God's plan.[36]

---

[32] John H. Walton, *Ancient Near Eastern Thought and the Old Testament: Introducing the Conceptual World of the Hebrew Bible* (Ada, MI: Baker Academic: 2006).

[33] Derek Kidner, *Genesis: An Introduction and Commentary* (Westmont, IL: InterVarsity Press, 1967).

[34] Richards, the *Pearl of Great Price.*

[35] James E. Talmage, *Articles of Faith* (Salt Lake City: Deseret Book Co., 2015).

[36] Blake Ostler, *Exploring Mormon Thought: The Attributes of God* (Sandy, UT: Greg Kofford Books: 2001).

From a scientific standpoint, the formation of landmasses and the beginning of plant life are significant events in Earth's history, but they did not occur in rapid succession, as suggested in the biblical account.

The process by which landmasses, or continents, are formed is known as plate tectonics. Over billions of years, Earth's lithosphere, broken into various plates, moved because of the convective currents in the mantle below. This movement caused landmasses to form through processes like volcanic activity and sediment accumulation.[37]

Vegetation's appearance on Earth is a landmark event in its evolutionary history. The earliest life forms were single-celled organisms,[38] and it took billions of years before multicellular plant life appeared.[39] The first land plants, resembling tiny mosses, are believed to have emerged around 500 million years ago.[40]

These simple plants paved the way for more complex plants that would eventually diversify into the wide variety of vegetation we see today.

The act of plants bearing seeds "in itself" can be seen in the light of plant evolution. Seed-bearing plants, or gymnosperms, appeared around 360 million years ago, allowing plants to reproduce efficiently in various environments.[41]

I delve deeper into the planet's age and processes in Chapter 4.

---

[37] Kent C. Condie, *Plate Tectonics and Crustal Evolution* (Oxford: Butterworth-Heinemann, 2016).

[38] Andrew H. Knoll, *Life on a Young Planet: The First Three Billion Years of Evolution on Earth* (Princeton: Princeton University Press, 2003).

[39] Stefan Bengtson, "Early Life on Earth: The Age of Prokaryotes," in *Evolution of Primary Producers in the Sea* (Cambridge, MA: Academic Press, 2007).

[40] Paul Kenrick and Peter R. Crane, *The Origin and Early Diversification of Land Plants: A Cladistic Study* (Washington, DC: Smithsonian Institution Press, 1997).

[41] Kathy Willis and Jennifer McElwain, *The Evolution of Plants* (Oxford: Oxford University Press, 2002).

In the creation narrative of the third day, whether viewed through a theological or a scientific lens, there's an undeniable emphasis on growth, order, and the continuity of life. The Christian perspective emphasizes God's role in introducing order and sustenance. While not diverging drastically from the mainstream Christian understanding, the LDS view offers nuances about organization and eternal progression. Simultaneously, the scientific viewpoint provides a detailed chronology and mechanism for these transformative events in Earth's history.

The Fourth Day – Genesis 1:14–19

> And God said, Let there be lights in the firmament of the heaven to divide the day from the night; and let them be for signs, and for seasons, and for days, and years:
>
> And let them be for lights in the firmament of the heaven to give light upon the earth: and it was so.
>
> And God made two great lights; the greater light to rule the day, and the lesser light to rule the night: he made the stars also.
>
> And God set them in the firmament of the heaven to give light upon the earth,
>
> And to rule over the day and over the night, and to divide the light from the darkness: and God saw that it was good.
>
> And the evening and the morning were the fourth day.

Ancient scripture paints a picture steeped in purpose. The celestial bodies are more than mere fixtures in the sky; they are divine tools governing time, seasons, and the dichotomy of day and night. Their importance to ancient civilizations as theological symbols and practical guides cannot be overstated. The annual flooding of the Nile, the timing of sowing and harvest, and even religious festivals were intricately tied to celestial events.[42]

To many Christian scholars, the specific reference to the lights being "for signs, and for seasons, and for days, and years" suggests a profound understanding of their cyclic nature and their role in marking time and guiding human activity. Their position as divinely ordained entities echoes the broader theme of Genesis: God as the grand architect, bringing forth order from chaos.[43]

In the LDS narrative, the heavens are alive with meaning and purpose. The account of creation in the Pearl of Great Price provides additional insights, with Abraham's recounting of God's instruction: "And I, God, said: Let there be lights in the firmament of the heaven to divide the day from the night, and let them be for signs and for seasons, and for days and for years."[44]

Beyond the text, LDS leaders have, over the years, provided added layers of interpretation. Brigham Young, for instance, expressed a belief that every star and planet was created by God for a purpose, reiterating the sentiment of the heavens as purposeful creations.[45] As noted earlier, Joseph Smith's expansive vision of the universe also encompasses the idea of worlds without limit, implying an eternal plan beyond our earthly sphere.[46]

While theological interpretations offer spiritual perspectives, scientific inquiry dives deep into the mechanics and origins of these celestial entities. The sun, our most immediate and influential star, is a giant ball of gas, predominantly made of hydrogen, undergoing nuclear fusion.[47] It has been

---

[42] Walton, *Ancient Near Eastern Thought and the Old Testament*.

[43] Kenneth A. Matthews, *Genesis 1–11:26* (Nashville: B&H Publishing Group, 1996).

[44] Richards, Pearl of Great Price, Abraham 4:14.

[45] Brigham Young, *Journal of Discourses*, vol. 13 (1870), 271.

[46] Joseph Smith, *Teachings of the Prophet Joseph Smith* (Salt Lake City: Deseret Book Company, 1938).

[47] Michael Zeilik, *Astronomy: The Evolving Universe*. 9th ed. (Cambridge: Cambridge University Press, 1992).

shining for about 4.6 billion years[48] and is pivotal in sustaining life on Earth. The sun's consistent radiation provides the necessary warmth and energy for photosynthesis, which is foundational to Earth's food chain.[49]

The moon, Earth's natural satellite, is pivotal in influencing our planet's dynamics. Rather than merely illuminating the night with reflected sunlight, the moon's gravitational force is crucial in regulating the ocean's tides. Scientific evidence indicates that the moon's origin can be traced back to the aftermath of a massive collision between Earth and a celestial body roughly the size of Mars.[50]

In their breathtaking variety, stars are nuclear furnaces, each with a unique life cycle determined by their mass and composition. Our understanding of stars has evolved from regarding them as mere pinpricks in the night sky to realizing they are suns, some with their own systems of planets, potentially teeming with life.[51]

Modern astronomy and space exploration have expanded our understanding of the universe. The Hubble Space Telescope, for instance, has sent back images of distant galaxies, each containing billions of stars, giving us a glimpse into the universe's vastness and beauty.[52]

The fascinating interplay between theology and science in understanding the fourth day of creation highlights humanity's quest for understanding. While ancient scripture and religious doctrines provide spiritual and moral guidance, scientific inquiry unravels the intricate workings and origins of

---

[48] Katharina Lodders, "Solar System Abundances and Condensation Temperatures of the Elements," *The Astrophysical Journal* 591, vol. 2 (2003): 1220–1247.
[49] Carl J. Hansen, Steven D. Kawaler, and Virginia Trimble, *Stellar Interiors: Physical Principles, Structure, and Evolution* (New York: Springer Science & Business Media, 2004).
[50] Robin M. Canup, "Forming a Moon with an Earth-like composition via a Giant Impact," *Science* 338, no. 6110 (2012): 1052–1055.
[51] Dina Prialnik, *An Introduction to the Theory of Stellar Structure and Evolution* (Cambridge: Cambridge University Press, 2000).
[52] Mario Livio, *The Hubble Space Telescope: New Views of the Universe* (New York: Harry N. Abrams, 2000).

the cosmos. The sun, moon, and stars stand as a testament to the Divine and the laws of nature.

In conclusion, the fourth day of creation, as described in Genesis 1:14–19, serves as a reminder of the universe's grandeur and complexity. Whether viewed through the lens of faith or the microscope of science, the celestial bodies inspire wonder and reverence. Their presence in the sky, guiding the rhythms of days, seasons, and years, reflects a cosmos infused with order, purpose, and beauty.

The Fifth Day – Genesis 1:20–23

> And God said, Let the waters bring forth abundantly the moving creature that hath life, and fowl that may fly above the earth in the open firmament of heaven.
>
> And God created great whales, and every living creature that moveth, which the waters brought forth abundantly, after their kind, and every winged fowl after his kind: and God saw that it was good.
>
> And God blessed them, saying, Be fruitful, and multiply, and fill the waters in the seas, and let fowl multiply in the earth.
>
> And the evening and the morning were the fifth day.

The Book of Genesis, cherished and revered by believers worldwide, serves as an intricate tapestry that recounts the unfolding of creation. These verses, in particular Genesis 1:20–23, are often viewed through a lens of awe and wonder, capturing the imagination of theologians, scholars, and the laity alike. Within these lines, Christians discern a crucial moment in God's creative process: the inception of animal life. The narrative meticulously unfolds, detailing the addition of marine and avian beings to Earth, a testimony to God's expansive vision for his creation.

For countless generations, these scriptures have illuminated the path of faith, serving as a constant reminder of God's omnipotence and his meticulous planning. The intricate details, ranging from the smallest marine organism to the largest avian species, underscore the Creator's intent: each life form, no matter its size or function, has been purposefully designed, bearing testament to God's grand design for the world.[53]

As Christians delve deeper into the narrative, the message becomes clear—this isn't just a moment of creation but an act of love, imbuing the world with a dazzling array of creatures, each playing its part in the divine symphony of life.

One cannot help but be captivated by the mention of "great whales" in this narrative. Delving into the etymology of this term, we encounter the Hebrew word *tannin*. Historically rich and varied in interpretation, *tannin* can evoke images of mythical sea serpents, legendary dragons, or simply colossal sea creatures. As translations evolved, it became commonplace to associate *tannin* with "whales," an interpretation widely accepted, given the whale's majesty and stature in the marine world. Their awe-inspiring presence in the vast oceans is a testament to God's ability to craft wonders.[54]

"Let the waters bring forth abundantly the moving creature that hath life, and fowl that may fly above the earth in the open firmament of heaven" (Gen 1:20). This verse beautifully encapsulates the Creator's command, illustrating the scope and the magnitude of life that he envisioned for the seas and the sky. Each creature, from the nimblest bird darting in the sky to the most graceful marine life gliding through the waters, reflects a facet of God's creativity.

The recurring theme in these passages is the celebration of life in its diverse forms. "And God created great whales, and every living creature that

---

[53] N. T. Wright, *Christian Origins and the Question of God,* Vol. 1 (London: SPCK Publishing, 1992).
[54] Victor P. Hamilton, *The Book of Genesis, Chapters 1–17* (Grand Rapids: Wm. B. Eerdmans Publishing, 1990).

moveth, which the waters brought forth abundantly, after their kind, and every winged fowl after his kind: and God saw that it was good" Gen 1:21). This affirmation not only underscores the value of every creature but also emphasizes God's satisfaction in his work, a world teeming with life, each species intricately designed and wonderfully made.[55]

This meticulous portrayal in Genesis, when juxtaposed against the vastness of the natural world, serves as a reminder of the bridge between scripture and nature. As believers ponder these verses, they are prompted to reflect upon God's boundless imagination, which envisioned whales navigating the depths of oceans and birds charting courses across the vast sky. It's a narrative that invites introspection, urging readers to acknowledge and appreciate the wonders of creation that surround them daily.[56]

Latter-Day Saints hold a nuanced, profound understanding of the scriptures, particularly concerning the creation narrative in Genesis 1:20–23. Within LDS doctrine, God's divine hand in the process of creation is undeniable. These verses, which depict the Lord's command to populate the waters and the sky with life, are deeply revered and taken to symbolize God's unwavering intent to bring life, diversity, and purpose to our world.

A central tenet of LDS belief is the principle of agency. This principle suggests that every great or small creation possesses an intrinsic purpose and is endowed with the freedom—or agency—to fulfill that divine purpose within the parameters defined by the Creator.[57]

Applying this principle to the creatures mentioned in Genesis 1:20–23 takes on a richer, more expansive meaning. The myriad of marine and avian life, from the majestic whales to the soaring eagles, aren't merely products of

---

[55] Bruce K. Waltke and Cathi J. Fredricks, *Genesis: A Commentary* (Grand Rapids: Zondervan, 2001).

[56] Karl Barth, *Church Dogmatics: The Doctrine of Creation* (London: T&T Clark, 1958).

[57] Dallin H. Oaks, "Free Agency and Freedom," LDS General Conference, Oct. 1987.

divine whim. From the LDS viewpoint, they are sentient beings with purpose, capable of exercising agency in their aquatic and aerial domains.

Intriguingly, one notices a departure from some traditional Christian views when examining the LDS approach to the creation process. While many Christian denominations might lean toward the belief in an instantaneous act of creation, Latter-Day Saint teachings offer a more layered, progressive interpretation. The Church suggests that the act of creation wasn't a singular, immediate event but instead a series of divinely orchestrated phases or sequences that unfolded over an extended period.[58] Rather than clashing with scientific accounts, this perspective might find some harmony with them, especially when considering geological and paleontological timelines.

Joseph Smith, the founder of the LDS Church, brought forth additional scriptures that complement and expand upon the biblical narrative. The Pearl of Great Price, particularly the Book of Moses, delves deeper into the creation story. It reaffirms God's role as the Creator while providing insight into the purpose and sequence of each creative act.[59] When read in conjunction with Genesis, these scriptures further elucidate the LDS Church's understanding of a deliberate, phased creation.

Furthermore, the Doctrine and Covenants, another canonized LDS work, provides teachings that harmonize with the idea of purposeful, organized creation. The revelations contained within emphasize God's forethought and meticulous planning in all His works.[60] For Latter-Day Saints, these additional scriptures serve to reinforce the idea that every creature, from the enormous whales of the sea to the myriad birds of the sky, was created with intention and divine design.

In summation, the LDS perspective on Genesis 1:20–23 is both profound and layered. While deeply rooted in a reverence for God's creative power,

---

[58] Russell M. Nelson, "The Creation," *Ensign*, May 2000.
[59] Smith, Pearl of Great Price.
[60] Smith, Doctrine and Covenants, 104:14–17.

it also embraces a more expansive, phased understanding of creation. This view not only underscores the divine agency vested in all of God's creations but also finds unexpected resonance with scientific timelines, bridging faith and reason in a uniquely harmonious manner.

From the perspective of modern science, Earth's biological history is a mesmerizing tale of resilience, diversification, and evolutionary marvels spanning billions of years. Genesis 1:20–23 portrays a divine mandate: life burgeoning from the waters and the sky. While metaphorical in nature, this scriptural depiction mirrors certain pivotal epochs in Earth's extensive paleontological record.

When Genesis refers to the waters teeming with life, it evokes the concept of the "primordial soup."[61] This term refers to the oceans of the young Earth, rich with organic molecules. Over eons, given the right conditions, these molecules merged and formed the building blocks of life, eventually leading to the birth of the first simple organisms.[62] These rudimentary life forms began a long, complex evolutionary journey that transformed our planet into the vibrant biosphere we observe today.

The verses that discuss the emergence and proliferation of marine life echo the phenomenon known as the Cambrian explosion. This monumental event, which unfolded approximately 541 million years ago, represents one of Earth's most significant evolutionary radiations.[63] Over a relatively short geological timespan, the world's oceans bore witness to an unprecedented burst of life, with most major animal phyla marking their debut in the fossil record. Rapid diversification reshaped marine ecosystems, laying the foundations for future evolutionary ventures.

---

[61] S. Tirard, "Oparin's Conception of Origins of Life," in *Encyclopedia of Astrobiology*, ed. M. Gargaud et al. (Berlin: Heidelberg, 2011), https://doi.org/10.1007/978-3-642-11274-4_1111.

[62] A. I. Oparin, *Origin of Life*, 1938.

[63] D. H. Erwin et al., "The Cambrian Conundrum: Early Divergence and Later Ecological Success in the Early History of Animals," *Science* 334, no. 6059 (2011): 1091–1097.

The scriptural mention of "great whales" and other large sea creatures is somewhat anachronistic when juxtaposed with the Cambrian period. In reality, these magnificent marine mammals trace their lineage back to terrestrial ancestors.[64] The evolutionary journey of whales is a testament to nature's adaptability. Around 50 million years ago, certain land mammals began a gradual yet profound transition.[65] These creatures adapted to aquatic environments, undergoing significant morphological and physiological changes over millennia to evolve into the majestic whales we observe today.

Equally captivating is the biblical reference to birds that fly "above the earth." Modern paleontology reveals that birds evolved from theropod dinosaurs during the Mesozoic Era.[66] A cascade of evolutionary innovations marked this transition: the emergence of feathers, initially for thermoregulation and later co-opted for flight; modifications in skeletal structures, making them lighter and adapted for aerial locomotion; and the development of endothermy or warm-bloodedness, a trait that enabled higher metabolic rates and enhanced muscular activity. Archaeopteryx, dating back around 150 million years, is a testament to this evolutionary transition.[67] With characteristics of dinosaurs and modern birds, it exemplifies the intricate pathways through which life evolves.

Furthermore, while the Genesis narrative presents the advent of marine and avian life in a condensed time frame, science paints a picture of gradual, often painstaking evolution. Ecosystems evolved, species emerged and went extinct, and life's tapestry grew richer and more complex. The fossil record

[64] J. G. M. Thewissen, L. N. Cooper, J. C. George et al., "From Land to Water: the Origin of Whales, Dolphins, and Porpoises," *Evo Edu Outreach* 2 (2009): 272–288, https://doi.org/10.1007/s12052-009-0135-2.

[65] M. D. Uhen, "Evolution of Marine Mammals: Back to the Sea After 300 Million Years," *The Anatomical Record* 290 no. 6 (2007): 514–522.

[66] X. Xu et al., "A Jurassic Avialan Dinosaur from China Resolves the Early Phylogenetic History of Birds," *Nature* 498 no. 7454 (2013): 359–362.

[67] T. G. Kaye, M. Pittman, and W. R. Wahl, "Archaeopteryx Feather Sheaths Reveal Sequential Center-out Flight-related Molting Strategy," *Communications Biology* 3, no. 1 (2020): 745.

provides a window into these ancient worlds, enabling us to piece together the grand story of life on our planet.

In summary, while the Book of Genesis offers a theologically rich account of the world's beginnings, the scientific narrative complements it with a detailed, evidence-based chronicle of Earth's biological history. Both perspectives, when examined side by side, provide a holistic understanding of our planet's vibrant legacy of life.

In its poetic and theological depth, the biblical narrative provides an account of creation that varies significantly from the empirical timelines and mechanisms outlined by modern science. However, both of these narratives, with their distinct orientations, converge on the awe-inspiring phenomena of life's emergence and diversification.

While the scriptural representation in Genesis is replete with symbolism and divine purpose, the scientific perspective delves into the intricate processes, evolutionary pathways, and the vast epochs that have sculpted the tapestry of life on Earth. For numerous devout believers, the precise modalities of *how* life came to be are secondary to the overarching question of *why*. Genesis serves as a spiritual compass, delineating humanity's intrinsic connection to the cosmos and underscoring a grand divine orchestration. It posits a universe teeming with purpose, where every creature, from the humblest microorganism to the most complex mammal, fits into a celestial blueprint.

Conversely, the scientific narrative thrives on inquiry, evidence, and a relentless pursuit of knowledge. It chronicles the gradual unfolding of life, the challenges faced, adaptations made, and the myriad factors contributing to the kaleidoscope of biodiversity we observe today. Through the fossil record, genetic studies, and various other methodologies, science pieces together a chronicle of life that is as wondrous as any divine tale.

For some, juxtaposing these two narratives might appear like an exercise in reconciling opposites. However, numerous individuals across the world find a harmonious intersection between the two. They perceive the Divine not as an antithesis to nature but as an inherent aspect of it. To them the laws of physics, evolutionary mechanisms, and the fortunate events that led to life are all manifestations of a higher design. The unfolding of life over billions of years doesn't diminish the role of the Divine; instead, it magnifies it, showcasing an intricate plan played out over eons.

Furthermore, this multifaceted understanding fosters a profound appreciation for the myriad forms of life around us. Recognizing the divine hand in the natural world can imbue individuals with a more profound sense of responsibility toward all living beings, fostering empathy and stewardship.

The depiction of the fifth day in Genesis is more than just a chronicle of creation; it's an ode to the marvels of life, a celebration of its myriad forms, and a call to cherish and protect it. Whether one interprets this through the lens of faith or the microscope of science, the essence remains unaltered: life is a precious gift, and it's incumbent upon us to honor, understand, and preserve it.

The Sixth Day (Creation of Man) – Genesis 1:24–31

> And God said, Let the earth bring forth the living creature after his kind, cattle, and creeping thing, and beast of the earth after his kind: and it was so.

> And God made the beast of the earth after his kind, and cattle after their kind, and every thing that creepeth upon the earth after his kind: and God saw that it was good.

> And God said, Let us make man in our image, after our likeness: and let them have dominion over the fish of the sea, and over the fowl of the air, and over the cattle, and over all the earth, and over every creeping thing that creepeth upon the earth.

So God created man in his own image, in the image of God created he him; male and female created he them.

And God blessed them, and God said unto them, Be fruitful, and multiply, and replenish the earth, and subdue it: and have dominion over the fish of the sea, and over the fowl of the air, and over every living thing that moveth upon the earth.

The declaration of God's intent to craft man "in our image, after our likeness" is symbolic in the biblical creation narrative. Historically, these verses have been viewed as denoting the pinnacle of God's creative work, imbuing humanity with a unique significance in the cosmic order.[68] Following the formation of the cosmos and the establishment of various life forms, the narrative crescendos as God bestows upon man a unique essence—that which resembles the Divine.

The phrase "in our image, after our likeness" has sparked theological inquiry and debate for millennia. Augustine of Hippo, a prominent early Christian theologian, interpreted this phrase as representing mankind's rational soul, allowing individuals to think and understand, differentiating them from other creatures.[69] Another significant interpretation comes from St. Thomas Aquinas, who viewed this as pointing toward man's capacity to know and love his Creator.[70]

Further, many theologians hold the perspective that being made in God's image imbues humans with inherent dignity, value, and worth. It is not merely about physical resemblance but is deeply rooted in spiritual, moral, intellectual, and relational capacities. This intrinsic value bestows upon humanity an unmatched status in creation.[71]

---

[68] G. J. Wenham, *Word Biblical Commentary: Genesis 1–15* (Waco: Word Books, 1987).
[69] Augustine of Hippo, the *City of God*, Book XII, Chapter 24.
[70] Thomas Aquinas, *Summa Theologica*, I, Q 93, Art. 4.
[71] Karl Barth, *Church Dogmatics III.1* (London: T&T Clark, 1958).

Moreover, the mandate to exercise "dominion" over all other creatures is both an honor and a responsibility. It's not a call for unchecked dominion or tyranny over nature but rather an invitation to stewardship, reflecting God's own care and governance of the universe.[72] Theologian John Walton contends that this dominion should mirror God's character: one of love, care, and righteousness.[73]

These verses offer profound insights into the Christian understanding of human nature, purpose, and responsibility. They underscore the belief that humans are not mere accidents of evolution but intentionally designed, bearing the image and essence of their Creator.

For LDS, the biblical narrative of the creation of man transcends mere historical recounting. It envelops vast stretches of time and existence, traversing premortal realms, our current mortal vacation, and looking forward to an eternal, post-mortal continuum.[74]

The pivotal statement "Let us make man in our image" forms a central theological nexus for LDS believers. This plurality in divine expression is deeply rooted in LDS teachings concerning the Godhead, which comprises the Father, the Son, and the Holy Ghost.[75] While other Christian traditions interpret this plurality differently, within LDS doctrine, it is seen as a direct reference to the council of the Gods, illuminating their teachings about the plurality of Gods.[76]

---

[72] Richard Bauckham, *The Bible and Ecology: Rediscovering the Community of Creation* (Waco: Baylor University Press, 2010).

[73] John H. Walton, *The Lost World of Adam and Eve: Genesis 2–3 and the Human Origins Debate* (Downers Grove, IL: IVP Academic, 2015).

[74] Bruce R. McConkie, "The Seven Deadly Heresies," in *1980 Devotional Speeches of the Year* (Salt Lake City: BYU Press, 1981).

[75] Dallin H. Oaks, "The Godhead and the Plan of Salvation," LDS General Conference, April 2017.

[76] Joseph Smith, *Teachings of the Prophet Joseph Smith* (Salt Lake City: Deseret Book Co., 1976), 348.

LDS doctrine asserts a premortal existence where every individual lived and learned as spirit offspring of heavenly parents.[77] This notion shifts the paradigm of the creation account. Instead of just the origin of humanity, it's the beginning of a crucial chapter in the eternal journey of every spirit child. Acquiring a physical body and experiencing mortality equips these spirit children with opportunities to grow, make choices, face adversity, and eventually progress toward their divine potential.

Furthermore, when God instructs Adam and Eve to "multiply, and replenish the earth, and subdue it" (Gen 1:28), LDS theology perceives deeper layers of meaning. Beyond a mere directive, it's an invitation to partake in the divine process. LDS teachings value families as eternal structures. Hence, this divine commandment is interpreted not just as a biological instruction but as an eternal principle—allowing God's spirit children to receive mortal bodies and progress through life's journey.[78]

Incorporating the idea of a physical creation with premortal existence results in a tapestry of profound implications. Every individual, being a literal spiritual progeny of divine beings, possesses inherent, infinite worth. This doctrine profoundly shapes LDS perspectives on the sanctity of life, morality, familial bonds, and the nature of our eternal identity.[79] Deep-seated beliefs impact LDS life and culture, from family-centered activities to missionary work, as believers strive to share this eternal perspective with others.[80]

Additionally, this emphasis on divine lineage and eternal potential underscores the Church's emphasis on personal revelation and continuous learning, both in a spiritual and a secular context.[81] By understanding our divine heritage, Latter-Day Saints are motivated to seek wisdom,

[77] Russell M. Nelson, "We Are Children of God," LDS General Conference, Oct. 1998.
[78] David A. Bednar, "We Believe in Being Chaste," LDS General Conference, April 2013.
[79] Dieter F. Uchtdorf, "You Matter to him," LDS General Conference, Oct. 2011.
[80] Russell M. Ballard, "The Importance of Family," *New Era Magazine*, Feb. 2005.
[81] Henry Eyring, "Education for Real Life," *Ensign*, Oct. 2002.

understanding, and personal growth throughout their lives, reflecting the eternal progression they believe is central to God's plan for his children.

The story of human evolution, as charted by modern science, is a journey of understanding that unfolds across an expansive temporal canvas, with every discovery offering more profound insights into our shared ancestry and history. While the Genesis narrative encapsulates the act of human creation in a few verses, the scientific account unravels a more intricate and protracted tale.

When Genesis speaks of God's creation of "living creatures after their kind: cattle and creeping things and beasts of the earth," it echoes a scientific truth of Earth's rich and varied tapestry of life evolving and diversifying over hundreds of millions of years.[82] The transition from aquatic to terrestrial life, symbolized by the first tetrapods setting foot on land around 375 million years ago, marked a significant evolutionary milestone.[83] This event set the stage for the subsequent rise of various species, with some facing extinction, paving the way for newer forms in a dynamically changing biosphere.

The Bible's assertion, "Let us make man in our image, after our likeness," establishes humanity's distinguished position within the vast spectrum of creation. Evolutionary biology also acknowledges this unique trajectory. While all life on Earth shares a common ancestry, the line leading to Homo sapiens has been marked by distinct evolutionary events. As members of the primate order, humans share a lineage with the great apes, including gorillas, orangutans, and chimpanzees.[84] The evolutionary divergence from

---

[82] Michael J. Benton, *Vertebrate Paleontology*, 4th ed. (Hoboken: Wiley Blackwell, 2014).
[83] Donald R. Prothero, *The Story of Life in 25 Fossils* (New York: Columbia University Press, 2015).
[84] David S. Strait and Frederick E. Grine, "Inferring Hominoid and Early Hominid Phylogeny Using Craniodental Characters: The Role of Fossil Taxa," *Journal of Human Evolution* 47 no. 6 (2004): 399–452.

our closest genetic relatives, the chimpanzees and bonobos,[85] began approximately 5–7 million years ago,[86] leading to a diverse range of hominins, each representing a different facet of the human evolutionary experiment.

The emergence of the Homo genus roughly 2.5 million years ago was characterized by several distinct features, such as an increasing cranial capacity, adaptations favoring bipedal locomotion, and the dexterity that enabled complex tool making.[87] Homo sapiens, the species we all belong to, emerged around 300,000 years ago. Their larger brains facilitated the development of symbolic thought, language, and an unprecedented ability for cultural and social organization not seen in other species. [88]

Modern genetics further enriches our understanding of human evolution. Advancements in DNA analysis have charted the migratory patterns of early humans out of Africa,[89] their interactions and interbreeding events with other hominins like Neanderthals and Denisovans,[90] and the genetic legacies these encounters have left in diverse populations today. Such insights have reshaped traditional anthropological views, underscoring humanity's interconnectedness and shared history.

This scientific narrative, grounded in empirical evidence, seeks to elucidate the mechanisms, processes, and pathways that have shaped human evolution.

---

[85] T. D. White, C. O. Lovejoy, B. Asfaw et. al., "Neither Chimpanzee Nor Human, Ardipithecus Reveals the Surprising Ancestry of Both," *Proceedings of the National Academy of Sciences of the United States of America* 112 no. 16 (2015): 4877–4884.

[86] Kay Prüfer et al., "The Bonobo Genome Compared with the Chimpanzee and Human Genomes," *Nature* 486, no. 7404 (2012): 527–531.

[87] Bernard Wood and Nicholas Lonergan, "The Hominin Fossil Record: Taxa, Grades, and Clades," *Journal of Anatomy* 212, no. 4 (2008): 354–376.

[88] Jean-Jacques Hublin et al., "New Fossils from Jebel Irhoud, Morocco and the Pan-African Origin of Homo sapiens," *Nature* 546, no. 7657 (2007): 289–292.

[89] S. López, L. van Dorp, L., and G. Hellenthal, "Human Dispersal Out of Africa: A Lasting Debate," *Evolutionary Bioinformatics Online* 11, Suppl 2 (2016): 57–68.

[90] K. H. Ko, "Hominin Interbreeding and the Evolution of Human Variation," *Journal of Biological Research (Thessalon)* 23 (2016): 17.

While the biblical narrative of human origins is brief and allegorical, the scientific account offers a nuanced, detailed exploration. Though differing in approach and details, both narratives ultimately celebrate the mystery, complexity, and wonder of human existence and our place in the vast expanse of life.

The Sixth Day (The Giving of Food) – Genesis 1:29–31

> And God said, Behold, I have given you every herb bearing seed, which is upon the face of all the earth, and every tree, in the which is the fruit of a tree yielding seed; to you it shall be for meat.
>
> And to every beast of the earth, and to every fowl of the air, and to every thing that creepeth upon the earth, wherein there is life, I have given every green herb for meat: and it was so.
>
> And God saw every thing that he had made, and, behold, it was very good. And the evening and the morning were the sixth day.

Genesis 1:29–31 defines God's dietary plan for his created beings and profoundly reflects the state of creation and its intricate interconnectedness. In this design, everything—from the tallest trees to the smallest herbs—played a role in sustaining life.

The emphasis on a herbivorous lifestyle hints at a world where harmony and nonviolence were paramount. By bestowing upon humans and animals alike a vegetarian diet, God seemed to establish a foundation where life did not necessitate the taking of another's life.[91] This contrasts markedly with

---

[91] John C. Collins, *Genesis 1–4: A Linguistic, Literary, and Theological Commentary* (Phillipsburg, NJ: P&R Publishing, 2006).

the natural world as we observe it today, pointing to profound theological debates about the introduction of death and predation following the Fall.

Furthermore, the specifics of God's provision—"every herb bearing seed" and "every tree yielding fruit"—highlights a system rooted in sustainability and regeneration. In God's design, not only were the plants provided as food, they were also given the means to reproduce, ensuring a continual supply.[92] This underscores a Creator who is not just powerful but also profoundly wise and foresightful.

For many theologians and Christian scholars, these verses also serve as a foundation for discussions on stewardship and sustainability. If the initial divine command was to consume sustainably, how much more should contemporary Christians be concerned about unsustainable consumption patterns and environmental degradation?[93]

Historically, various Christian movements have drawn inspiration from these verses to advocate for vegetarianism, citing it as God's original plan for humanity and the animal kingdom.[94] While mainstream Christianity doesn't mandate vegetarianism, the ethical considerations derived from these passages certainly influence discussions on food, ethics, and sustainability.

The declaration that God saw everything and proclaimed it "very good" carries profound theological implications. This wasn't a mere nod to creation's aesthetic or functional aspects but a profound assertion of its moral and spiritual goodness. This proclamation challenges believers to view every part of creation—down to the food they consume—as imbued with divine goodness and purpose.[95]

---

[92] Kenneth A. Matthews, *Genesis 1–11:26* (Nashville: B&H Publishing Group, 1996).

[93] Norman Wirzba, *Food and Faith: A Theology of Eating* (Cambridge, MA: Cambridge University Press, 2011).

[94] Stephen H. Webb, *Good Eating* (Ada, MI: Brazos Press, 2011).

[95] Craig G. Bartholomew and Michael W. Goheen, *The Drama of Scripture: Finding Our Place in the Biblical Story* (Ada, MI: Baker Academic, 2004).

In the broader context of biblical theology, these verses lay the groundwork for understanding humanity's role not as exploiters but as stewards entrusted with the responsibility of caring for and preserving Earth in all its abundance.[96]

Latter-Day Saint beliefs are deeply rooted in the understanding that God's teachings are eternal and consistent across ages. The ancient and modern scriptures provide a continuous tapestry of divine counsel, emphasizing the care and precision with which God has designed His children's physical and spiritual lives. This consistent divine concern is profoundly evident in the dietary guidelines provided to humanity.

The Genesis account of God endowing the first humans with seeds, herbs, and fruits for sustenance is reminiscent of a divine design aiming for holistic well-being. This idea gains further clarity and depth in Latter-Day Saint teachings through the Word of Wisdom, a set of health guidelines in the Doctrine and Covenants, a modern-day scripture that is unique to the faith.[97] This connection bridges ancient instruction and contemporary revelation, emphasizing the Church's belief in God's ongoing involvement in human affairs.

Delving deeper into the Word of Wisdom, we notice its detailed guidelines on meat consumption. While meat is not prohibited, it should be consumed "sparingly" and ideally in times of "winter, or of cold, or famine."[98] This counsel resonates with the Edenic harmony described in Genesis, suggesting a time when humans and animals coexisted peacefully. This alignment between ancient scripture and modern revelation

---

[96] Christopher J. H. Wright, *Old Testament Ethics for the People of God* (Downers Grove: IVP Academic, 2011).

[97] James E. Talmage, *The Word of Wisdom: A Modern Interpretation* (Salt Lake City: Deseret Book Co., 1937).

[98] Smith, Doctrine and Covenants, 89:12–13.

symbolizes the Church's belief in God's eternal principles and how they manifest across different times and contexts.[99]

Grains, often termed the "staff of life" in LDS teachings, form a cornerstone of the dietary guidelines in the Word of Wisdom.[100] The emphasis on grains reflects the Genesis account, reinforcing the idea that God's dietary counsel has remained consistent over millennia. This consistency points toward the timeless nature of divine instruction and its adaptability to different eras.[101]

For Latter-Day Saints, the intersection of the Genesis account and the Word of Wisdom serves as a testament to the unity and harmony of God's teachings. They are not disparate doctrines from different eras but are harmonious parts of an eternal whole, consistently guiding God's children toward physical and spiritual prosperity.

From a scientific basis, Genesis 1:29–31 puts forth an interesting proposition, suggesting that humans and animals were destined to be herbivores in the initial stages of creation. In examining this assertion through the lens of science, particularly the fields of paleontology, anthropology, and evolutionary biology, we encounter a captivating tapestry of evidence detailing the dietary evolution of life on Earth.

Beginning with early hominids, dental fossils are critical in deciphering dietary habits.[102] The structures of teeth—the shape of molars, the wear patterns, and even the chemical makeup of tooth enamel—can offer a window into the dietary preferences of long-extinct species. Early hominids, with their broader, flatter molars, were seemingly adapted for a diet

---

[99] Gordon B. Hinckley, "The Wondrous and True Story of Christmas," *Ensign*, Dec. 2000.

[100] Smith, Doctrine and Covenants, 89:14.

[101] Russell M. Ballard, "What Matters Most Is What Lasts Longest," LDS General Conference, Oct. 2005.

[102] Peter S. Ungar and Matt Sponheimer, "The Diets of Early Hominins," *Science* 334 no. 6053 (2011): 190–193.

primarily composed of fruits and other soft plant materials.[103] However, it's important to note that these early dietary habits were, over time, influenced by various ecological factors, including environmental shifts and interspecies competition.

With the advent of tools, some hominids began incorporating more meat into their diet. Tool marks on animal bones and the presence of animal remains at hominid sites provide evidence for this shift.[104] This dietary expansion, combined with the added nutritional value of meat, is hypothesized by some experts to have been a catalyst in the enlargement of the hominid brain, which paved the way for developing the more cognitively advanced Homo sapiens.[105]

Parallel to the hominid trajectory, the large animal kingdom experienced diverse dietary evolutions. For instance, certain modern-day herbivores stem from ancestral lines that once included carnivorous or omnivorous members. Consider the evolutionary journey of whales. Their terrestrial ancestors were, by some accounts, carnivorous before re-entering aquatic environments, eventually leading to the diverse cetacean dietary habits we see today.[106]

Plant life underwent significant evolutionary shifts, shaping the dietary choices of herbivores. Developing defensive mechanisms in plants, such as thorns, toxins, and chemical deterrents, influenced herbivorous behaviors

[103] David S. Strait and Frederick E. Grine, "Inferring Hominoid and Early Hominid Phylogeny Using Craniodental Characters: The Role of Fossil Taxa," *Journal of Human Evolution* 47, no. 6 (2004): 399–452.

[104] Manuel Dominguez-Rodrigo and Rebeca Barba, "New Estimates of Tooth Mark and Percussion Mark Frequencies at the FLK Zinj Site: The Carnivore-Hominid-Carnivore Hypothesis Falsified," *Journal of Human Evolution* 50, no. 2 (2006): 170–194.

[105] Leslie C. Aiello and Peter Wheeler, "The Expensive-Tissue Hypothesis: The Brain and the Digestive System in Human and Primate Evolution," *Current Anthropology* 36, no. 2 (1995): 199–221.

[106] J. G. Thewissen et al., "Whales Originated from Aquatic Artiodactyls in the Eocene Epoch of India," *Nature* 450, no. 7 (2007): 173.

and adaptations.[107] In response, some herbivores developed specialized digestive systems, like the four-chambered stomachs of ruminants, to extract maximum nutrients from plants.

Then there's the broader picture of the plant-based food web. The pioneering process of photosynthesis, which evolved over 3 billion years ago, laid the foundation for the planet's diverse ecosystems.[108] This groundbreaking adaptation allowed plants to harness the sun's energy, producing oxygen and forming the bedrock of the food chain upon which herbivores and carnivores depend.

When juxtaposed against the biblical account of Genesis 1:29–31, the scientific narrative is less a contradiction and more a deeper dive into the intricate nuances of life's dietary journey. While the Bible offers a broad, philosophical perspective on creation and sustenance, science delves into the mechanisms and adaptations that underpin these grand themes.

---

[107] Thomas Hartmann, "From Waste Products to Ecochemicals: Fifty Years Research of Plant Secondary Metabolism," *Phytochemistry* 68, no. 22–24 (2007): 2831.
[108] Peter H. Raven, et al, *Biology of Plants*, 7th ed. (New York: W. H. Freeman and Company, 2005).

Chapter 2: Adam and Eve vs. Evolution.

Chapter 1 delved into the intricate tapestry of creation as described in the Book of Genesis, covering the initial six days. As we transition past the sixth day, where God created man, our attention shifts to the mesmerizing narrative of the Garden of Eden and the introduction of Adam and Eve. This biblical portrayal, juxtaposed with the scientific theory of human evolution, offers two profound yet seemingly divergent perspectives on humanity's origins. While they may appear at odds, each narrative brings forth its own depth, insights, and challenges, encapsulating diverse facets of human comprehension and belief.

In the Judeo-Christian tradition, Adam and Eve's story is a profound allegory for human nature, free will, and moral responsibility. It offers a spiritual understanding of human existence, giving believers a sense of purpose and a connection to the Divine. For centuries this narrative has shaped cultural, ethical, and societal norms and values. As the Book of Genesis illustrates, "So God created man in his own image, in the image of God created he him; male and female created he them" (Gen 1:27). For centuries this narrative has shaped cultural, ethical, and societal norms and values.

Genesis 2:21–25: The Creation of Eve

> And the Lord God caused a deep sleep to fall upon Adam, and he slept: and he took one of his ribs, and closed up the flesh instead thereof;
>
> And the rib, which the Lord God had taken from man, made he a woman, and brought her unto the man.
>
> And Adam said, This is now bone of my bones, and flesh of my flesh: she shall be called Woman, because she was taken out of Man.

Therefore shall a man leave his father and his mother, and shall cleave unto his wife: and they shall be one flesh.

And they were both naked, the man and his wife, and were not ashamed.

The Book of Genesis, especially the segment discussing the creation of Eve, remains a cornerstone in biblical literature, revered for its rich narrative and theological implications. This particular portion is unparalleled in its depth and has captivated theologians, scholars, and lay believers alike for millennia. Its essence illuminates the divine wisdom and intention behind the profound relationship between man and woman.

When the narrative describes God inducing a profound slumber upon Adam, it sets the stage for a monumental act of divine creation. This deep sleep can be interpreted as a literal state of unconsciousness and perhaps as a symbolic precursor to a new awakening or a new beginning. Following this, God's decision to craft Eve from Adam's rib rather than from the earth, as He did with Adam, serves multiple symbolic purposes. It underscores the organic bond between the two and suggests a kind of equality and mutual dependence. The rib, positioned close to the heart, can be seen as a metaphorical representation of love, companionship, and the deeply intertwined destinies of man and woman.

When Adam beholds Eve for the first time, his declaration, "This is now bone of my bones, and flesh of my flesh," is not merely an acknowledgment of their shared physicality. It profoundly affirms recognition, kinship, and a mirrored identity.[109] The subsequent verses elegantly emphasize the sanctity and depth of the marital bond, suggesting a union so intense and sacred that it is envisioned to be even more profound than the ties binding a child to their parents. The portrayal of them becoming "one flesh" is a

---

[109] Gordon J. Wenham, *Word Biblical Commentary Vol. 1, Genesis 1–15* (Waco: Word Books, 1987).

powerful allegory for the spiritual, emotional, and physical unity ordained by God for married couples.

The narrative's culmination, which draws attention to the unashamed nakedness of Adam and Eve, is an evocative reflection of their initial purity. In this Edenic state, they existed in perfect harmony, untouched by guile, deceit, or the shadow of sin.[110] Their transparent and untarnished relationship starkly contrasts the complexities that would ensue following the Fall.

The Dilemma of Literalism vs. Science

However, interpreting the story of Adam and Eve literally can lead to conflicts with scientific evidence, particularly concerning human evolution and genetics. The idea of a single original human couple from whom all humans descended clashes with the findings of paleontology and genetic studies, which point to a gradual evolution of Homo sapiens from ancestral species over millions of years. As paleontologist Stephen Jay Gould explains, "Humans are not the end result of predictable evolutionary progress, but rather a fortuitous cosmic afterthought."[111] This perspective emphasizes the randomness and complexity of evolution rather than a linear or preordained process leading to humans.

At first glance, the story of Adam and Eve, which conveys the divine creation of humans, is at odds with certain peculiarities present within human anatomy. A case in point is the non-recurrent laryngeal nerve. More commonly referred to as the recurrent laryngeal nerve in most mammals, this nerve offers a tantalizing glimpse into our evolutionary past, presenting a puzzle that has intrigued scientists for years.

In humans and various other mammals, the laryngeal nerve doesn't follow what one might consider the "logical" or shortest path from the brain to the

---

[110] Kenneth A. Matthews, *Genesis 1–11:26* (Nashville: Holman Reference, 1986).
[111] Stephen Jay Gould, *Wonderful Life: The Burgess Shale and the Nature of History* (New York: W. W. Norton & Company, 1989).

larynx. Instead of traversing the few centimeters directly, the nerve dives down into the chest, looping around the aorta close to the heart, only to climb back up to the larynx. This seemingly redundant detour becomes even more pronounced in creatures like the giraffe, where the nerve takes a journey of several extra meters. Such a lengthy and indirect path might initially appear counterintuitive, and it begs the question: why would an "intelligent design" feature such an anatomical oddity?

In the nineteenth century, anatomist Richard Owen was among the first to detail this nerve's path in various animals, noting the curious route it takes.[112] His observations laid the groundwork for future biologists to delve deeper into the significance of this anomaly.

The circuitous route of the laryngeal nerve can be understood better when we trace back the evolutionary history of vertebrates. Early in vertebrate evolution, when our distant ancestors resembled fish, this nerve traveled directly from the brain to the gills without detours.[113] However, as evolution sculpted and changed these early vertebrates, the heart and its associated vessels, including the aorta, shifted positions. Instead of being re-routed, the laryngeal nerve got "caught" in this evolutionary transition, leading to the roundabout pathway we see in modern mammals.

Unlike an architect, evolution doesn't have the luxury of starting from scratch. It builds upon existing structures, adapting and modifying them for new purposes, even if it leads to what might seem like design flaws. Biologist and writer Neil Shubin noted that "Nature is a tinkerer, not an engineer."[114] The story of the laryngeal nerve exemplifies this notion,

---

[112] Richard Owen, *On the Anatomy of Vertebrates* (London: Longmans, Green and Co., 1866).

[113] Kenneth V. Kardong, *Vertebrates: Comparative Anatomy, Function, Evolution* (New York: McGraw-Hill, 2018).

[114] Neil Shubin, *Your Inner Fish: A Journey into the 3.5-Billion-Year History of the Human Body* (New York: Pantheon Books, 2008).

highlighting the patchwork and incremental nature of evolutionary changes.

Richard Dawkins has often showcased this nerve as compelling evidence for evolution. He said, "No engineer would ever make a mistake like that."[115] Instead of debunking a grand design, this nerve's seemingly illogical pathway reinforces the marvels of natural selection and the unpredictability of evolutionary paths.

For many, these anatomical quirks provide a deeper understanding of life's interconnectedness and the profound processes that have sculpted every living organism over eons. The laryngeal nerve is but one chapter in the vast and intricate narrative of evolution—a narrative that need not conflict with religious beliefs but can enrich our appreciation for the complexity and beauty of life.

Moreover, the genetic diversity observed in modern human populations is inconsistent with a literal interpretation of Adam and Eve as the only human progenitors. Geneticists have shown that the genetic variation in human populations indicates a common ancestry spread across a population of several thousand individuals, not just two.

Embryonic Development and the Intricacies of Sex Determination

While our exploration of the intricacies of the natural world, such as the remarkable journey of the laryngeal nerve, underscores evolution's complex dance, we find yet another layer of wonder when delving into the realm of human embryonic development. The narrative of evolution, which spotlights nature's myriad marvels and perceived idiosyncrasies, parallels our journey to understanding the very beginnings of human life. Just as the laryngeal nerve provides a glimpse into the evolutionary tapestry of life,

---

[115] Richard Dawkins, *The Blind Watchmaker: Why the Evidence of Evolution Reveals a Universe Without Design* (New York: W.W. Norton & Company, 1986).

embryology offers a window into the sophisticated processes that shape human beings even before birth.

Human embryonic development is fascinating, revealing intricate pathways that challenge and expand our understanding of biological sex. One of the most captivating insights from developmental biology is the trajectory of sex differentiation in human embryos, a process that appears in contrast with certain biblical accounts.

At conception, an embryo receives one chromosome from each parent, determining its genetic sex. An XX chromosome configuration results in a female, while an XY configuration results in a male. And yet, all embryos, whether genetically XX or XY, begin their development with undifferentiated structures that are the precursors to female internal and external reproductive organs.[116]

For the first six to seven weeks post-fertilization, these embryonic structures remain indistinguishable between genetic males and females. The presence of the Y chromosome and, specifically, the SRY gene on it triggers the differentiation of these gonadal structures into testes around the seventh week.[117] If this Y chromosome is absent, as in typical female (XX) embryos, the undifferentiated structures default to becoming ovaries.

Hormones heavily influence this transformation. The developing testes in a genetically male (XY) embryo release testosterone, stimulating the formation of male reproductive anatomy. In contrast, the absence of testosterone allows the embryo to maintain its original, female-oriented developmental pathway.[118]

---

[116] Gerald R. Cunha et al., "Development of the External Genitalia: Perspectives from the Spotted Hyena," *Differentiation* 87 (2004): 4–22.

[117] Peter Koopman, "Sry and Sox9: Mammalian Testis-Determining Genes," *Cellular and Molecular Life Sciences* 55, vol. 6-7 (1999): 839–856.

[118] Dennis McFadden, "Masculinization of the Mammalian Cochlea," *Hearing Research*, 250, vol. 1–2 (2017): 37–48.

Dr. David Page of the Whitehead Institute stated, "It's as if we're all female, and then some of us count ourselves as male at the end."[119] This remark underlines the biological notion that male differentiation is a process overlaying a default female template.

The embryological evidence suggests a "female-first" developmental model. This contrasts with the biblical narrative in Genesis, where Adam is formed before Eve. While the Genesis account has profound theological and symbolic implications, the scientific understanding underscores the intricacies and nuances of human development.

When examining the stages of embryogenesis, we find a narrative that is not only profound in its intricacies but which also offers a perspective that may seem at odds with traditional biblical stories. This does not necessarily diminish the reverence associated with religious texts but instead adds depth to our understanding, invoking a sense of awe for the natural processes that have been at play for millennia.

Attempting to merge or juxtapose these scientific and religious frameworks can be challenging. It underscores the broader conversation about the relationship between sacred texts and evolving scientific knowledge. Both domains offer profound insights into human existence and understanding but operate on different premises and methodologies.[120]

Interpreting religious narratives in light of contemporary scientific findings necessitates a nuanced approach, encouraging dialogues that respect religious beliefs and scientific evidence.

Diverse Christian Perspectives

The different religious traditions also complicate matters, as they interpret the story of Adam and Eve in varying ways. While some fundamentalist

---

[119] David Page, Lecture at the Whitehead Institute.
[120] Alister E. McGrath, *Science & Religion: A New Introduction* (Hoboken: Wiley-Blackwell, 2009).

Christian groups might insist on a literal reading, other Christian denominations, Jewish and Islamic traditions, and LDS members see the story as allegorical or symbolic.[121] These interpretations reflect different theological understandings of creation, sin, redemption, and human nature, leading to diverse views on original sin and the nature of human responsibility and free will.

Scientific discoveries and religious beliefs have often found themselves on intersecting paths, with areas of convergence and divergence. While science provides tangible evidence about our physical existence, religion offers insights into life's spiritual dimension. For members of the Church of Jesus Christ of Latter-day Saints, this intersection creates a rich tapestry of understanding about humanity's origins.

The Church stands firmly on the foundation that Adam and Eve were historical figures, molded by God's hand and placed within the sanctity of the Garden of Eden.[122] Their spiritual significance cannot be overstated, particularly given President Ezra Taft Benson's assertion, "The fall of Adam and Eve is one of the most important occurrences of all time, next to the atonement of the Lord Jesus Christ."[123] This profound religious assertion, however, doesn't inherently preclude acceptance of evolutionary processes.

The scientific understanding of our evolutionary journey, underscored by phenomena like the non-recurrent laryngeal nerve's path, paints a compelling story of our anatomical past.[124] When contemplating this alongside LDS teachings, an intriguing perspective emerges: the physical forms of Adam and Eve might have been a product of evolutionary processes, but their spiritual inception marked the birth of modern humans

---

[121] Ibid, *The Science of God: An Introduction to Scientific Theology* (Grand Rapids: Eerdmans, 2004).

[122] *The Family: A Proclamation to the World*, Church of Jesus Christ of Latter-day Saints, 1995.

[123] Ezra Taft Benson, "The Book of Mormon and the Doctrine and Covenants," *Ensign*, May 1987.

[124] Neil Shubin, *Your Inner Fish: A Journey into the 3.5–Billion-Year History of the Human Body* (New York: Pantheon Books, 2008).

with divine souls as spiritual descendant children of God, distinguishing them from their biological predecessors.

James E. Talmage, a luminary within the Church, elegantly married these concepts. He posited that while "[the soul of] Man is the child of God.. . . He is born in the lineage of Deity, not in the posterity of the brute creation."[125] This encapsulates the duality of our existence: our bodies, shaped by millennia of evolution and our souls by divine provenance. Further reflecting on the creation of Adam and Eve, Talmage mused, "The creation . . . was a step plainly foreseen and definitely planned from the beginning. As to whether the physical bodies were evolved . . . or whether they appeared within the brief scope of one of the creative days, is a question of no vital consequence."[126]

LDS philosopher and theologian Blake Ostler expanded on this duality, emphasizing that "Adam and Eve are viewed in Latter-Day Saint theology not only as historical persons but also as symbolizing every man and every woman. Their choices and their consequences are representative of our own existential situation."[127] This underscores the universality of the Adam and Eve narrative as a recounting of humanity's beginnings and a reflection of every individual's spiritual journey.

The LDS Church, while steadfast in its belief in the historical existence of Adam and Eve, also values the symbolic resonance of the narrative, emphasizing themes like agency, obedience, and redemption. This rich tapestry of interpretations within the Church serves as a testament to the ongoing dialogue between faith and reason, sacred scriptures, and empirical discoveries.

---

[125] James E. Talmage, "The Earth and Man," address delivered in the Tabernacle, Salt Lake City, Utah, Aug. 9, 1931.
[126] James E. Talmage, "The Origin of Man," *Improvement Era* 13, no. 1, 1909.
[127] Blake Ostler, *Exploring Mormon Thought: The Problems of Theism and the Love of God* (Sandy, UT: Greg Kofford Books, 2006).

The convergence of scientific and LDS views provides a holistic understanding of humanity's origins. It underscores the beauty of our evolutionary journey while celebrating the divine essence that makes us uniquely human.

Across the broad spectrum of mainstream Judeo-Christianity, theological disagreements and inconsistencies can add to the difficulty of reconciling religious beliefs with scientific evidence. While some religious scholars and theologians argue that the story of Adam and Eve can coexist with the theory of evolution, others find the two irreconcilable. This tension between literal interpretations and allegorical or symbolic readings continues to be a significant topic of debate and reflection within religious communities as scholars and believers seek to harmonize faith with reason. It opens a complex discussion beyond mere historical or scientific considerations, touching the core of our understanding of existence, morality, and the Divine.

On the other side, the scientific theory of evolution provides a detailed and empirically supported explanation for the gradual development of life on Earth, including the emergence of Homo sapiens. Charles Darwin's insights continue to shape this understanding, as he once wrote, "It is not the strongest of the species that survives, nor the most intelligent that survives. It is the one that is most adaptable to change."[128] This serves as a foundational concept in biology and has led to advancements in various fields, such as medicine and agriculture. The theory offers a cohesive explanation for the diversity of life and connects diverse phenomena across biological sciences. Richard Dawkins encapsulates this understanding: "We are survival machines—robot vehicles blindly programmed to preserve the selfish molecules known as genes."[129]

---

[128] Often attributed to Darwin, this quote may be a paraphrase of his ideas rather than a direct quote. See Michael Shermer's *Why Darwin Matters* (2006) for a detailed discussion.
[129] Richard Dawkins, *The Selfish Gene* (London: Oxford University Press, 1976).

Despite the insights it offers, the theory of evolution has been controversial, particularly in its perceived conflict with certain religious beliefs about human creation. Misinterpretations of the theory have sometimes led to harmful ideologies or policies. However, some religious leaders, like Pope John Paul II, have acknowledged the scientific merit of evolution, stating, "New knowledge leads to the recognition of the theory of evolution as more than a hypothesis."[130]

Some Christian theologians argue that evolution does not contradict faith despite these challenges. As Augustine of Hippo wrote, "In matters that are so obscure and far beyond our vision, we find in Holy Scripture passages which can be interpreted in very different ways without prejudice to the faith we have received."[131] Moreover, in the LDS tradition, there is an acknowledgment that science and religion can coexist, as Brigham Young stated, "In these respects, we differ from the Christian world, for our religion will not clash with or contradict the facts of science in any particular."[132]

As I grappled with these two perspectives, I realized they were not necessarily at odds. Rather than a literal account, the story of Adam and Eve could be understood as a symbolic narrative that captures essential truths about human consciousness, ethics, and spirituality. It does not necessarily conflict with the scientific understanding of human development but can complement it by addressing the "why" rather than the "how" of human existence.

Meanwhile, the scientific theory of evolution offers valuable insights into humanity's physical and biological aspects. It provided a framework for

---

[130] Pope John Paul II, "Message to the Pontifical Academy of Sciences: On Evolution," Oct. 22, 1996, https://rb.gy/gfv8m.
[131] Augustine of Hippo, *The Literal Interpretation of Genesis*. Ancient Christian Writers Series, trans. John Hammond Taylor, 1982.
[132] Brigham Young, *Discourses of Brigham Young*, selected by John A. Widtsoe (Salt Lake City: Deseret Book Company, 1954).

understanding our biological heritage without negating the spiritual dimension explored in religious narratives.

In reconciling these two views, I found a more nuanced and integrated understanding of humanity that honored faith and reason. The seeming contradictions between the symbolic meaning of the biblical account and the empirical evidence supporting evolution began to dissolve, replaced by a harmonious and multifaceted worldview. It was a journey of discovery that led me to appreciate the complexity of our scientific and spiritual understanding, recognizing that they are not mutually exclusive but complementary parts of a greater whole.

Chapter 3: The Great Flood and Noah's Ark

The story of the Great Flood and Noah's Ark is among the most well-known and widely misunderstood tales across various cultures and religious traditions. This narrative, filled with dramatic imagery, has been a source of inspiration and a subject of scrutiny. The story presents several challenges when examined through the lens of modern science, particularly geology and paleontology.

What I find compelling is how flood myths are a recurring motif in religious and cultural traditions across the globe, appearing in everything from the Mesopotamian epic of Gilgamesh[133] to the biblical account of Noah. These stories often serve as cautionary tales about cosmic resets, reflecting a phenomenon that historian and mythographer Mircea Eliade describes as follows: "The flood is not just a dissolution; it is also regeneration and purification."[134]

Many scholars believe these stories are rooted in localized yet significant flood events. These tales, reverberating through oral traditions, might have evolved into narratives that signify a moral, cultural or spiritual paradigm.[135] A case in point is the Black Sea deluge hypothesis, which points to a colossal inundation event circa 7,500 years ago that dramatically expanded the Black Sea's boundaries.[136]

The universality of flood myths often encompasses deep symbolism and meaning. Historian Ian Wilson explains that these myths may represent a cultural memory of actual events imaginatively expressed in allegorical form. He asserts that floods are not merely destructive forces but are seen as

---

[133] Stephanie Dalley, *Myths from Mesopotamia: Creation, the Flood, Gilgamesh, and Others* (Oxford: Oxford University Press, 2000).

[134] Mircea Eliade, *The Myth of the Eternal Return* (Princeton: Princeton University Press, 1971).

[135] Alan Dundes, *The Flood Myth* (Los Angeles: University of California Press, 1988).

[136] William Ryan and Walter Pitman, *Noah's Flood: The New Scientific Discoveries about the Event That Changed History* (New York: Simon & Schuster, 1998).

tools of renewal, cleansing, and divine judgment, reflecting humanity's fear and awe of the uncontrollable natural world.[137]

The widespread occurrence of flood myths has also attracted the attention of scientists. Geologist David Montgomery argues that such stories might have originated from actual flooding events passed down through generations and growing in the retelling.[138] The prevalence and persistence of these myths point to a universal human experience with floods, transformed into meaningful narratives.

Religious scholars have further explored the theological significance of flood myths. Theologian John Walton emphasizes the unique perspective in the ancient Near East, stating that "the flood account is not about the judgment of all humankind, but the re-creation of the cosmic order."[139] In various religious traditions, flood myths often reflect a higher moral order and the Divine's interaction with humanity.

This narrative highlights the multifaceted nature of flood myths and their resonance across cultures. From their symbolic meaning to their literal interpretations and theological implications, flood myths have an enduring significance in human civilization.

The Pervasiveness of Deluge Myths

Throughout human history, the narrative of a cataclysmic flood—a deluge of such magnitude that it reshapes civilizations and landscapes—has resonated across diverse cultures. The efforts of pioneering scholars such as Richard Andree, Hermann Usener, and Sir James George Frazer have

---

[137] Ian Wilson, *Before the Flood: The Biblical Flood as a Real Event and How It Changed the Course of Civilization* (New York: St. Martin's Press, 2004).
[138] David R. Montgomery, *The Rocks Don't Lie: A Geologist Investigates Noah's Flood* (New York: W. W. Norton & Company, 2012).
[139] John H. Walton, *Ancient Near Eastern Thought and the Old Testament: Introducing the Conceptual World of the Hebrew Bible* (Ada, MI: Baker Academic, 2009).

illuminated this phenomenon, documenting the expansive reach and variations of these flood myths.[140]

In human psychology and mythology, water holds a place of awe and fear. It is a life bringer but also a harbinger of destruction. The frequent occurrence of flood myths in disparate cultures, portraying this duality of destruction and rebirth, speaks to our species' shared experience with, and reverence for, the forces of nature.[141]

Andree's meticulous compilation, the *Flood Legend Considered Ethnographically*, is a detailed examination of the global spread of these myths. While highlighting the absence of such tales in Africa, he brought attention to their rich presence in the Americas, Asia, and especially the Middle East.[142]

Ancient Mesopotamia in particular provides some of the earliest written records of flood narratives. Tales such as that of King Ziusudra from the Sumerian tradition and Utnapishtim from the Akkadian tradition narrate the survival of a chosen individual, forewarned by a deity about an impending divine deluge.[143] [144] Given their age, such accounts suggest Mesopotamia as a potential starting point for the dissemination of the flood myth.

India also boasts a storied tradition of flood myths, including the tale of Manu. As recounted in ancient Vedic texts, Manu is warned of a deluge by a fish, which he saves. The fish, an incarnation of the god Vishnu,

[140] James George Frazer, *Folk-lore in the Old Testament: Studies in Comparative Religion, Legend, and Law.* Vol. 1 (New York: Macmillan and Company, 1918).

[141] Mircea Eliade, *The Myth of the Eternal Return: Cosmos and History.*

[142] Richard Andree, *The Flood Legend Considered Ethnographically* (New York: Macmillan and Company, 1891).

[143] A. R. George, *The Epic of Gilgamesh: The Babylonian Epic Poem and Other Texts in Akkadian and Sumerian* (New York: Penguin Classics, 1999).

[144] Jeffrey H. Tigay, *The Evolution of the Gilgamesh Epic* (Philadelphia: University of Pennsylvania Press, 2022).

reciprocates by guiding Manu to safety, a narrative echoing the elements found in other flood stories.[145]

Such tales, born possibly from actual events and then enriched by the layers of time and tradition, underscore humanity's universal effort to understand and narrate the unpredictable forces of nature. These stories serve as cautionary tales, moral lessons, and reminders of life's cyclical patterns of creation, destruction, and rebirth.[146]

While symbolic, the universality of these stories might also hint at genuine historical events. Cataclysmic floods, once etched into the collective memories of ancient civilizations, might have evolved into myths that crossed cultural and geographical boundaries, echoing humanity's shared experiences.

Did a Global Flood Actually Occur?

The idea of a global flood that submerged every inch of Earth's terrestrial surface, as depicted in scriptures, struggles to find validation within the scope of modern geological evidence. Renowned Geologist David R. Montgomery affirms that "geologists have found no evidence of such a catastrophe in the planet's sedimentary record."[147] This is a critical statement, as sedimentary rocks provide a vital record of the planet's history, chronicling events from thousands to billions of years ago.

Understanding the magnitude of a global flood requires examining the sheer volume of water needed. Consider Mount Everest, an emblem of Earth's natural grandeur, peaking at 8,848 meters (29,029 feet) above sea level. A flood of such magnitude that it could swallow even this towering monument would necessitate an amount of water that exceeds the collective

---

[145] Wendy Doniger, *Hindu Myths: A Sourcebook Translated from the Sanskrit* (New York: Penguin Books, 1975).
[146] David A. Leeming, *The Oxford Companion to World Mythology* (New York: Oxford University Press, 2005)
[147] David R. Montgomery, *The Rocks Don't Lie: A Geologist Investigates Noah's Flood* (New York: Norton & Company, 2012).

volume of our current oceans, lakes, and rivers. Our planet's hydrosphere, comprising all water forms, is roughly 1.332 billion cubic kilometers (319.294 million cubic miles).[148] To suggest that an additional, unaccounted-for volume could suddenly appear to inundate the entire landmass strains our current scientific understanding.

To drive home this point, let's do a bit of math.

$$\text{Surface Area of New Earth} = 4\pi(R + h)^2$$

R = Radius of the Earth (approximately 3,959 miles or 6,371 km)
h = Height of Mount Everest above the current sea level (approximately 5.5 miles or 8.848 km)

$$\text{Volume of New Earth} = 34\pi(R + h)^3$$
$$\text{Volume of Current Earth} = 34\pi R^3$$
$$\text{Volume of Extra Water} = \text{Volume of New Earth} - \text{Volume of Current Earth}$$

$$=$$

$$\text{Volume of Extra Water} = 34\pi(3959 + 5.5)^3 - 34\pi(3959)^3$$
$$\text{Volume of Extra Water} \approx 34\pi(3964.5)^3 - 34\pi(3959)^3$$
$$\text{Volume of Extra Water} \approx 2.6 \times 10^8 \text{ cubic miles (rounded)}$$

So, roughly, an additional 260 million cubic miles of water would be needed to cover the planet's surface up to the height of Mount Everest, or slightly over double the current amount of water. This is a simple and theoretical calculation. In reality, factors like erosion, displacement, and other complexities would affect the exact number.

Even if all the polar ice caps from Greenland and Antarctica were to melt, it would result in approximately 7.04 million cubic miles of water.[149] The effect of the polar ice caps melting would be a rise in sea level of an estimated 60–70 meters (around 200–230 feet).[150]

[148] Peter H. Gleick, *Water in Crisis: A Guide to the World's Fresh Water Resources* (New York: Oxford University Press, 1993).
[149] E. Rignot, E. and P. Kanagaratnam, "Changes in the velocity structure of the Greenland Ice Sheet," *Science,* 311 (5763) (2006): 986–990.
[150] J. A. Church and P. U. Clark, et. al., "Sea level change," *Climate Change,* 5 (2013): 1137–1216.

However, only some of this water would add to the ocean's volume straightforwardly due to factors like displacement (remember the principle of buoyancy from Archimedes' principle).[151]

Given the vast expanse of our planet, the question of how so much water could appear and subsequently disappear presents a formidable puzzle. Setting aside these logistical concerns, and for the sake of argument, let's assume an omnipotent deity possesses the capacity to conjure such a colossal volume of water instantaneously. With that presumption in mind and recognizing the awe-inspiring power that such an act would demonstrate, it is crucial to examine additional scientific facets and conundrums intertwined with this ancient narrative. It's also essential to avoid oversimplifying or overlooking the myriad of other considerations that come into play when discussing such a monumental event.

The study of Earth's strata provides significant insights. In the context of a global flood, one would anticipate finding a universally consistent layer of flood deposits. Instead, Earth's crust presents intricate and varied sedimentary layers, many of which tell tales of epochs where life thrived, landscapes evolved, and environments transitioned.[152] For instance, fossilized sand dunes and ancient river valleys indicate arid and fluvial environments, respectively. Coral reef fossils hint at stable, shallow marine settings over extended periods—not conditions associated with a tumultuous global flood event.[153]

Furthermore, ice cores, often referred to as the "time machines" of climatology, offer sequential climatic data across millennia. Extracted from the polar ice caps, these cores contain trapped air bubbles, particulates, and isotopes that chronicle Earth's climatic tale. If a global flood occurred in the

---

[151] Archimedes of Syracuse, "On Floating Bodies," in *The Works of Archimedes, Edited in Modern Notation with Introductory Chapters,* Vol. 2. (Cambridge: Cambridge University Press, 1897).
[152] Donald R. Prothero, *The Story of Life in 25 Fossils: Tales of Intrepid Fossil Hunters and the Wonders of Evolution* (New York: Columbia University Press, 2015).
[153] Peter M. Sadler, "Sediment Accumulation Rates and the Completeness of Stratigraphic Sections," *Journal of Geology* 89, no. 5 (1981): 569–584.

relatively recent past, it would undoubtedly register as a stark anomaly within these records. However, meticulous studies have revealed a continuity in these ice layers, betraying no sign of such a catastrophic watery event.[154]

Two of Every Species—Is that Possible?

The account of Noah's Ark, a vessel that reportedly housed a pair of every animal species on Earth, raises numerous questions and complexities when examined in the light of contemporary scientific knowledge.

To begin with, the sheer number of species is staggering. Current estimates posit around 8.7 million distinct species, which doesn't account for the countless species yet to be discovered.[155] When confronted with this staggering biodiversity, prominent evolutionary biologist Jerry Coyne observes, "The space and sustenance required for even a fraction of these species makes the Ark's capacity seem untenable."[156] Consider also the sheer physiological diversity among these species. From the tiniest insects to the colossal blue whales, the range in size, dietary needs, and habitat requirements is astounding.

Beyond just space considerations, the dietary requirements of so many distinct species pose another logistical problem. Every creature has evolved its unique dietary patterns adapted to its native environment. For instance, the panda's diet predominantly consists of bamboo, with certain species of bamboo preferred over others. Would the Ark have had the provisions to cater to such specific needs throughout the flood's duration?[157] And it's not just about food. Certain animals have evolved in particular ecological niches

---

[154] Jean Jouzel et al., "Orbital and Millennial Antarctic Climate Variability over the Past 800,000 Years," *Science* 317, no. 5839 (2007): 793–796.

[155] Camilo Mora et al., "How many species are there on Earth and in the ocean?" *PLoS Biology* 9, no. 8 (2011).

[156] Jerry Coyne, *Why Evolution Is True* (New York: Penguin, 2010).

[157] George B. Schaller et al., "The feeding ecology of giant pandas and Asiatic black bears in the Tangjiahe Reserve, China," in *Biology and Management of Giant Pandas* (Washington, DC: Smithsonian Institution Press, 1998).

with unique conditions. The tuatara, for instance, is a reptile native to New Zealand that requires cool burrows for incubation. Such specific ecological conditions would have been challenging to replicate on the Ark.[158]

Following the flood, the reintroduction of species poses another scientific conundrum. For example, marsupials, such as kangaroos and wallabies, are predominantly found in Australia.[159] As anthropologist and author Dr. Alice Roberts notes, "The lack of any traceable path of marsupial fossils from the Middle East to Australia is a profound puzzle if we take the Ark narrative at face value."[160] The same applies to other unique species in isolated regions: the lemurs in Madagascar, the myriad of unique creatures in the Galápagos Islands, or the countless endemic species in the Amazon rainforest.

Furthermore, ecosystems worldwide are intricately balanced and fine-tuned over millennia of evolutionary processes. Introducing pairs of every species into a singular environment, followed by their dispersal, would have catastrophic ecological consequences. Dr. Jane Goodall, a primatologist, comments on this delicate balance, saying, "Every species has a role in its ecosystem. A sudden mass extinction and subsequent repopulation would disrupt this balance, potentially leading to ecological chaos."[161]

Historical Large-Scale Floods: Nature's Testament

While not encompassing the whole Earth as the biblical Flood narrative suggests, the cataclysmic episodes of large-scale floods have nonetheless played crucial roles in shaping the physical landscapes and cultural tales of human history. These geologically and anthropologically significant events

---

[158] Charles H. Daugherty et al., "Age-specific reproductive success: evidence for the selection hypothesis," *Evolution* 44, no. 3 (1990): 679–686.
[159] Sascha Brune et al., "Oblique Plate Tectonic Movement," *Scientific Reports* 6 (2016): 14677.
[160] Alice Roberts, *The Incredible Unlikeliness of Being: Evolution and the Making of Us* (Sheridan, OR: Heron Books, 2014).
[161] Jane Goodall, *Seeds of Hope: Wisdom and Wonder from the World of Plants* (New York: Grand Central Publishing, 2014).

offer insights into the dynamic interplay between nature's might and human resilience.

In the Pacific Northwest of the present-day United States, one finds evidence of a series of remarkable flooding events known as the Missoula Floods, which occurred between 13,000 and 15,000 years ago.[162] These floods were not singular events but rather a sequence of cataclysms resulting from the periodic rupturing of the ice dam containing Glacial Lake Missoula.[163] With each breach, colossal volumes of water, at times discharging up to fifteen times the flow of the present-day Amazon River, rushed out, carving deep channels and redefining landscapes.[164] "The cataclysmic floods of Lake Missoula . . . represent the power of nature to shape our world in a geological instant,"[165] observes geologist Richard B. Waitt Jr. Today's Channeled Scablands—a maze of buttes, basins, and coulees—are living testament to these ancient deluges.[166]

Concurrently, on the other side of the world in Southeast Asia, a different kind of flood story was unfolding between 7,000 and 15,000 years ago.[167] As the Pleistocene epoch waned, the planet warmed, and melting glaciers caused sea levels to rise precipitously.[168] This gradual inundation dramatically transformed the region, turning expanses of plains into the

---

[162] David Alt, *Glacial Lake Missoula and Its Humongous Floods* (Missoula, MT: Mountain Press Publishing, 2001), 197.

[163] Robert J. Carson and Kevin R. Pogue, "Flood Basalts and Glacier Floods: Roadside Geology of Parts of Walla Walla, Franklin, and Columbia Counties, Washington," *Washington Division of Geology and Earth Resources Information Circular* 90, 1996.

[164] Victor R. Baker, *Channeled Scablands of Eastern Washington: The Geomorphology of Planet Earth* (Cambridge: Cambridge University Press, 1978).

[165] Richard B. Waitt Jr., "Case for periodic, colossal jökulhlaups from Pleistocene glacial Lake Missoula," *Geological Society of America Bulletin* 96, no. 10 (1985): 1271–1286.

[166] Harlen J. Bretz, "The Lake Missoula Floods and the Channeled Scabland," *Journal of Geology* 77 (1969): 505–543.

[167] Michael I. Bird et al., "Palaeoenvironments of insular Southeast Asia during the Last Glacial Period: a savanna corridor in Sundaland?" *Quaternary Science Reviews* 24, vol. 20–21 (2005): 2228–2242.

[168] Edlic Sathiamurthy and Harold K. Voris, "Maps of Holocene sea level transgression and submerged lakes on the Sunda Shelf," *Natural History Journal of Chulalongkorn University Supplement* 2 (2006): 1–44.

intricate archipelagos of today. Dr. Michael I. Bird notes that these inundations were significant enough to "alter not just landscapes but the very way of life of ancient communities residing in these regions."[169] The rising waters, encroaching upon ancient human settlements, may have given rise to enduring myths and legends passed down through millennia.

Though vast and transformative, these historical flood events were regional in scope. They provide a testament to the power of nature to reshape our world in relatively short geological time spans. When comparing these localized events with global flood narratives, however, it's imperative to delineate between these ancient floods' regional impacts and the biblical account's all-encompassing nature. In doing so, we gain a deeper appreciation for the nuances of our planet's geological history and the rich tapestry of human storytelling it inspired.

Native American Flood Myths and Parallels with Noah's Ark

Native American cultures, with their vast tapestry of oral traditions and myths, include tales of great floods that resemble the story of Noah's Ark from the Judeo-Christian tradition. In light of the teachings of Latter-Day Saints, these parallels offer intriguing interpretations of the universality and transmission of the flood narrative.

The Ojibwa, an indigenous tribe from the northeastern US and Canada, has a flood tale that resonates deeply with the biblical account. As their legends go, an enraged serpent causes the waters to rise, swallowing the land and its creatures. However, a figure named Nanabozho, akin to a cultural hero, finds refuge atop a mountain, where various animal species join him. This sanctuary amidst destruction parallels Noah's Ark. As the floodwaters retreat, Nanabozho sends a bird to survey the land, echoing the biblical scene where Noah releases the dove.[170] An Ojibwa elder recounted, "As the

---

[169] Michael I. Bird, interview, June 15, 2021.
[170] Frances Densmore, *Chippewa Customs* (Minneapolis: Minnesota Historical Society Press, 1979).

water ebbed, so did the sorrow in Nanabozho's heart, and he knew the world would be reborn."[171]

Venturing southward, the flood myth of the Choctaw tribe echoes a similar theme. Their legends tell of a wise prophet who, foreseeing a deluge, warned his people. The ones who heeded the forewarning constructed a raft, mirroring Noah's efforts, and endured the floodwaters. When calm returned, they, too, dispatched a bird to ascertain the situation, symbolizing hope and renewal.[172] A Choctaw saying goes, "From water's depth to mountain's height, our stories span and bridge the sight."[173]

While these parallels are fascinating, the LDS Church offers an additional layer of interpretation. The Book of Mormon chronicles Christ's visitation to the ancient Americas post-resurrection. Latter-Day Saints believe Christ conveyed age-old Israelite narratives during this visit, including the Flood story. As the Book of Mormon records, "And it came to pass that Jesus spake unto them and expounded all the scriptures unto them which they had received, and he expounded them unto them from the beginning until he came" (3 Nep 23:6). This passage implies a comprehensive recounting of ancient events and teachings, possibly including the Flood.

Given this, it's conceivable that these flood narratives were introduced or re-emphasized during Christ's visit and later intertwined with pre-existing indigenous myths, resulting in stories combining biblical and native elements. LDS Apostle Elder Jeffrey R. Holland remarked, "The Savior's visit to the New World was a testament to his teachings and his atonement. The stories shared, including that of the flood, serve as a binding narrative, bridging the old and new worlds."[174]

---

[171] *Ojibwa Elder's Tales,* Oral Narratives Collection, American Folklore Society.

[172] Clara Sue Kidwell, *Choctaws and Missionaries in Mississippi, 1818–1918* (Norman, OK: University of Oklahoma Press, 1997).

[173] *Choctaw Oral Tradition Archive,* Mississippi Choctaw Cultural Center.

[174] Jeffrey R. Holland, *Christ and the New Covenant: The Messianic Message of the Book of Mormon* (Salt Lake City: Deseret Book Company, 1997).

The Latter-Day Saints' View of the Great Flood

While the tale of Noah's Ark remains an integral and profound narrative in various religious traditions, providing moral and spiritual lessons, it's imperative to distinguish between the metaphorical wisdom it offers and the empirical, logistical, and ecological challenges it presents when taken literally.

However, the story's paradoxes with scientific understanding do not necessarily diminish its value or significance. Latter-Day Saints scholar James E. Faulconer explains that scriptural narratives like Noah's Ark convey spiritual truths rather than literal historical events.[175]

The Great Flood symbolizes a fresh start, a washing away human corruption and wickedness. It's a narrative of divine judgment but also of divine mercy, where a faithful few are spared to begin anew. Noah's obedience and trust in the face of an incomprehensible task reflect virtues held dear across religious traditions.

The Ark can be seen as a metaphor for the Church or the community of believers, providing safety and guidance through turbulent times. The gathering of animals might symbolize the inclusiveness and universality of divine love and care. This metaphor parallels the Allegory of the Olive Tree from the Book of Mormon, particularly in the Book of Jacob, chapters 5 to 6.

In this allegory, the olive tree represents the house of Israel, and its various states of growth, decay, pruning, and nourishment symbolize God's constant care and interaction with his people. The master of the vineyard, who is laboring to preserve the tree, is an image of Christ, working tirelessly to cultivate faith and righteousness.

---

[175] James E. Faulconer, "Scripture as Incarnation," in *Faith, Philosophy, Scripture* (Provo, UT: Neal A. Maxwell Institute, 2010).

Just as the Ark was constructed to withstand the chaos of the flood, the olive tree's strong roots symbolize a firm faith that can endure life's trials and tribulations. The olive tree's roots need to be nourished and tended to ensure the tree's growth and fruitfulness. Similarly, the construction of the Ark required precise obedience to divine instructions, reflecting how adherence to God's word builds a spiritual refuge.

The olive tree's branches, which were grafted in and pruned to produce good fruit, can be seen as a symbol of the inclusiveness of God's love, mirroring the gathering of different animals in the Ark. Jacob 5:11 states, "For it grieveth me that I should lose this tree; wherefore, that perhaps I might preserve the roots thereof that they perish not, that I might preserve them unto myself, I have done this thing."

The combined imagery of the Ark and the Allegory of the Olive Tree illustrate the nature of faith, obedience, divine care, and the universality of God's love. Both metaphors serve to teach the necessity of staying rooted in faith, following God's guidance, and embracing the inclusiveness of divine love to navigate the storms of life.

Recognizing the allegorical richness of the Great Flood story, the conflicts with scientific evidence become less problematic. The narrative is no longer constrained by historical or logistical scrutiny but is free to speak to more profound spiritual and moral truths.

Ultimately, the story of the Great Flood transcends the question of historical accuracy. It becomes a timeless and universal tale that resonates across cultures and beliefs, reflecting shared human values and aspirations. Whether seen as myth or metaphor, the story continues to inspire, challenge, and enlighten, a testament to the enduring power of storytelling and human thought.

Chapter 4: The Age of the Planet

For centuries Earth's age has been a pivotal point of contention and wonder, weaving a complex tapestry of science, faith, and philosophy. At its core, this topic is more than just an attempt to chronicle the planet's lifespan; it reflects humanity's enduring desire to locate its position within the vast expanse of cosmic time and uncover its profound mysteries.

Historically, diverse civilizations have crafted their narratives of the world's genesis. Many of these stories are deeply rooted in religious or cultural beliefs, offering moral lessons and cosmological insights. In Judeo-Christian traditions, for instance, Earth's age has often been calculated using genealogies and events mentioned in the Bible. Early theologians and scholars, such as James Ussher, meticulously analyzed biblical texts and posited that Earth was created in 4004 BCE, a perspective that held considerable influence for centuries.[176]

However, as the lens of inquiry shifted with the advent of the Scientific Revolution, a new paradigm emerged. Geological studies, advancements in the field of radiometric dating, and the pioneering work of figures like Charles Lyell and Charles Darwin suggested that Earth was far older than previously believed.[177] [178] The study of strata, rock formations, and fossils painted a world that evolved over billions of years.

This disparity between religious interpretations and scientific findings instigated profound debates and reflections. For some it intensified the perceived rift between faith and reason. For others, it offered a chance to reconcile and reinterpret religious texts in a manner that complemented emerging scientific revelations. Many theologians began to view religious

---

[176] James Ussher, *The Annals of the World* (Master Books, 1658).

[177] Charles Lyell, *Principles of Geology* (London: John Murray, 1880–1883).

[178] Charles Darwin, *On the Origin of Species by Means of Natural Selection* (London: John Murray, 1859).

texts as allegorical or symbolic rather than strictly literal, embracing the idea that the essence of divine truths might be metaphorical and multifaceted.[179]

Deciphering Earth's Age through Radiometric Dating

Radiometric dating, often described as Earth's chronological compass, provides a remarkable avenue to deduce the age of our planet. This technique, rooted in the realm of atomic physics, leverages the principles of radioactive decay, wherein specific atomic nuclei undergo spontaneous disintegration, shedding particles and emitting energy. This meticulous and consistent progression of decay has become an invaluable asset in the chronology of geologic formations and, by extension, estimating Earth's age.

The fundamental idea behind radiometric dating is this: radioactive "parent" isotopes degrade over time to form stable "daughter" isotopes. By assessing the ratio of parent to daughter isotopes in a rock sample and understanding the established rate of decay for the parent isotope (its half-life), scientists can determine the time since that rock solidified.[180] Dr. Henry Faul, a noted geochemist, posits, "The time-clocks of radioactive decay act like hourglasses that start when molten rocks solidify and offer a window into the chronology of Earth's tapestry."[181]

Uranium-lead dating stands as a pillar in the arena of radiometric methods. Specific isotopes of uranium decay into lead at steady rates, presenting a timescale spanning several hundred thousand years to multiple billion years. Zircon crystals, frequently found within igneous rocks, are particularly valuable in this methodology. Their resistance to post-formational changes and inherent traces of uranium make them excellent chronological

---

[179] Stephen Jay Gould, *Rocks of Ages: Science and Religion in the Fullness of Life* (New York: Ballantine Books, 1999).

[180] G. Faure and T. M. Mensing, *Isotopes: Principles and Applications* (Hoboken: John Wiley & Sons, 2005).

[181] Henry Faul, *Ages of Rocks, Planets, and Stars* (New York: McGraw-Hill Book Company, 1966).

markers.[182] According to a groundbreaking study by John W. Valley and colleagues, dating ancient zircon crystals has led to the consensus that Earth is approximately 4.5 billion years old.[183]

Potassium-argon dating offers another tool, particularly potent for dating volcanic materials. As potassium-40 decays into argon-40, the emergent argon, being a gas, is often expelled from molten rock. However, as the rock solidifies and ages, the argon gas becomes trapped, and its quantity becomes a reliable timestamp of the rock's age.[184] Dr. Ian McDougall asserts, "The beauty of potassium-argon dating, especially for volcanics, is its ability to provide exacting dates for events we thought were merely recent in geological terms."[185]

Numerous other radiometric techniques, including the rubidium-strontium and carbon-14 methods, augment our toolkit. While each method is tailored to specific materials and timescales, collectively, they render a multi-faceted approach to decoding Earth's vast history.[186]

While radiometric dating is a formidable asset in geochronology, it's also challenging. Ensuring accuracy often mandates rigorous laboratory procedures. Over vast timescales, samples might face contamination or undergo changes due to geothermal events.[187] In his comprehensive study on isotope geology, Dr. A. P. Dickin elaborates on these challenges but also

---

[182] John W. Valley et al., "Hadean Age for a Post-Magma-Ocean Zircon Confirmed by Atom-Probe Tomography," *Nature Geoscience* 7 (2014): 219–223.

[183] Brent G. Dalrymple, *The Age of the Earth* (Redwood City, CA: Stanford University Press, 1991).

[184] Ian McDougall and T. Mark Harrison, *Geochronology and Thermochronology by the $^{40}Ar/^{39}Ar$ Method* (Oxford: Oxford University Press, 1999).

[185] Ian McDougall, "The Role of K-Ar Age Dating in Geological Investigations," *Journal of the Geological Society* (1975).

[186] A. P. Dickin, *Radiogenic Isotope Geology* (Cambridge: Cambridge University Press, 2005).

[187] Ibid.

emphasizes, "By corroborating findings across methods, we've been able to craft a coherent timeline of our planet's evolution."[188]

Tracing Earth's Age Through Plate Tectonics

Estimating Earth's age using plate tectonics involves examining the historical movements and transformations of Earth's lithospheric plates and the supercontinents they've formed over eons. Plate tectonics revolves around the movement of massive plates of Earth's lithosphere atop the more fluid asthenosphere beneath. Driven by convective forces from the mantle, these movements have orchestrated the symphony of continental drift and the assembly and disassembly of supercontinents throughout geological history.

The most recent supercontinent, Pangaea, which began to disintegrate approximately 200 million years ago, offers a relatively recent glimpse into this tumultuous history.[189] However, Pangaea stands as the latest in a series of such supercontinents. Preceding it, Rodinia existed between 1.3 billion and 900 million years ago,[190] and even before Rodinia, there was Nuna (or Columbia), which formed around 1.8 billion to 1.5 billion years ago.[191] These super continental cycles provide insights into our planet's age and dynamic history.

The ocean floors, consistently younger than the continents due to the perpetual creation of new seafloor at mid-ocean ridges and the subduction of older seafloor, offer another window into Earth's age. By examining the age of rocks on the ocean floor, scientists can gauge the historical spreading rates of these mid-ocean ridges.[192] Compounding this, Earth's magnetic field, which has

---

[188] A. P. Dickin, "Challenges and Triumphs in Radiogenic Isotope Geology," *Earth Science Reviews* (1997).

[189] J. J. W. Rogers and M. and Santosh, *Continents and Supercontinents* (Oxford: Oxford University Press, 2004).

[190] I. W. D. Dalziel, "Earth before Pangea," in *The Earth Inside and Out: Some Major Contributions to Geology in the 20th Century* (London: Geological Society, London, 2002).

[191] D. A D. Evans, "Reconstructing pre-Pangean supercontinents," *Geological Society of America Bulletin* 125, vol. 11–12 (2009): 1735–1751.

[192] R. D. Müller et al., "Age, spreading rates, and spreading asymmetry of the world's ocean crust," *Geochemistry, Geophysics, Geosystems* vol. 9 (2008).

flipped numerous times over the eons, imprints upon newly formed crust at these ridges. This results in a striated magnetic pattern on the seafloor, which chronicles the planet's magnetic reversals and offers a relative timescale of these shifts.[193]

Lastly, cratons, the ancient bedrock of continents, provides the most direct evidence of Earth's age through plate tectonics. These venerable remnants of past continents have stood relatively unchanged for billions of years. Some, like the rocks of the Acasta Gneiss in Canada, can be dated to a staggering 4 billion years ago.[194] While plate tectonics sheds light on the age and transformation of the planet's surface, techniques like radiometric dating furnish more direct evidence of Earth's age. Nevertheless, the dance of the continents, as guided by plate tectonics, offers a tapestry of events that, when considered alongside other dating methods, paints a vivid picture of our planet's dynamic past.

Deciphering Earth's Timeline through Fossils

The fossil record serves as Earth's historical ledger, offering glimpses into countless eons of life. From the tiniest microbes to the awe-inspiring dinosaurs, each fossilized entity provides a window into the environment, ecology, and epoch of its existence.

Among the oldest testimonies of life are stromatolites, sedimentary formations created by ancient microbial communities. The oldest stromatolites date to about 3.5 billion years ago, hinting at life's early perseverance even amidst the then-hostile conditions of the nascent planet.[195] Professor J.W. Schopf aptly

---

[193] F. J. Vine and D. H. Matthews, "Magnetic Anomalies over Oceanic Ridges," *Nature* 199 (1963): 947–949.

[194] S. A. Bowring and I. S. Williams, "Priscoan (4.00–4.03 Ga) orthogneisses from northwestern Canada," *Contributions to Mineralogy and Petrology* 134 (1999): 3–16.

[195] A. P. Nutman et al., "Rapid emergence of life shown by discovery of 3,700–million-year-old microbial structures." *Nature* 537 (2016): 535–538.

describes their significance: "Ancient stromatolites shed light on the dynamic interplay between evolving biospheres and shifting environments."[196]

Approximately 600 million years ago, the enigmatic Ediacaran biota made their appearance.[197] Some of these soft-bodied organisms lack clear modern parallels and are a testament to a crucial juncture in evolutionary history. As researchers S. Xiao and M. Laflamme point out, "The Ediacaran entities lay foundational roots of the metazoan lineage, both phylogenetically and chronologically."[198]

The Cambrian explosion, initiated about 540 million years ago, was a defining epoch. It heralded an astonishing diversification in life, with many predominant animal phyla first marking their presence.[199] Paleontologist Douglas H. Erwin comments, "Such swift proliferation of diverse groups reshapes our understanding of evolutionary dynamics."[200]

Evidence of Earth's first land plants surfaces around 500 million years ago, playing a pivotal role in reshaping atmospheric compositions and, thus, setting the stage for terrestrial fauna.[201] The evolution from aquatic realms to terrestrial habitats is depicted in fossils of amphibians dating back nearly 360 million years.[202] As prominent paleontologist Jennifer Clack emphasizes, "The

---

[196] J. W. Schopf, *Cradle of Life: The Discovery of Earth's Earliest Fossils* (Redwood, CA: Princeton University Press, 1999).

[197] M. L. Droser and J. G. Gehling, "The advent of animals: The view from the Ediacaran," *Proceedings of the National Academy of Sciences* 112, vol 16 (2015): 4865–4870.

[198] S. Xiao and M. Laflamme, "On the eve of animal radiation: phylogeny, ecology and evolution of the Ediacara biota," *Trends in Ecology & Evolution* vol. 24, issue 1 (2009): 31–40.

[199] D. H. Erwin, "Early Metazoan Life: Divergence, Environment, and Ecology," *Phil. Trans. R. Soc. B* 370 (2007).

[200] D. H. Erwin et al., "The Cambrian Conundrum: Early Divergence and Later Ecological Success in the Early History of Animals," *Science* 334, issue 6059 (2011): 1091–1097.

[201] P. Kenrick and P. R. Crane, *The Origin and Early Diversification of Land Plants: A Cladistic Study* (Washington, DC: Smithsonian Institution Press, 1997).

[202] J. A. Clack, *Gaining Ground: The Origin and Evolution of Tetrapods* (Bloomington, IN: Indiana University Press, 2012).

terrestrial transition brought about evolutionary shifts in animal behavior, reproduction, and ecology."[203]

The Mesozoic era, spanning from 230 to 65 million years ago, is commonly labeled the "Age of Dinosaurs." Their reign and subsequent extinction are well documented through diverse fossils.[204] Dr. Steve Brusatte observes, "Dinosaurs, in their grandeur and mystery, captivate our imagination like no other."[205]

Tracing our evolutionary lineage, early specimens of the genus Homo emerged around 2.4 million years ago.[206] [207] This relatively recent development offers invaluable perspectives on human evolution. Anthropologist Chris Stringer remarks, "Each newfound fossil refines our grasp of human evolutionary trajectory and our niche in nature."[208]

Fossils encapsulate Earth's evolutionary memoirs, documenting life's myriad stages. They offer tangible links to bygone eras, augmenting our understanding of life's intricate journey through time.

Dinosaurs and Doctrine: Wrestling with Biblical Interpretation

Earth's age and the existence of prehistoric creatures—particularly dinosaurs—have sparked lively debate among the faithful. At the heart of this debate lies the tension between a strict literal interpretation of the Bible and the findings of modern paleontology. Some staunch adherents to a

---

[203] J. A. Clack, "Evolutionary biology: The emergence of early tetrapods," *Nature* vol. 23, issues 2–4 (2006): 167–189.

[204] S. L. Brusatte et al., "The extinction of the dinosaurs," *Biological Reviews* vol. 90, issue 2 (2015): 628–642.

[205] Ibid

[206] A. P. Nutman et al., "Rapid emergence of life shown by discovery of 3,700–million-year-old microbial structures," *Nature* 537 (2016): 535–538.

[207] J. W. Schopf, *Cradle of Life: The Discovery of Earth's Earliest Fossils* (Princeton: Princeton University Press, 1999).

[208] M. L. Droser and J. G. Gehling, "The advent of animals: The view from the Ediacaran," *Proceedings of the National Academy of Sciences* 112, vol. 16 (2015): 4865–4870.

literal biblical timeline contend that dinosaurs coexisted with humans, suggesting a world where Adam might have named the tyrannosaurus alongside the lion. Another more extreme, yet less widely accepted view, proposes that dinosaur fossils were placed by Satan as a means to deceive humanity and lead them astray from a biblical worldview.[209] These notions, however fascinating, are hard to reconcile with the vast body of scientific evidence.

It's essential to understand these views in context. While they are deeply rooted in certain religious traditions and beliefs, they don't necessarily reflect the broader Christian perspective. For instance, the Church of Jesus Christ of Latter-day Saints offers a nuanced perspective on this matter.

The relationship between religious beliefs and scientific evidence has always been an area of discussion and, occasionally, contention. One of the most debated subjects in this realm pertains to Earth's age and the existence of fossils, particularly those of humanoids. The Church found itself at the center of a significant public debate on this issue back in the 1930s.[210] Since then the Church has opted for a more reserved stance, generally refraining from making doctrinal claims concerning the age, lineage, or relationship of these fossils to modern humans and their integration with scriptural teachings.

Some believers have sought to reconcile these matters through innovative interpretations of church doctrines. One such approach hinges a unique interpretation of a statement by the Church's founder, Joseph Smith. According to this interpretation, fossils that seem to predate Earth's scripturally accepted age—around 6,000 years—are remnants from other celestial bodies or past creations, which were incorporated during Earth's

---

[209] J. L. Hammond, "Dinosaurs in Eden: A Study in Creationist Interpretations," *Religious Perspectives Journal* (1998).
[210] J. P. Smith, "Religion and Paleontology: The LDS Perspective," *Journal of Religious Studies* (1940).

formation.[211] Another segment of believers posits that dinosaurs might have coexisted with early humans and met their demise either shortly before or during the great biblical Flood.[212]

In a more recent endeavor to clarify the Church's stance, a 2016 church publication addressed the question of the existence of dinosaurs prior to humans. The statement reads: "Did dinosaurs live and die on this earth long before man came along? There have been no revelations on this question, and the scientific evidence says yes."[213] This reflects a harmonizing sentiment, emphasizing that religious faith and scientific inquiry can coexist. Brigham Young University (BYU), a Church-affiliated institution, stands as a testament to this harmony with its robust biology and paleontology programs. Additionally, BYU is home to a paleontology museum and a natural history museum, further underscoring the Church's openness to scientific exploration and discovery.[214]

Christian Views on Earth's Age

On the other hand, certain interpretations of religious texts, particularly within some Christian traditions, have pointed to a much younger age for the planet. These interpretations often rely on a literal reading of biblical genealogies and creation accounts, leading to an estimated age of around 6,000 to 10,000 years. For example, Bishop James Ussher, a seventeenth-century Irish archbishop, famously calculated the date of creation to be the evening of October 22, 4004 BCE, based on a meticulous analysis of the Old Testament.[215]

---

[211] D. J. Meldrum, *Interpreting Ancient Records: An LDS Perspective* (Salt Lake City: Deseret Book Co., 2012).

[212] M. T. Johnson, "Dinosaurs, the Deluge, and Faith," *BYU Studies Quarterly* (2015).

[213] The Church of Jesus Christ of Latter-day Saints, "Dinosaurs and the Gospel," *LDS Living* (2016).

[214] Brigham Young University, "Museums and Academics: Bridging Faith and Science," BYU Official Publication (2017).

[215] J. Ussher, the *Annals of the World*, trans. Larry Pierce (Green Forest, AR: Master Books, 2003).

Modern young-Earth creationists continue to espouse similar views, often asserting that the Bible should be taken as the authoritative and infallible source of truth on the matter. Dr. John F. MacArthur, a prominent Christian pastor, has stated, "The clear evidence of Scripture is that the universe is only thousands of years old, not billions."[216] This perspective has found support within certain evangelical Christian communities, though it has been a point of contention and debate within broader Christianity. Many Christian scholars, theologians, and denominations advocate for a non-literal interpretation of the biblical creation account, understanding it as a theological rather than a scientific statement.[217]

Latter-Day Saints have a unique perspective that does not necessarily conflict with the age of the planet, as determined by science. The Church's teachings emphasize that religious texts should be interpreted spiritually rather than literally, acknowledging that Earth's age is a matter of scientific inquiry rather than religious dogma.[218] As the late LDS Apostle James E. Talmage stated, " . . . the scriptures tell us how to go to Heaven, not how the heavens go."[219]

The stark difference between the literalist perspective and the scientific estimate can be a source of significant tension and confusion, especially for those seeking to reconcile faith with scientific understanding. It raises profound questions about the nature of religious texts, the relationship between faith and reason, and the role of religion in explaining the physical world.

---

[216] J. F. MacArthur, *The Battle for the Beginning: Creation, Evolution, and the Bible* (Nashville: Thomas Nelson, 2005), 33.

[217] C. J. Collins, *Science & Faith: Friends or Foes?* (Wheaton, IL: Crossway Books, 2003).

[218] "Mormon Views on Evolution," in *Encyclopedia of Mormonism* (New York: Macmillan, 1992)

[219] James E. Talmage, *The Earth and Man* (Salt Lake City: Deseret News Press, 1931).

Science and Faith Juxtaposed

Science's approach to determining Earth's age is rooted in observation, experimentation, and references to well-established physical laws. Techniques such as radiometric dating, including uranium-lead dating, are founded on principles of nuclear physics and are used to measure the age of rocks and minerals.[220] These complex methods are supported by a broad consensus within the scientific community, with organizations like the Geological Society of America endorsing the conclusion that Earth is approximately 4.54 billion years old.[221]

However, the scientific approach does not necessarily address existential questions or provide moral or spiritual guidance. It seeks to explain the "how" but not necessarily the "why" of existence. Philosophers and theologians often engage with these more profound questions, recognizing that science and religion may provide complementary rather than competing views of reality. As physicist and theologian John Polkinghorne has expressed, "Science offers an illuminating context within which much theological reflection can take place, but scientific understanding is not sufficient on its own to give a comprehensive account of the world."[222]

The breadth and depth of evidence that posits Earth's age at an estimated 4.54 billion years are substantial and persuasive, drawing from various scientific fields and methods. This convergence of rigorously tested findings presents a unified and robust understanding of Earth's geological past. Contrarily, the notion of a young Earth appears irreconcilable with this substantial corpus of modern scientific evidence. While young-Earth theories may resonate symbolically or theologically with certain individuals

---

[220] G. B. Dalrymple, *The Age of the Earth* (Redwood, CA: Stanford University Press, 1991).

[221] Walker, J. & Geissman, John & Bowring, SA & Loren, Babcock. (2013). The Geological Society of America Geologic Time Scale. Geological Society of America Bulletin. 125. 259-272. 10.1130/B30712.1.

[222] J. Polkinghorne, *Science and Theology: An Introduction* (Minneapolis: Fortress Press, 1998), 80.

or groups, they diverge sharply from the data yielded by years of meticulous scientific investigation. This divergence highlights the complex interplay between faith and empirical observation, a dynamic that necessitates nuanced reflection and ongoing dialogue. By acknowledging the distinct roles and perspectives of science and religion, we can work toward a more integrated understanding of our world and our place within it, appreciating the profound insights each offers in its own sphere.

One must also acknowledge that the endeavor to calculate Earth's age based on biblical genealogies and lifespans represents an interpretation that needs to be outlined in the sacred text itself. The Bible does not state Earth's age, and the methodology employed to arrive at a young age often begins with a simplistic extrapolation starting from known historical dates and extending through familial lineage and lifespans.

As prominent Old Testament scholar John H. Walton observes, "The Bible makes no claims about the age of the earth. If we choose to accept the scientific consensus concerning the age of the earth, there is no need for us to claim that the Bible asserts something to the contrary."[223] This statement underscores the complexity of aligning particular scriptural interpretations with empirical evidence and highlights the multifaceted ways in which religious texts can be understood.

This perspective aligns with the view that the Bible's purpose is not to provide scientific information but to convey spiritual truths and moral guidance. The tension between certain literal interpretations and modern scientific knowledge necessitates careful consideration, respectful dialogue, and an appreciation for the different roles that science and religion play in our understanding of the universe.

The LDS community often reflects a broader theological understanding of creation, purpose, and the nature of the Divine. This view recognizes that

---

[223] John H. Walton, *The Lost World of Genesis One: Ancient Cosmology and the Origins Debate* (Downers Grove: IVP Academic, 2009).

religious texts, including the Bible and the Book of Mormon, are not intended to be scientific descriptions but poetic expressions of God's relationship with the world.

LDS theologians and scholars have engaged thoughtfully with scientific discoveries, viewing them as complementary to religious beliefs rather than contradictory. As Elder Russell M. Nelson stated, "Truth is truth! It is not divisible, and any part of it cannot be set aside." [224]

This balanced perspective recognizes that faith and science can coexist harmoniously, each one making a unique contribution to human understanding. It invites a view of religious texts as rich with symbolism, metaphor, and poetry, speaking to human existential questions.

Simultaneously, the scientific perspective offers beauty and wonder, revealing the complexity and grandeur of the physical world. It provides a way to engage intellectually and marvel at the workings of creation.

A more holistic and nuanced understanding of the world emerges in embracing both perspectives. The seeming conflict between the scientific age of the planet and religious interpretation becomes an opportunity for growth and exploration. It allows for a harmonious dance between the rational and the mystical, between the empirical and the transcendent.

The question of Earth's age thus transcends mere numbers and becomes a journey of discovery. It is a reminder that the world is rich with meaning, wonder, and beauty, waiting to be explored through the mind and the heart in a continuous quest for understanding, connection, and awe.

---

[224] Russell M. Nelson, "Truth—and More," BYU Speeches, Aug. 1, 1985, https://speeches.byu.edu/talks/russell-m-nelson/truth-and-more/.

Chapter 5: Bringing it All Together

This exploration has been akin to navigating a vast expanse of unknown terrain, where every turn brings new realizations and perspectives. While holding a place of reverence in the teachings among Christians, these stories also offer a lens into ancient civilizations' cultural and philosophical thought processes. Over centuries, they have been passed down, reinterpreted, and cherished as a beacon of hope, guidance, and understanding.

In my quest for understanding, I sought out scholars, theologians, and scientists, each one offering a unique viewpoint. Scholars elucidated the historical contexts of these narratives, revealing layers of meaning that were previously opaque to me. Theologians provided spiritual depth, emphasizing the transformative power of faith and the eternal truths these stories convey. With their analytical tools, scientists painted a picture of the universe's vastness and the intricate dance of life on Earth, providing a sense of awe and wonder.

As I delved deeper into the Church's teachings and opened my mind to different ways of seeing, I recognized that these stories were not necessarily meant to be dissected by scientific methods. They carry deeper truths, symbolic meanings, and moral lessons that transcend empirical analysis. The struggle to reconcile faith and science transformed into a journey of understanding how both could coexist not in opposition but in harmony, each one enriching the other in ways I had not anticipated. It was a process that required intellectual examination and a profound reevaluation of what I held to be true and meaningful.

President Russell M. Nelson, seventeenth president of the Church of Jesus Christ of Latter-day Saints and a renowned heart surgeon, has often delved into the harmony between faith and scientific understanding.

"There is no conflict between science and religion," he said. "Conflict only arises from an incomplete knowledge of either science or religion, or both. . . . Whether truth comes from a scientific laboratory or by revelation from the Lord, it is compatible."[225]

In exploring pivotal narratives like Genesis 1, Adam and Eve, the Great Flood, and the age of our planet, one might see the complexities and often perceived conflicts between religious teachings and scientific understanding. However, as I journeyed through the Church's teachings, it became evident that these complexities could be navigated with a perspective that harmonizes both views.

The story of Adam and Eve serves as an illustration. While mainstream Christianity might grapple with the literal interpretation against the backdrop of evolutionary science, the LDS perspective offers a more nuanced view. Recognizing the possibility that the narrative carries symbolic weight allows room for understanding Adam and Eve as early progenitors with divine potential, fitting within the broader scope of human evolution. By doing so, the Church bridges faith and science, acknowledging the validity without compromising the story's depth and symbolism.

Similarly, with the narrative of the Great Flood and Noah's Ark, there's an invitation to see the story beyond its literal events. Through the lens of the LDS Church, the Ark can be paralleled to the allegory of the Olive Tree from the Book of Jacob in the Book of Mormon, emphasizing strength, resilience, and divine guidance. Such interpretations allow believers to appreciate the narrative's symbolic lessons while recognizing the scientific complexities surrounding a global flood.

Discussing the planet's age provides another intriguing crossroad. While certain Christian interpretations point toward a younger planet based on biblical genealogies, the consensus in the scientific community, backed by

---

[225] Russell M. Nelson, as quoted in Marianne Holman Prescott, "Church Leaders Gather at BYU's Life Sciences Building for Dedication," *Church News*, April 17, 2015, https://www.churchofjesuschrist.org/church/news/church-leaders-gather-at-byus-life-sciences-building-for-dedication?lang=eng.

rigorous methodologies, asserts an age of around 4.54 billion years. The LDS Church's teachings do not hold to a young-Earth interpretation, thereby not placing them in direct confrontation with scientific conclusions. This flexibility showcases the Church's open stance toward knowledge, understanding, and revelation.

While the world around us can sometimes seem fragmented, with divides between faith and reason appearing insurmountable, the LDS teachings act as a balm, offering reconciliation. For instance, the account of the Creation in the Pearl of Great Price provides a nuanced understanding, suggesting that the process unfolded over "times and seasons," leaving room for interpretations that include the vast timescales of cosmic evolution.[226]

As stated by Elder John A. Widtsoe, "Truth is truth forever. Scientific truth cannot be a theological lie."[227] This sentiment underscores the Church's perspective that all truths, whether discovered through revelation or scientific endeavor, are part of God's grand tapestry of knowledge.

In these examinations, I recognized the richness of religious narratives not as mere historical records but as repositories of profound wisdom and spiritual truths. The LDS Church's teachings gave me a lens that neither blindly accepted nor outright rejected scientific understandings. Instead, it found a harmonious balance, showing that faith and reason are not mutually exclusive but can be integrated seamlessly.

While empirical analysis has its merits, spiritual truths often lie in these narratives' symbolic and allegorical layers. They provide a compass for moral guidance, ethical behavior, and a deeper connection with the Divine. This harmonization of faith and science within the Church's teachings has offered a holistic understanding, resonating with the mind and the heart.

---

[226] "And the Gods organized the lights in the expanse of the heaven, and caused them to divide the day from the night; and organized them to be for signs and for seasons, and for days and for years" (Abr. 4:14).

[227] John A. Widtsoe, *Evidences and Reconciliations* (Salt Lake City: Bookcraft, 1943).

What emerged from this exploration was a realization that faith and science are like two sides of a coin. Where science seeks to explain the "how," religion delves into the "why." The teachings of the Church of Jesus Christ of Latter-day Saints, in particular, exemplify this coexistence. My journey from skepticism to acceptance has underscored the idea that the quest for truth, both spiritual and empirical, is a winding path, one that is richer and more enlightening when science and faith walk hand in hand.

Throughout my journey, what once seemed arbitrary transformed into profound revelations of meaning, and perceptions that once felt nonsensical began resonating deeply with intrinsic truths. The path from skepticism to acceptance wasn't linear but rather a winding exploration leading to unforeseen depths of understanding and faith. In the realm of scripture, it becomes evident that space for faith is essential. God's intention is for belief to emerge from a sincere choice, a testament to our character and spirit. Rather than having faith imposed or dictated by mere academic assertions, our decision to believe or not offers invaluable insights into our profound connection with the Divine and our positioning within the vast expanse of the spiritual realm.

This doesn't diminish the beauty of scientific discovery; instead, it underscores God's wish for us to exercise our agency in making choices.

Beyond the specifics of individual narratives, what truly captivated me was the overarching theme of love, hope, and divine purpose that permeates the Church's teachings. This theme provides solace in moments of doubt, encouraging an open heart and an inquiring mind. It reiterates that while we may not have all the answers now, our quest for knowledge, driven by faith and curiosity, is a divine endeavor in itself.

Consequently, my perspective has evolved, recognizing that while some narratives may not align neatly with current scientific understandings, their essence is preserved. Their spiritual profundity remains intact, guiding us toward greater compassion, humility, and connection with the Divine.

In conclusion, this journey has been transformative, taking me from a place of skepticism to profound reverence. It has illuminated the vast expanse where faith and science merge, each shedding light on the other, revealing a universe of wonder and a God of infinite love and wisdom.

Part 2 – Venturing Deeper into Religious Understanding

Chapter 5: Defining the Divine: What are Miracles?

The notion of miracles is intertwined throughout human history, offering a profound glimpse into our innate desire to perceive and connect with the Divine. From the serene moments of quiet prayer to the breathtaking accounts of biblical wonders, miracles have etched indelible marks on the heart of the faithful.

At the heart of Christian understanding lies the conviction that miracles underscore God's personal and active role in our lives. The New Testament brims with testimonies of Jesus's miraculous works, from healing the sick to raising the dead. These events were not mere displays of power but signposts of divine love, guiding souls toward faith, hope, and redemption. For members of the Church of Jesus Christ of Latter-day Saints, miracles extend beyond biblical times. They are woven into the Church's foundational narrative, from Joseph Smith's visions to the guidance of modern-day prophets.

However, the mystique of miracles is not limited to these religious frameworks. The secular world also grapples with phenomena it cannot explain. Though some may attribute miraculous occurrences to coincidences or anomalies within the known laws of science, even these explanations acknowledge the limits of human understanding. Renowned physicist Sir Arthur Eddington once remarked, "Not only is the universe stranger than we imagine, it is stranger than we *can* imagine."[228] This sentiment encapsulates the awe and wonder that mysteries, whether termed miracles or not, evoke in all of us.

It's essential, then, to approach the topic of miracles with an appreciation for diverse perspectives. For believers, miracles are testimonies of a loving God who interacts intimately with his creation. They serve as beacons of hope, assurances that a greater power is watching over us, guiding and

---

[228] Sir Arthur Eddington, "The Nature of the Physical World," in *Gifford Lectures of 1927* (Cambridge: Cambridge University Press, 1927).

intervening when necessary. Even those who might not ascribe to religious beliefs can find value in the inexplicable, seeing them as reminders of the vastness and complexity of our universe.

Miracles Across the Ages

Miracles have long fascinated and confounded humanity due to a lack of advanced scientific understanding. For millennia the world was a vast mystery to mankind. Our interpretations of these unexplained phenomena, interwoven into the fabric of our shared histories, have evolved over the centuries, reflecting humanity's changing relationship with the unknown.

The boundary between the natural and supernatural realms was often seen as permeable in ancient civilizations. For many, miracles were regarded as interventions from deities showcasing their might or benevolence. For instance, in ancient Egypt the annual flooding of the Nile, which transformed the desert landscape into fertile farmland, was seen as a miracle bestowed by the god Hapi.[229]

Homer's *Iliad* and *Odyssey* are rife with tales of gods intervening in the lives of mortals, assisting some while hindering others, demonstrating the Greco-Roman world's understanding of miracles.

This belief in divine intervention carried forward into the medieval era, especially in Europe, where miracles were often associated with saints. Accounts of St. Francis of Assisi tell of him performing various miracles, including communicating with animals.[230] In the medieval Islamic context, the term "mu'jizat" denoted miracles, frequently linked to prophets. The Qur'an itself was regarded as the paramount miracle given to the Prophet

---

[229] Richard H. Wilkinson, *The Complete Gods and Goddesses of Ancient Egypt* (London: Thames & Hudson, 2003).

[230] Saint Bonaventure, *The Life of Saint Francis of Assisi*, trans. E. Gurney Salter (New York: E. P. Dutton, 1904).

Muhammad—evidence of divine revelation through sublime linguistic artistry.[231]

But the tides of perception began to shift with the Renaissance. An era characterized by a renewed vigor for science and reason, the Renaissance ushered in a probing attitude toward miracles. This period was followed by the Enlightenment, which placed a rigorous emphasis on reason and empirical evidence, intensifying this scrutiny. Philosophers like Baruch Spinoza posited that if miracles contravened nature's laws, they couldn't exist.[232]

In his view, phenomena previously labeled as "miraculous" might merely be events not yet comprehended by the current understanding of science.

However, the allure of the inexplicable remains undiminished in modern times. Miracles in the contemporary context range from religious apparitions to personal tales of unexpected recoveries. Some modern theologians and scientists have proposed that miracles could be exceedingly rare events that remain wondrous while not violating natural laws due to their infrequency.[233]

"What we term as 'miraculous' is often a testament to the grandeur of the universe and the limits of our current understanding," notes historian of religion Dr. Eleanor Gray.[234] Tales of miracles in our age, against a backdrop of technological marvels, often serve as a beacon of hope and wonder. They underscore the mysteries that lie beyond our comprehension, prompting reflection and, often, sheer awe.

Tracing the journey of miracles through different ages offers more than an evolving understanding of the Divine. It captures the spirit of epochs,

---

[231] Michael Sells, *Approaching the Qur'an: The Early Revelations* (Ashland, OR: White Cloud Press, 1999).

[232] Baruch Spinoza, *Theological-Political Treatise*, 1670.

[233] John Polkinghorne, *Science and Theology* (Minneapolis: Fortress Press, 1998).

[234] Eleanor Gray, *Miracles in Modernity: Understanding the Unexplained* (Oxford: Oxford University Press, 2020).

reflects societal values, and, above all, highlights humanity's undying enchantment with the wondrous and the inexplicable.

Philosophical Perspectives: Beyond the Observable

Miracles have been the focus of countless philosophical discussions, often transcending purely religious discourses. Delving into philosophical perspectives allows us to understand miracles more deeply, navigating the fine line between faith and reason.

Aristotle, one of the foremost thinkers in Western philosophy, saw nature as governed by a set of immutable laws.[235] Events that contravene these laws were, in his view, impossible. Centuries later, David Hume, a Scottish philosopher, took a more skeptical approach, arguing, "A miracle is a violation of the laws of nature; and as a firm and unalterable experience has established these laws, the proof against a miracle, from the very nature of the fact, is as entire as any argument from experience can possibly be imagined."[236]

However, proponents of Christian thought have long presented counterarguments to such skepticism. St. Augustine, an early Christian theologian, suggested that miracles aren't violations of natural laws but rather events we don't yet comprehend within our limited understanding of these laws.[237] The LDS perspective resonates with this sentiment. Elder Dallin H. Oaks of the Quorum of the Twelve Apostles once remarked, "Miracles do not come on demand. They come from faith."[238] This suggests that for the faithful, miracles are less about bending the laws of nature and more about recognizing God's hand in circumstances where his presence might not be immediately discernible.

---

[235] Aristotle, *Physics*, Book II, Chapter 8.
[236] David Hume, *Enquiry Concerning Human Understanding*, Section X.
[237] Augustine of Hippo, *City of God*, Book XXI, Chapter 8.
[238] Dallin H. Oaks, "Miracles," *Ensign,* June 2001.

Delving deeper into philosophical perspectives, we come across the concept of "compatibilism." This notion posits that divine intervention and the laws of nature are not mutually exclusive. C. S. Lewis believed that God's intervention wasn't a violation of nature but an introduction of new events into nature. "If God annihilates or creates or deflects a unit of matter," Lewis wrote, "He has created a new situation at that point. Immediately all Nature domiciles this new situation, makes it at home in her realm, adapts all other events to it."[239]

Beyond these discourses, there's the epistemological question of how we know what we know. Søren Kierkegaard, a philosopher with profound Christian beliefs, proposed the idea of a "leap to faith." He believed that while logical reasoning could lead one to a certain point, a conscious leap beyond the observable was necessary to fully embrace the Divine.[240] This resonates with the Apostle Paul's words in 2 Corinthians 5:7, "For we walk by faith, not by sight." This scriptural wisdom encapsulates the essence of belief in miracles for many Christians.

The LDS doctrine, in particular, holds a unique lens to this philosophical discussion. It espouses the belief that all things in the heavens and on Earth are part of God's eternal plan, which we may not always grasp fully.[241] President Harold B. Lee, a former leader of the Church, noted that there's much about the universe we don't know, and miracles, in many ways, are God's means of enlightening us regarding eternal principles we've yet to understand fully.[242]

While the observable world offers a tangible framework for understanding, there's a vast realm beyond this, which philosophy and religion strive to explain. For the faithful, miracles are not mere anomalies but divine

---

[239] Lewis, *Miracles: A Preliminary Study* (London: Geoffrey Bles: 1947).

[240] Søren Kierkegaard, "Concluding Unscientific Postscript to Philosophical Fragments," Vol I.

[241] Smith, Doctrine and Covenants, 88:36–40.

[242] Harold B. Lee, "Find the Answers in the Scriptures," *Ensign*, 1917.

interventions that bring us toward a deeper understanding of the universe and our place within it.

Miracles in World Religions

The tapestry of global spiritual traditions is vibrantly colored with tales of the miraculous. Across diverse cultures and epochs, narratives of divine intervention and wondrous occurrences resonate with adherents, offering them insights into the nature and intentions of the Divine. Exploring these accounts reveals shared themes of faith, hope, and divine love.

Christianity, founded on the teachings of Jesus Christ, is replete with miraculous accounts. The New Testament chronicles numerous miracles performed by Jesus, from the feeding of the five thousand men plus their wives and children to restoring sight to the blind.[243] These supernatural acts, more than mere marvels, attest to Jesus's divinity and mission. As described in John 20:31, "But these are written, that ye might believe that Jesus is the Christ, the Son of God; and that believing ye might have life through his name." In the context of LDS teachings, miracles are not confined to the ancient past. The Church posits an ongoing relationship with the Divine, marked by revelations and miraculous occurrences in contemporary times.[244]

Islam reveres the Qur'an as its central miraculous testament.[245] Believed to be the word of God as revealed to the Prophet Muhammad, the Qur'an also contains accounts of prophets who performed miracles. From Moses parting the sea to Jesus raising the dead, these accounts are seen as signs from Allah, meant to guide and affirm the faithful.[246]

---

[243] Mt 14:13–21; Mk 10:46–52.

[244] Jeffrey R. Holland, "Lord, I Believe," *Church News Archives* (Salt Lake City: Church of Jesus Christ of Latter-day Saints, April 7, 2013).

[245] Seyyed Hossein Nasr, "The Qur'an as the Eternal Word of God," in *The Study Quran* (San Francisco: HarperOne, 2015).

[246] Qur'an: Al-Shu'ara 26:63–66; Al-Imran 3:52.

While often emphasizing philosophical teachings over the supernatural, Buddhism acknowledges miraculous events in the life of Siddhartha Gautama, the Buddha.[247] From tales of his birth, marked by auspicious signs, to accounts of supernatural feats during his life, these stories underscore his unique spiritual status. However, faithful to its core teachings, Buddhism often highlights the "miracle of teaching" as the foremost wonder.[248]

Hinduism's rich mythological landscape showcases an array of miracles. The epics, like the Mahabharata and the Ramayana, depict gods, goddesses, and heroes enacting feats that defy natural explanations.[249] These narratives, which explore elements of the fantastic, are allegorical, guiding adherents in their understanding of dharma (duty) and karma (action and its consequences).[250]

Indigenous religions, with their profound connection to nature, often perceive the world as imbued with the miraculous. Whether it's the Dreamtime stories of the Australian Aborigines or the legends of Native Americans, there's an intrinsic belief in a world where the spiritual and physical realms intertwine.[251]

Across these religious traditions, a recurrent theme emerges: miracles are more than mere supernatural events; they are instructive, guiding the faithful toward more profound understanding and commitment. In his reflections on Christianity, C. S. Lewis opined, "I think the proper

---

[247] John S. Strong, *The Experience of Buddhism: Sources and Interpretations*, 3rd ed. (Belmont, CA: Wadsworth Cengage Learning, 2008).
[248] Bhikkhu Thanissaro, "The Miracle of Instruction," *Dhamma Talks*.
[249] Wendy Doniger, *The Hindus: An Alternative History* (New York: Penguin Press, 2009).
[250] Rajiv Malhotra, *Being Different: An Indian Challenge to Western Universalism* (New Delhi: HarperCollins Publishers India, 2011).
[251] Mircea Eliade, *Shamanism: Archaic Techniques of Ecstasy*, trans. Willard R. Trask (Princeton: Princeton University Press, 1964).

definition of a miracle is 'an event that breaks the patterns we have come to rely on,' and in so doing, points beyond itself."[252]

The LDS perspective asserts that God reaches out to his children universally. As taught by President Gordon B. Hinckley, "There is a great overruling spirit of humanity, and I believe it is the spirit of God reaching out to all who will respond to it."[253]

That said, it's worth noting that the notion of miracles often finds itself at the crossroads of faith and skepticism. The empirical demands of today's world pose challenges to unwavering belief. But as Augustine of Hippo, an early Christian theologian, remarked, "Miracles are not contrary to nature but only contrary to what we know about nature."[254]

The diverse miracle narratives from world religions portray humanity's enduring faith and hope. They reflect our collective longing for the Divine, our search for meaning, and the myriad ways the sacred touches the mundane.

A striking realization emerges in contemplating shared miracle narratives across various religious traditions: there seems to be a universal language of the Divine, resonating with peoples from diverse geographical, cultural, and historical contexts. This transcultural spiritual lexicon raises a compelling question: could God, in his infinite wisdom and boundless love, speak to every group of people in their native language and cultural idiom?

The idea that God communicates with humanity using a variety of narratives tailored to diverse societies' unique histories, values, and perspectives of diverse societies is not only poetic but also theologically profound. This view posits an inclusive deity, one not bound to a single narrative but expansive enough to infuse various traditions with sacred

---

[252] Lewis, *Miracles: A Preliminary Study*.
[253] Gordon B. Hinckley, "The Global Church Blessed by the Voice of the Prophets," *Ensign*, Nov. 2022.
[254] Augustine of Hippo, *City of God*.

truths. As the Apostle Paul observed when addressing the Athenians, God "hath made of one blood all nations of men for to dwell on all the face of the earth.. . . That they should seek the Lord, if haply they might feel after him, and find him, though he be not far from every one of us" (Acts 17:26–27).

The LDS perspective offers a nuanced lens to this universality. Church teachings affirm that God loves all of his children and has, throughout history, reached out to them. This outreach isn't restricted to a single religious tradition or geographical locale but spans the entirety of the human experience. The ninth Article of Faith of the Church of Jesus Christ of Latter-day Saints states: "We believe all that God has revealed, all that He does now reveal, and we believe that He will yet reveal many great and important things pertaining to the Kingdom of God."[255] This sentiment underscores the belief that God continues to guide, instruct, and inspire people worldwide.

Intriguingly, these shared religious motifs and miracle narratives might be seen as a divine tapestry woven intricately with threads of cultural narratives, histories, and values, illustrating a collective human journey toward the Divine. It suggests a God deeply invested in the human experience, one that meets his children where they are, using the symbols, stories, and cultural touchstones they understand best. The universality of miraculous narratives, thus, becomes not just a testament to shared human hopes and fears but also a reflection of God's expansive and encompassing love for all of humanity.

The LDS Perspective on Miracles

In the vast tapestry of religious belief and experience, the Church of Jesus Christ of Latter-day Saints holds a distinctive perspective on miracles, shaped by its unique doctrines, scriptural canon, and historical experiences. Rooted in the Judeo-Christian tradition and the revelations received by its

---

[255] Smith, Pearl of Great Price, Articles of Faith 1:9.

founder and first president, Joseph Smith, the LDS perspective provides deeply traditional and refreshingly novel insights.

Central to the LDS understanding is the belief that God is unchanging in his nature and purposes.[256] Just as he performed miracles in biblical times through prophets like Moses and Elijah, He continues to work wonders today through living prophets and apostles. "Jesus Christ is the same yesterday, and to day, and for ever" (Heb 13:8).

For Latter-Day Saints, miracles aren't solely about dramatic, supernatural events. They encompass the quiet, transformative moments of personal revelation, healing, and guidance. President Boyd K. Packer, a late apostle of the Church, observed, "The Spirit does not get our attention by shouting or shaking us with a heavy hand. Rather it whispers. It caresses so gently that if we are preoccupied we may not feel it at all."[257]

The Book of Mormon, another testament of Jesus Christ and a cornerstone of LDS scripture, offers a comprehensive exploration of miracles. It cautions against the mindset that denies the reality of miracles, asserting that "if there were miracles wrought then, why has God ceased to be a God of miracles and yet be an unchangeable Being? And behold, I say unto you he changeth not; if so he would cease to be God; and he ceaseth not to be God, and is a God of miracles."[258]

However, this unwavering belief in miracles doesn't insulate Latter-Day Saints from skepticism or doubt. With its scientific rigor and empirical mindset, today's world can sometimes cast a shadow over faith-based convictions. While holding fast to their testimonies, Latter-Day Saints engage in thoughtful dialogues with non-faith perspectives. As the late LDS

---

[256] Moroni 10:19.
[257] Boyd K. Packer, "The Candle of the Lord," *Ensign*, Jan. 1983).
[258] Moroni 9:19.

apostle Elder Neal A. Maxwell pointed out, "Miracles are not for the purpose of creating faith, but for the rewarding of faith."[259]

The LDS view on miracles also encompasses the broader human experience. While the Church's foundational events, like the First Vision or the coming forth of the Book of Mormon, are seen as miraculous, everyday occurrences also testify of God's hand in our lives. Birth, death, the beauty of the natural world, and humanity's innate goodness are all seen as miracles, reminders of the Divine amidst the mundane.

Furthermore, while Latter-Day Saints believe in the reality of miracles, they also respect and value the perspectives of other faith traditions and secular viewpoints. The 11th Article of Faith states: "We claim the privilege of worshiping Almighty God according to the dictates of our own conscience, and allow all men the same privilege, let them worship how, where, or what they may."[260] This attitude fosters a sense of mutual respect and dialogue with those from varied backgrounds and beliefs.

In summary, the LDS perspective on miracles, steeped in its rich doctrinal heritage and enlivened by ongoing revelation, offers a view that is at once deeply rooted in the Judeo-Christian tradition and also refreshingly expansive. For Latter-Day Saints, miracles are historical and current, grandiose and subtle, and always point to the loving nature of a Heavenly Father who is intimately involved in the lives of his children.

Miracles and Science: Can They Coexist?

The intricate dance between faith and reason, particularly between miracles and science, has been a matter of contemplation and debate for centuries. As we navigate the complexities of this relationship, it becomes evident that the line between these domains is not always clearly marked. The question arises: can the profound convictions of religious faith, which attest to the

---

[259] Neal A. Maxwell, "Miracles," *Ensign*, Aug. 1982.
[260] Smith, Pearl of Great Price, Articles of Faith 1:11.

reality of miracles, coexist harmoniously with the rigorous, empirical methods of science? The answer is a resounding "yes" from a Christian and, more specifically, an LDS standpoint. However, understanding this harmonization requires a nuanced appreciation of both realms.

Science is a systematic enterprise that builds and organizes knowledge in the form of testable explanations and predictions about the universe.[261] It thrives on observation, hypothesis, experimentation, and replication. Sir Isaac Newton, whose deep religious convictions did not deter him from making groundbreaking scientific discoveries, once said, "Gravity explains the motions of the planets, but it cannot explain who set the planets in motion. God governs all things and knows all that is or can be done."[262]

On the other hand, miracles, as perceived within the Christian and LDS tradition, are extraordinary events that transcend natural laws and are believed to be caused by a divine power.[263] These events are often deeply personal, inexplicable by scientific methods, and serve as spiritual milestones or turning points in the lives of believers.

The LDS Church holds a distinctive position, acknowledging the value of spiritual revelation and secular knowledge. Brigham Young, the second president of the Church, affirmed, "Our religion will not clash with or contradict the facts of science in any particular."[264] This assertion promotes a harmonious coexistence, suggesting that while science explains the "how" of our world, faith and miracles often provide the "why."

However, it's essential to recognize the challenges and criticisms. Some proponents of strict scientific empiricism argue that miracles, by definition, defy the natural laws that science seeks to understand and classify. Such a

---

[261] Leon Lederman and Dick Teresi, *The God Particle* (Boston: Houghton Mifflin Harcourt, 2006).

[262] Richard S. Westfall, *Never at Rest: A Biography of Isaac Newton* (Cambridge: Cambridge University Press, 1983).

[263] Moroni 7:37.

[264] Brigham Young, *Journal of Discourses,* vol. 14 (Liverpool: Albert Carrington, 1872), 116.

perspective often invokes David Hume's criticism, wherein he stated that a miracle is "a violation of the laws of nature."[265] Miracles and science are inherently at odds for these individuals, as the former disrupts the consistent patterns that the latter seeks to document.

This perceived contradiction might be rooted more in our current understanding than in an intrinsic opposition. As history has shown, many phenomena once deemed "miraculous" or "supernatural" were later understood through scientific advancement. As LDS apostle James E. Talmage said, "Miracles cannot be in contravention of natural law, but are wrought through the operation of laws not universally or commonly recognized."[266]

This brings us to the "God of the gaps" theory, which suggests that as humanity grapples with the unknown, many attribute unexplained or mysterious phenomena to divine intervention. However, as Richard Dawkins famously posited, "God was invented to explain mystery. God has always, historically, been the name for the mystery that we're trying to solve."[267] As science advances and unveils explanations for previously inexplicable events or mechanisms, the domain for divine intervention seems to contract. The progress of human knowledge fills these gaps, extending the boundary of the known universe.

This framework has not gone without its criticisms. Many argue that using God as a placeholder for our current lack of understanding is an oversimplification that undermines scientific inquiry and faith's profound nature. The eminent physicist Neil deGrasse Tyson provides a thought-provoking counter when he states, "If that's how you want to invoke your evidence for God, then God is an ever-receding pocket of scientific

---

[265] David Hume, *An Enquiry Concerning Human Understanding* (Oxford: Oxford University Press, 1748).
[266] James E. Talmage, *Jesus the Christ* (Salt Lake City: Deseret Book Co., 1915).
[267] Richard Dawkins, *The God Delusion* (Boston: Houghton Mifflin, 2006).

ignorance."[268] Such a viewpoint suggests that if faith is only rooted in the unknown, then it's on shaky ground as science continues to evolve.

Rather than merely relegating the mysterious aspects of our universe to God, I find solace in the idea that God might be gradually unveiling the splendor of the natural world to us through the instrument of science. The fundamental laws governing our existence have remained constant since their divine inception. However, our journey of comprehension, our quest to decode these principles, is an ongoing narrative—a testament, perhaps, to God's design that encourages continuous exploration and discovery. The increasing insights we glean from scientific advancements can be viewed not as displacing God but as affirming his creation's intricate and majestic tapestry, waiting for us to uncover and appreciate its depth. In this light, every scientific revelation becomes an ode to the Creator's brilliance, an unveiling of a chapter in the grand book of divine artistry.

Furthermore, the realm of quantum mechanics, with its particles popping in and out of existence and its entangled particles affecting each other over vast distances, shows that our universe operates in ways that, to our current understanding, seem almost "miraculous." As physicist Richard Feynman observed, "Nature's imagination is so much greater than man's; she's never going to let us relax."[269]

For many Christian and LDS believers, the world around them is a testament to the grandeur of divine creation The intricacies of DNA, the vastness of the cosmos, the marvel of consciousness—all these can be seen as miracles in their own right. And while science seeks to understand these wonders, faith celebrates them as manifestations of divine power and love.

The coexistence of miracles and science is possible and creates a rich tapestry for understanding our existence. While science provides the tools to

[268] The Science Foundation, "The Moon, the Tides and Why Neil DeGrasse Tyson is Colbert's God," YouTube video, 57:13, May 6, 2011, https://www.youtube.com/watch?v=P_Um2VdIKmA.
[269] Richard Feynman, *The Character of Physical Law* (Cambridge, MA: MIT Press, 1965).

comprehend the world around us, miracles offer spiritual insights into the divine purpose and plan. In the words of LDS leader John A. Widtsoe, "The man of science and the man of religion are the same man, seeking the same end, and they will understand each other when they stand on common ground."[270]

Stories of Modern-Day Miracles

Miracles, for many, are not merely tales from ancient scriptures or relics of a bygone era. Even in our technologically advanced age, countless individuals, both within and outside the Christian and LDS communities, attest to having witnessed or experienced events that they deem miraculous. These modern-day miracles range from inexplicable medical recoveries to timely interventions in desperate situations. While skeptics might attribute such occurrences to mere coincidence or explain them away through scientific means, for many believers, these are divine manifestations, signaling God's ongoing presence and concern for his children.[271]

Among the many tales of modern miracles celebrated within the LDS community, the narrative of Elder John H. Groberg stands out as a testament to divine intervention and the indomitable spirit of faith. Dispatched to the remote islands of Tonga in the mid-1950s, this young missionary encountered myriad trials that tested the limits of his endurance and faith.[272]

The stark cultural shift, linguistic barriers, and periodic scarcities were just the tip of the iceberg. There were times he grappled with life-threatening situations, such as violent storms that threatened to drown him or natives who were initially suspicious and unwelcoming. Groberg's memoir, *In the Eye of the Storm,* paints a vivid picture of his challenges, encapsulating the

---

[270] John Widtsoe, *Evidences and Reconciliations* (Salt Lake City: Bookcraft, 1943).
[271] Lewis, *Miracles: A Preliminary Study.*
[272] John H. Groberg, *In the Eye of the Storm* (Salt Lake City: Deseret Book Co., 1993).

physical, emotional, and spiritual upheavals that became a part of his daily life in Tonga.[273]

In one particularly harrowing episode, Groberg found himself marooned on a remote island, devoid of sustenance and parched from lack of water. An overwhelming sense of isolation amplified the anguish of hunger and dehydration. However, in his darkest hour, Groberg recalls a profound spiritual experience—an overwhelming sensation of divine presence that fortified him. He writes of feeling a comforting warmth, an inexplicable assurance that he wasn't alone.[274]

The climax of this ordeal came when, driven by a potent mix of desperation and faith, Groberg felt inspired to explore an unlikely part of the island. Miraculously, he stumbled upon a source of fresh water—a discovery that he attributes to divine guidance. For Groberg, this wasn't just a matter of physical survival; it was a spiritual affirmation, a palpable instance of God's protective embrace, even in the most adverse conditions.[275]

Beyond LDS circles, numerous Christians worldwide share stories that they believe showcase divine intervention. Consider the case of a family trapped in a car during a blizzard in Nevada. After several hours, the mother, weakened and desperate, prayed earnestly for deliverance. Soon after, a stranger approached on foot, guiding them to a nearby refuge. When they later attempted to thank him, the man was nowhere to be found, leading them to believe he was an angel sent in response to their prayers.[276]

One modern-day miracle touched my life when I was a volunteer EMT in a tight-knit rural Virginia community. This call inspired me to continue my education and become my community's only volunteer paramedic to provide a higher level of care when tragedy strikes.

---

[273] Ibid.

[274] Ibid.

[275] Ibid.

[276] Eric Metaxas, *Miracles: What They Are, Why They Happen, and How They Can Change Your Life* (New York: Dutton, 2014).

In the early morning hours, when most households were still nestled in the embrace of sleep, the stillness was shattered by an urgent distress call. Fierce flames were consuming a family home. The acrid scent of smoke was palpable even before the looming, fiery glow painted the pre-dawn sky, an alarming testament to nature's unpredictable fury. I lived less than a mile away, and the burning silhouette became hauntingly vivid as I rushed from my house to theirs. My heart raced with a mixture of adrenaline and dread, knowing lives hung in the balance. I arrived less than two minutes after the 911 call from a concerned neighbor, just moments behind an off-duty firefighter who had spotted the inferno during his early commute to work. The severity of the situation bore down heavily when we realized the family was trapped within the burning house.

Later, as the ashy remnants of that harrowing morning cooled, husband and wife Aaron and Amy Weakly recounted an extraordinary experience. With tears glistening in her eyes, Amy spoke of a sensation of being lifted and guided as if by angels. These unseen forces navigated her through the fire-ravaged hallways, down a staircase that had succumbed to the blaze, and ultimately to the sanctuary of the outside world.[277] Her heartfelt recollection was laden with raw emotion. In that dire moment of unimaginable terror, their beacon, their singular focus, was the safety and well-being of their cherished children. Aaron had already rescued two of their daughters, and it was up to Amy to get the last girl out of the inferno. Higher powers, heeding her fervent prayers, seemed to echo her maternal instincts.

In the aftermath, our community's true spirit shone brightly. Neighbors, friends, and even strangers rallied together, a testament to the close-knit bonds that characterize our small Virginia town. They united in solidarity, providing comfort, support, and basic necessities to the family.

---

[277] CBN, "Through the Fire: A Family's Story of Loss & Survival," YouTube video, 7:53, Nov. 20, 2015, https://www.youtube.com/watch?v=6SOsvGXP3FQ.

The incident etched an indelible mark on all who witnessed it. While the devastating blaze showcased nature's might, the family's testimony stood as a radiant beacon, a poignant reminder of the unwavering flames of faith and divine protection that can pierce our darkest moments.

In the aftermath of the fire, Tony, the off-duty firefighter who had arrived at the fire just minutes before me, underwent a profound spiritual transformation. He heeded the divine call, embracing faith anew, and becoming a born-again Christian. Intriguingly, he joined the very church that the Weakleys attended. As for me, for years I rejected the Lord's persistent calls, metaphorically directing them to voicemail. Then, in due course, I succumbed to a profound spiritual awakening, culminating in my baptism in the Church of Jesus Christ of Latter-day Saints.

Reflecting upon these synchronous spiritual journeys, it's remarkable to consider how both of us—positioned by fate or divine will at that harrowing scene—were ultimately guided to the Lord. Though we went in slightly different directions, our paths converged under the vast umbrella of devotion to our Lord Jesus Christ.

While writing this book, I shared a draft of this section with Aaron Weakley. He observed with wonder, "It's quite the irony, isn't it? That both you and Tony—the initial responders to our crisis—would come to embrace Jesus, with our fire serving as a pivotal chapter in your spiritual narratives."[278]

Of course, miracles aren't limited to life-threatening situations. There are accounts of individuals praying for clarity on life decisions, from career changes to family challenges, and receiving insights or encountering circumstances they believe were orchestrated from above. The Apostle James reminds us, "If any of you lack wisdom, let him ask of God, that

---

278 Aaron Weakly, Facebook Messenger message to author, Sept. 11, 2023.

giveth to all men liberally, and upbraideth not; and it shall be given him" (James 1:5).

Even so, it's essential to address the skepticism that surrounds such accounts. Many within the scientific and secular communities might argue that these are mere coincidences, cognitive biases, or instances of people seeing patterns they want to see.[279] And indeed, in an age of reason and empirical evidence, it's worth considering these viewpoints. It's possible that some interpreted miracles could have natural explanations, and believers and non-believers alike should approach such accounts with both faith and reason.

From the LDS perspective, President Dallin H. Oaks has said, "Miracles, by definition, are extraordinary events that surpass all known human or natural powers. Although they are usually ascribed to God, this need not be so. Some miracles come from a source other than God."[280] The LDS stance encourages discernment and understanding that while God does indeed work miracles, not everything inexplicable or extraordinary necessarily stems from the Divine.

But what of these stories? Can we find a balance between faith and skepticism? Perhaps the true value in modern-day miracle accounts lies not in their empirical verifiability but in the hope, strength, and inspiration that they provide to countless individuals. For many, these stories are a testament to a loving God who is involved in the minutiae of our lives and ready to intervene in moments of need.

President Russell M. Nelson of the LDS Church has shared numerous accounts of divine guidance and intervention in his life, both in his capacity as a church leader and as a heart surgeon. In one incident, while attempting a complicated heart surgery procedure, he felt an unmistakable prompting

---

[279] Michael Shermer, *The Believing Brain: From Ghosts and Gods to Politics and Conspiracies—How We Construct Beliefs and Reinforce Them as Truths* (New York: Times Books, 2011).
[280] Dallin H. Oaks, "Miracles," *Ensign*, June 2001.

to modify his approach. Following this impression led to the successful completion of the surgery and the patient's recovery.[281]

However, a critical aspect to note is that while many believe in and attest to miracles, there are countless others whose prayers seemingly go unanswered or who face inexplicable hardships. This dichotomy often raises profound theological questions. Nevertheless, the stories of modern-day miracles serve as a beacon of hope and a testament to the idea that even in a rapidly evolving world, some phenomena remain beyond human comprehension.

For believers, these narratives aren't just coincidental events but are emblematic of an ever-present God who intervenes in the lives of his children, whether through grand gestures or subtle nudges. In a world often dominated by skepticism, these stories serve as a potent reminder of God's intercession and the continuous unfolding of miracles in the tapestry of human existence.

---

[281] Russell M. Nelson, *Accomplishing the Impossible: What God Does, What We Can Do* (Salt Lake City: Deseret Book Company, 2015).

Chapter 6: Why Does God Allow Evil to Happen?

In the annals of theological debate, few topics are as widely discussed, deeply felt, and persistently perplexing as the issue of divine justice. Many have grappled with intense emotions and philosophical quandaries when contemplating the coexistence of an omnipotent, benevolent God juxtaposed with the undeniable presence of evil and suffering. This juxtaposition forms a profound paradox that has shaped theological discourse and personal beliefs for millennia.

The foundation of the Christian faith rests upon the belief in a God who is omniscient, omnipotent, and omnibenevolent.[282] This belief stems from numerous biblical passages that speak to God's limitless power and unwavering love for his creation. "The earth is the Lord's, and the fullness thereof; the world, and they that dwell therein" (Ps 24:1). And in the New Testament, John poignantly captures the essence of God's nature: "God is love" (1 Jn 4:8). The underpinning notion is clear: God is both the Creator and Sustainer of the universe, a being of boundless love and unmatched power.

For all its beauty and wonder, the world is also a theater of heartache, tragedy, and sometimes inexplicable suffering. Natural disasters claim innocent lives, diseases ravage communities, and man-made atrocities often leave scars that persist through generations. The stark reality of all this suffering raises profound questions. If God possesses the power to prevent evil and the love to desire the well-being of all his creatures, why does suffering prevail?

This enduring question isn't solely a Christian or even a religious dilemma. The secular world also wrestles with the complexities of justice, fairness, and

---

[282] David Bentley Hart, *The Doors of the Sea: Where Was God in the Tsunami?* (Notre Dame, IN: University of Notre Dame Press, 2011).

the seemingly randomness of suffering. Many atheists and agnostics have pointed to the problem of evil as a significant challenge to religious belief. For them the magnitude of pain and suffering in the world offers evidence against the existence of an all-good and all-powerful deity.

In the context of LDS theology, the issue of divine justice takes on unique dimensions. The Church maintains a deep belief in God's eternal purposes and plans. "For behold, this is my work and my glory—to bring to pass the immortality and eternal life of man" (Moses 1:39). This perspective views mortal life as a brief but essential phase in an eternal journey, wherein individuals gain experience, make choices, and undergo challenges that shape their eternal progression.[283]

From this viewpoint, earthly suffering can be seen as part of a divine pedagogy, a means of testing, refining, and teaching God's children. However, this doesn't diminish the genuine pain and questions that arise. The Book of Mormon, another testament of Jesus Christ, recognizes these struggles when Alma, a prophet, grapples with sorrow and pleads, "O Lord, wilt thou grant unto me that I may have strength" (Alma 31:31).

To some, the explanations of faith, divine pedagogy, and external perspectives offer solace. For others, they might seem inadequate in the face of profound suffering. At its core, however, the question of divine justice revolves around our limited mortal understanding and the eternal mysteries of God's plans.

Throughout this chapter, we will embark on a balanced exploration of this topic, which requires recognizing the profound depths of faith and doubt it evokes, understanding the historical and theological contexts from which these questions arise, and approaching them with humility and empathy. For in the heart of this dilemma lie some of the most profound questions of existence, purpose, and the nature of God himself.

---

[283] "The Purpose of Life,"
https://www.churchofjesuschrist.org/comeuntochrist/africacentral/beliefs/purpose-of-life.

The Age-Old Question of Theodicy

Theodicy, a term derived from the Greek words "theos" (God) and "dike" (justice), grapples with reconciling God's goodness and omnipotence with the existence of evil and suffering in the world.[284] It's a philosophical and theological challenge that has been pondered by scholars, theologians, and everyday believers throughout the ages.

In the annals of Christianity, the Book of Job stands as an emblematic exploration of this challenge.[285] Job, a man "perfect and upright" who "feared God and eschewed evil," is beset with calamities, losing his wealth, his children, and his health in rapid succession.[286] His profound suffering, seemingly unmerited, leads to poignant dialogues with his friends and a direct conversation with God himself. Through these discourses, the text delves deep into questions of divine justice, human suffering, and the nature of God's relationship with his creations.

Job's friends, with their varying perspectives, offer interpretations that resonate even today. Some argue that suffering is a direct consequence of individual sin, implying a straightforward equation of misdeeds with divine retribution.[287] Others suggest that human understanding is inherently limited, and we cannot fathom the depths of divine wisdom.[288] While the Book of Job does not provide definitive answers, it emphasizes the importance of unwavering faith in God, even amid profound suffering and mystery.[289]

For Latter-Day Saints, the challenge of theodicy is viewed within the broader context of God's eternal plan for his children. Life on Earth is but a fragment of our eternal existence, a proving ground where our faith is

---

[284] John Hick, *Evil and the God of Love* (New York: Palgrave Macmillan, 2010).
[285] Gustavo Gutiérrez, *On Job: God-Talk and the Suffering of the Innocent* (Maryknoll, NY: Orbis Books, 1987).
[286] Job 1:1.
[287] Job 4:7–9.
[288] Job 11:7–9.
[289] Job 42:1–6.

tested and refined.[290] The Church's teachings stress the importance of agency or the freedom to choose, even if those choices lead to evil or suffering. For without the ability to choose, there can be no true righteousness or growth.[291] In this view, while deeply painful, evil and suffering test our resilience, mold our character, and draw us closer to our Heavenly Father.[292]

However, these explanations can sometimes seem unsatisfying, even troubling to those outside the fold of faith or some within. Prominent atheists, such as Richard Dawkins, argue that evil and suffering in the world challenge the traditional concept of an all-loving and all-powerful God.[293] In his words, "The universe we observe has precisely the properties we should expect if there is, at bottom, no design, no purpose, no evil, no good, nothing but pitiless indifference."[294]

There are also philosophical arguments that engage with the question of theodicy. The free will defense posits that God has given humans free will, and it's this free will that accounts for moral evils in the world.[295] God, in his omnibenevolence, values freedom and, in granting it, allows for the possibility of evil acts by his creations.[296]

Alternatively, the soul-making theodicy, rooted in the teachings of Saint Irenaeus, suggests that God allows evil to exist as it plays a role in developing souls, bringing about greater goods such as courage, patience, and

---

[290] "Plan of Salvation," https://www.churchofjesuschrist.org/study/manual/gospel-topics/plan-of-salvation.

[291] 2 Nephi 2:27

[292] Alma 14:10–11

[293] Richard Dawkins, *The God Delusion.*

[294] Ibid.

[295] Alvin Plantinga, *God, Freedom, and Evil* (Grand Rapids: Eerdmans Publishing Co., 1977).

[296] Ibid.

resilience.[297] Through experiencing and overcoming challenges, human beings mature spiritually and morally.[298]

The question of theodicy remains ever-relevant in the modern age, with its myriad of complexities and challenges. As the world grapples with natural disasters, man-made atrocities, and personal tragedies, believers and skeptics alike search for understanding and meaning. While answers may vary, and complete resolution might remain elusive, the journey through these questions deepens our understanding of faith, humanity, and the Divine. The human spirit is refined in seeking, pondering, and wrestling, and its relationship with the Divine is forged anew.

Biblical Insights on Suffering and Evil

The cornerstone of the Christian faith, the Holy Bible, offers profound insights into the complex tapestry of divine intent, human frailty, and the existence of suffering and evil. While distinctively rooted in the Judeo-Christian tradition, these biblical interpretations resonate with universal lessons that transcend denominational boundaries, echoing the broader human experience.

The early chapters of Genesis provide us with the narrative of Adam and Eve in the Garden of Eden.[299] Despite God's explicit caution, Adam and Eve introduced physical and spiritual death into the world by choosing to partake of the forbidden fruit.[300] However, this narrative signifies more than mere disobedience. It encapsulates the inherent human journey—the inevitable allure of temptation, the invaluable gift of agency, and the ensuing consequences of choice.[301]

---

[297] John Hick, *Soul-Making and Suffering* (London: Anvil Press, 1981).
[298] Ibid.
[299] Gen 2—3.
[300] Gen 3:22–24.
[301] C. S. Lewis, *The Problem of Pain* (New York: HarperOne, 2009).

From the LDS vantage point, the Fall isn't a lamentable accident but a crucial juncture in God's eternal design. At this stage, humanity learns, evolves, and ultimately discerns the path to salvation.[302]

The life of Jesus Christ, chronicled with deep reverence in the New Testament, stands as a testimony to the intertwining of divine essence with worldly suffering.[303] The Garden of Gethsemane bore witness to his anguished pleas and immense suffering as he vicariously bore the weight of all human sins.[304] His eventual crucifixion, a heart-wrenching tableau of sacrifice, revealed a God willing to undergo profound physical and emotional agony for his creation.[305] This culmination of Christ's earthly mission wasn't an end but a beginning, symbolizing the ultimate victory of good over malevolence, of hope over despair.[306]

The transformation of the Apostle Paul from a fierce opponent of Christianity to one of its most ardent proponents provides yet another dimension to this exploration.[307] Through his epistles, Paul delves into the juxtaposition of earthly suffering against a divine narrative.[308] In his poignant words, "And we know that all things work together for good to them that love God, to them who are the called according to his purpose" (Rom 8:28). For Paul, earthly travails aren't random or senseless; they play a pivotal role in a grander orchestration, serving to refine the human spirit and drawing souls closer to their Creator.[309]

For members of the Church of Jesus Christ of Latter-day Saints, canonical texts like the Book of Mormon and Doctrine and Covenants offer additional insight into the dialectics of suffering. Within these pages, Alma,

---

[302] "Fall of Adam and Eve," https://www.churchofjesuschrist.org/study/manual/gospel-topics/fall-of-adam-and-eve.

[303] Lk 22–24.

[304] Mt 26:39.

[305] Mk 15:34.

[306] 1 Cor 15:55–57.

[307] Acts 9:1–19.

[308] 2 Cor 1:3–7.

[309] Rom 5:3–5.

a revered prophet, explains that Christ, in his boundless compassion, took upon himself human infirmities so he might "know according to the flesh how to succor his people according to their infirmities" (Alma 7:12). This perspective presents a God who doesn't merely observe from a distance but deeply empathizes, intimately comprehends human pain, and offers unparalleled solace.[310]

From a secular vantage point, these narratives often resonate as allegorical or mythical.[311] While the ethical and moral lessons remain acknowledged, a literal interpretation often presents a problem for many, especially when juxtaposed with the tangible realities of suffering. However, for the devout, these scriptures transcend mere tales. They are divine truths that shape, guide, and fortify. They offer a compass in the turbulent voyage of life, providing solace, purpose, and a radiant hope that outshines the transient storms of existence.

Free Will: Humanity's Blessing and Curse

Free will remains one of the most intricate threads woven into the theological tapestry of Christian faith. It signifies the divine gift of agency—liberty to choose and, by extension, the capacity to love, create, destroy, and, above all, determine our destiny.[312] But with such freedom, there is also the ever-looming shadow of malice, mistakes, and suffering. Like the broader Christian context, the LDS doctrine grapples with this double-edged sword of human agency, trying to reconcile it with the benevolence and omnipotence of God.

The theological emphasis on free will isn't just an abstract concept; it embodies God's loving nature. A God who, in his boundless love, grants humanity the gift of choice, even if that means the possibility of them

---

[310] Smith, Doctrine and Covenants, 121:7–8.
[311] Bart D. Ehrman, God's Problem: How the Bible Fails to Answer Our Most Important Question—Why We Suffer (New York: HarperOne, 2009).
[312] Thomas Aquinas, Summa Theologica, Question 83: The Freedom of Will

choosing contrary to his will.[313] As expressed in Deuteronomy 30:19, "I have set before you life and death, blessing and cursing: therefore choose life, that both thou and thy seed may live."

The concept of free will finds profound resonance in the New Testament, particularly in the parable of the Prodigal Son (Lk 15:11–32). Having squandered his inheritance, the wayward son realizes his folly and returns to his father. Rather than a tale of mere redemption, this parable comments on the beauty of choice, repentance, and the overwhelming mercy of a loving God waiting with open arms.[314]

While the principle of agency is central to LDS doctrine, Latter-Day Saints do not view God as a distant observer, uninvolved in human affairs.[315] The Church believes that God respects agency but also continually extends his love, guidance, and, when sought, intervention to his children.[316] This delicate balance between divine involvement and respect for human agency is beautifully encapsulated in the words of a revered LDS hymn: "Know this, that every soul is free, to choose his life and what he'll be; for this eternal truth is given, that God will force no man to heaven."[317]

However, the existence of free will also begs an uncomfortable question: Why, if God is all-loving, would he allow such freedom when it can lead to immense pain, evil, and suffering? For many, the horrors of war, crime, prejudice, and natural disasters become almost insurmountable barriers to belief in a benevolent deity.[318]

Growth, genuine love, and moral authenticity can only arise in a realm where free will exists.[319] A world devoid of choice would also be devoid of

---

[313] C. S. Lewis, *The Problem of Pain.*
[314] Jeffrey R. Holland, "The Other Prodigal," *Ensign*, May 2002.
[315] Smith, Doctrine and Covenants, 130:20–21.
[316] Henry B. Eyring, "God Helps the Faithful Priesthood Holder," *Ensign*, Nov. 2007.
[317] "Know This, That Every Soul Is Free," in *Hymns of The Church of Jesus Christ of Latter-day Saints*, (Salt Lake City: Church of Jesus Christ of Latter-day Saints, 1983).
[318] Hume, *Dialogues Concerning Natural Religion.*
[319] Plantinga, *God, Freedom, and Evil.*

virtues born out of that choice. There would be no courage in the absence of danger, patience without tribulation, and genuine love without the freedom to hate.[320] Elder James E. Talmage, a notable LDS theologian, posited that "the Father's plan called for the ultimate realization of the highest blessings by His children, but it also provided for the free agency of men."[321]

For many secularists and skeptics, such explanations may seem inadequate, often citing them as rationalizations of evident contradictions.[322] However, for believers, free will's profound implications reaffirm faith, enriching the human-divine relationship. It presents a God who respects humanity enough to allow them self-determination and yet loves them enough to provide paths of redemption when they falter.[323]

The notion of free agency, both a blessing and a curse, remains one of the most profound theological deliberations in the Christian and LDS traditions. It symbolizes God's unyielding love and respect for human agency while also explaining the inherent challenges of the mortal experience. As we navigate this earthly journey with its amalgamation of joy, sorrow, choices, and consequences, the understanding of divine agency serves as a beacon, guiding, illuminating, and forever pointing toward eternal horizons.

Religious and Philosophical Responses to Theodicy

Theodicy, the justification of a benevolent and omnipotent deity in the face of evil and suffering in the world, is a theological challenge that dates back millennia. Christian thinkers and their counterparts from other philosophical and religious traditions have wrestled with this conundrum, attempting to understand and elucidate God's role in the presence of evil.

---

[320] C. S. Lewis, *Mere Christianity* (San Francisco: HarperSanFrancisco, 2023).
[321] James E. Talmage, *Articles of Faith*.
[322] Dawkins, *The God Delusion*.
[323] Dieter F. Uchtdorf, "The Merciful Obtain Mercy," *Ensign*, May 2012.

In the Christian tradition, the Fall in the Garden of Eden narrative stands as a foundational explanation. As recounted in Genesis, humanity's disobedience introduced sin and suffering into the world.[324] This "original sin" delineates the inherent human capacity to commit wrong, reflecting on the broader theme of free will.[325] Augustine of Hippo, one of the foremost theologians of early Christianity, posited that evil results from humanity's misuse of free will.[326] However, even amidst suffering, the Christian narrative offers hope: through Christ's atonement, redemption and healing become attainable.[327]

Mortality is deemed necessary for individual growth and progression with its associated trials and tribulations.[328] In this worldview, adversity becomes an opportunity to draw nearer to God, learn, and grow.[329]

Christian responses to theodicy extend beyond the narrative of the Fall. The concept of "soul-making," introduced by the theologian John Hick, posits that earthly challenges foster spiritual and moral growth. Thus, a world without pain or challenges would also lack virtues like courage, patience, or resilience.[330] Earthly life becomes a crucible, refining souls and nurturing virtues that draw individuals closer to the Divine.[331]

Contrasting with this, other religious traditions offer alternative insights into the problem of evil. In Buddhism, the Four Noble Truths identify suffering (*dukkha*) as an intrinsic aspect of existence. The source of such suffering is attachment and desire, and the path to its cessation is the Eightfold Path, a set of ethical and mental practices.[332]

---

[324] Gen 3.
[325] Rom 5:12.
[326] Augustine of Hippo, *City of God*.
[327] Rom 5:19.
[328] Bruce R. McConkie, "Fall of Adam," *Mormon Doctrine*.
[329] Alma 34:32.
[330] John Hick, *Evil and the God of Love*.
[331] Ja 1:2–4
[332] Walpola Rahula, *What the Buddha Taught* (New York: Grove Press, 1974).

Hinduism attributes suffering to karma, the law of action and reaction. Actions (good or bad) in one's life or past lives influence one's current state of existence.[333]

Many philosophical traditions outside religious frameworks have also delved into the theodicy dilemma. Existentialist philosophy, with figures like Jean-Paul Sartre and Albert Camus at its helm, acknowledges the inherent absurdity of life. Rather than seeking an external divine justification for suffering, existentialism propounds the idea of creating one's own meaning amidst the apparent chaos.[334]

A significant critique comes from the atheistic or agnostic front, contending that the evident malaise in the world is incompatible with a loving, omnipotent deity.[335] British philosopher J. L. Mackie famously argued that an all-good God wouldn't allow needless suffering, and an all-powerful God could prevent it. Hence, the existence of gratuitous evil stands at odds with traditional theistic beliefs.[336]

In response to such critiques, some Christian thinkers have propounded the "greater good defense." While certain evils may appear gratuitous, they might be instrumental in realizing higher-order goods inaccessible to human comprehension.[337] In his "free will defense," Alvin Plantinga posits that it might not be logically possible for God to create a world where free beings always choose rightly.[338]

The LDS perspective resonates with many of these views but also adds distinctive elements. Central to this is the eternal perspective, viewing mortal life as a mere blip in the continuum of eternal existence.[339] Through

---

[333] *The Bhagavad Gita*, trans. Eknath Easwaran (Tomales, CA: Nilgiri Press, 2007).

[334] Jean-Paul Sartre, *Existentialism is a Humanism* (Cleveland, World Publishing Company, 1956).

[335] Dawkins, *The God Delusion*.

[336] J. L. Mackie, "Evil and Omnipotence," *Mind* 64, vol. 254 (1955): 200–212.

[337] Richard Swinburne, *The Existence of God* (Oxford: Clarendon Press, 2004).

[338] Plantinga, *God, Freedom, and Evil*.

[339] Smith, Doctrine and Covenants, 76:94

this lens, trials, however harrowing, are temporal and purposeful, shaping souls for eternal glory.[340]

The question of theodicy remains one of the most profound mysteries of existence. While no single response can encapsulate the vastness of the issue, the myriad of religious and philosophical perspectives enriches the tapestry of understanding. The Christian and LDS viewpoints, rooted in scriptures and revelation, offer hope, redemption, and purpose amidst the chaos, perpetually pointing toward a loving God orchestrating a grand, eternal symphony.

Modern Theological Views and Critiques

Emerging from the crucible of the two World Wars, the Holocaust, and numerous other twentieth-century tragedies, many theologians were driven to re-examine classical theodicies. The visceral horrors of these events pushed the theodicy discourse into areas of profound depth. For instance, the post-Holocaust theology contended with the profound problem of God's silence during the extermination of six million Jews.[341] This led to a spectrum of responses, from the "death of God" theology, which posits God's literal death or abandonment, to perspectives that see the Holocaust as a mysterious element of divine providence.[342]

In the Christian ambit, the liberation theology movement, which emerged primarily in Latin America, centered its discourse on the suffering of the oppressed.[343] This theology seeks to understand suffering and also combat it, viewing God as standing in solidarity with the marginalized. Through the lens of liberation theology, Jesus's crucifixion is not just a distant

---

[340] Dieter F. Uchtdorf, "The Hope of God's Light," *Ensign*, May 2013.

[341] Richard L. Rubenstein, *After Auschwitz: History, theology, and Contemporary Judaism.* Indianapolis: (Indianapolis: The Bobbs-Merrill Company, 1966).

[342] Jürgen Moltmann, *The Crucified God: The Cross of Christ as the Foundation and Criticism of Christian Theology* (New York: Harper & Row, 1974).

[343] Gustavo Gutiérrez, *A Theology of Liberation: History, Politics, and Salvation* (Maryknoll, NY: Orbis Books, 1973).

theological event but also a mirror to the everyday crucifixions faced by the oppressed.[344]

In parallel fashion, the prosperity gospel, particularly influential in American evangelical circles, suggests that faith and righteousness can lead to material prosperity and health.[345] This viewpoint, however, has garnered critiques, including from within Christian circles, that it oversimplifies the complexities of suffering and tends to blame victims for their adversities.[346]

The LDS perspective on suffering in modern times is deeply rooted in the foundational narratives of persecution faced by early members.[347] The travails faced by pioneers crossing the American plains, the extermination orders, and other episodes of violence are seen as historical events and testamentary episodes that shaped the LDS identity. This framework views suffering as an individual and a collective refining process.[348] Adversities, though challenging, are perceived as tools that carve out a resilient and faithful community.

However, as we venture further into the twenty-first century, newer critiques emerge, particularly from the intersections of science and philosophy. The increasing understanding of neurology, genetics, and the socio-biological roots of behavior challenge the traditional notions of free will.[349] If our biology and environment significantly determine our actions, then how does one reconcile this with the idea of a just God punishing or rewarding those actions?[350]

---

[344] Jon Sobrino, *Christ the Liberator: A View from the Victims* (Maryknoll, NY: Orbis Books, 2001).

[345] Kate Bowler, *Blessed: A History of the American Prosperity Gospel* (New York: Oxford University Press, 2013).

[346] Miroslav Volf, *Exclusion and Embrace: A Theological Exploration of Identity, Otherness, and Reconciliation* (Nashville: Abingdon Press, 1996).

[347] Terryl L. Givens, *The Viper on the Hearth: Mormons, Myths, and the Construction of Heresy* (New York: Oxford University Press, 1997).

[348] Smith, Doctrine and Covenants, 121:7–8.

[349] Sam Harris, *Free Will* (New York: Free Press, 2012).

[350] Daniel M. Dennett, *Freedom Evolves* (New York: Viking, 2003).

On a philosophical front, secular humanism argues for ethical frameworks independent of divine command.[351] This worldview critiques traditional theodicies by suggesting that ethical behavior and the alleviation of suffering need not be rooted in religious narratives or divine mandates.

In response to such challenges, modern Christian apologists have striven for a more nuanced understanding of divine justice. In his seminal work, *The Problem of Pain*, C. S. Lewis delineates between the idea of a loving God and an "all-nice" God.[352] According to Lewis, God's love may sometimes manifest as challenges, much like a sculptor chiseling a stone to create a masterpiece.[353]

Personal Faith Amid Suffering

The radiant lighthouse of personal faith often penetrates the dense fog of human suffering. The eternal question reverberates through the hearts of many: how can a loving, omnipotent God seemingly stand by as his creations endure such anguish? This enigma has long perplexed theologians, philosophers, and laypeople, driving believers and non-believers to deep introspection.

To better understand the depths of this question, it is essential to approach it through the lens of personal experience, for such struggles are not mere abstract concepts but lived realities for countless individuals. I grappled with this very question during my journey toward understanding faith, influenced by the harrowing scenes I encountered as a paramedic. In the ambulance's white-knuckle embrace, while the siren's wail permeated the night air, I bore witness to a vast array of human suffering.

One particularly haunting memory stands out. While in paramedic school, seeking to broaden my experience, I served several shifts in a trauma center hospital. There, the weight of a single choice and the consequences of a

---

[351] Paul Kurtz, *In Defense of Secular Humanism* (Buffalo, NY: Prometheus Books, 1983).
[352] Lewis, *The Problem of Pain*.
[353] Rom 5:3–5.

fleeting judgment lapse became heartbreakingly clear. Having succumbed to the haze of intoxication, a woman took to the wheel with her three young children in tow. Tragically, none of them were safely secured with seat belts or child-safety seats. The inevitable crash that followed inflicted grievous harm upon these innocent souls. I remember my hands shaking, anger boiling at the pit of my stomach, as I wondered, why? Why must these children suffer for their mother's grave miscalculation? Why wouldn't a loving God intervene?

As I dove deeper into the realms of faith, however, especially within the Christian and LDS traditions, a nuanced understanding began to emerge.[354] Both traditions firmly uphold the principle of free agency or free will. This concept is foundational for Latter-Day Saints, as our Heavenly Father's plan emphasizes the importance of agency for our growth and progression.[355] Agency ensures that our mortal existence is a period of testing and growth, allowing us to make choices and thereby learn from the consequences, whether joyous or sorrowful.[356]

Indeed, if God intervened in every circumstance where poor decisions were made, it would negate the essence of agency itself. While potentially free of suffering, such a world would also be devoid of the growth, learning, and soul-shaping experiences that arise from our choices and their repercussions.[357]

But what about the innocents? Those, like the children in the car crash, who suffer not due to their own choices but the choices of others? It is here that Christian teachings provide solace. The Savior's words resonate: "Come unto me, all ye that labor and are heavy laden, and I will give you rest" (Mt 11:28). Christianity posits that earthly suffering is real and

---

[354] Lewis, *Mere Christianity.*
[355] Smith, Doctrine and Covenants, 58:27–28
[356] Ezra Taft Benson, "The Plan of Salvation," LDS General Conference, Oct. 1985.
[357] Richard Swinburne, *Providence and the Problem of Evil* (Oxford: Clarendon Press, 1998).

profound but also transient. Eternal justice will prevail, and those who have suffered will find solace and redress in God's embrace.[358]

On the other hand, the non-faith viewpoint tends to approach such situations from a purely naturalistic and deterministic perspective.[359] This view posits that actions and their consequences, including suffering, result from a complex web of prior causes devoid of divine orchestration or ultimate purpose.

Amidst these diverse perspectives, the anguished cries of those who suffer, like the children in that fateful car, serve as a call for compassion, understanding, and action. Whether one attributes their existence to divine design or mere chance, the imperative remains: to alleviate suffering, uphold justice, and make this world a place where stories of unwarranted pain become fewer and farther between.

While the whys of suffering might remain shrouded in mystery, the responsibility of our response remains clear. Our agency, whether viewed as a divine gift or a natural phenomenon, endows us with the power to shape our destinies and, more importantly, to make a difference in the lives of those who cross our paths.

Conclusion: The Journey of Faith Amid Shadows

In the expansive tapestry of human experience, the juxtaposition of light and shadow, of good and evil, emerges as one of its most poignant and inescapable motifs. The challenge posed by theodicy—reconciling the existence of an omnipotent, benevolent God with the reality of suffering and evil—has beckoned generations into a deep introspection on the nature of divinity, morality, and the human spirit.

In its rich and multifaceted tradition, Christianity holds at its core the profound belief in a loving God whose ways, though sometimes

---

Lewis, *The Problem of Pain.*
[359] Dennett, *Freedom Evolves.*

incomprehensible, always bend toward justice and love.[360] The crucifixion and resurrection of Jesus Christ stand as a potent emblem of this debate, encapsulating the deepest abyss of suffering and the triumphant zenith of redemptive love.[361] The cross, a symbol of anguish, also emerges as an emblem of hope, indicating that light finds a way even in the heart of darkness.

The LDS tradition adds further layers to this narrative. Through episodes such as Joseph Smith's profound existential question, "O God, where art thou?", amidst the vexing trials of Liberty Jail, the LDS tradition resonates deeply with the experience of seeking God in moments of profound darkness.[362] The subsequent assurance that "all these things shall give thee experience, and shall be for thy good" speaks to a theology that views adversity not merely as a test but also as an instrument of divine pedagogy.[363]

However, the journey of faith is not without its moments of profound doubt, especially in a world that is increasingly interconnected and exposed to many worldviews. Many contemporary thinkers, influenced by the secular humanist tradition, question the very premise of theodicy, arguing that moral frameworks can, and should, be constructed independent of any divine mandate.[364] The rise of the "nones"—those who identify as religiously unaffiliated—in many parts of the Western world is a testament to this shifting spiritual landscape.[365]

Many Christians find the most profound connection with the Divine in this space of not knowing, of faith. As the Apostle Paul noted, "For now we

---

[360] John Stott, *The Cross of Christ* (Downers Grove, IL: InterVarsity Press, 1986).
[361] N. T. Wright, *The Resurrection of the Son of God* (Minneapolis: Fortress Press, 2003).
[362] Joseph Smith, Doctrine and Covenants, 121:1–2.
[363] Ibid, 122:7.
[364] Paul Kurtz, *In Defense of Secular Humanism* (Buffalo, NY: Prometheus Books, 1983).
[365] Pew Research Center, "The Rise of the 'Nones' and Religious 'Unaffiliated,'" Pew Research Center's Religion & Public Life Project.

see through a glass, darkly; but then face to face: now I know in part; but then shall I know even as also I am known" (1 Cor 3:12).

The journey is not about arriving at neat answers but wrestling with profound questions. It is about finding God not just in the comforting embrace of a sunset or the innocent laughter of a child but also in the problematic shadows of a world fraught with pain and injustice. In this journey, the Christian and LDS narratives offer a compass—not of clear-cut answers but of a promise that beyond the night awaits the light of dawn.

The question of theodicy, while intellectually challenging, also offers a profound spiritual journey. For believers, it beckons a deeper dive into the nature of God, the purpose of life, and the pathways of faith. It also allows skeptics to explore ethical, philosophical, and existential vistas. Together, they create a dialogue—a symphony of voices that seek to understand the enigma of our existence and the profound mystery of the Divine.

Chapter 7: Prayer, Song, and Connecting with God

Throughout history, humankind's intrinsic longing to connect with something greater, with the Divine, remains a prevalent theme. This enduring quest to understand and relate to the source of life, love, and existence often propels individuals to adopt diverse paths. From the tranquil whispers of a secluded monk to the collective, harmonious voices of a Sunday congregation, the avenues leading to God are as varied as the souls who treat them.

At the heart of this journey is the question: how can one foster a closer relationship with God? The Judeo-Christian traditions offer profound insights into this query. "Draw nigh to God, and he will draw nigh to you," states the Book of James, encapsulating the principle that our efforts to approach God are reciprocated by him (Ja 4:8).

From this Christian perspective, the entire narrative of the Bible can be seen as God's constant effort to bridge the gap between the Divine and humanity. God walked with Adam in the Garden of Eden (Gen 3:8), spoke through prophets like Moses and Isaiah,[366] and ultimately, in the profound act of love, sent his Son, Jesus Christ, to provide a tangible, human experience of the Divine (Jn 3:16). The LDS Church further expounds upon these biblical narratives, adding layers of understanding through the Book of Mormon and the teachings of modern-day prophets.

Even so, one might question, in an increasingly secular world characterized by scientific discovery and skepticism, where does faith fit in? Non-religious perspectives often frame these spiritual pursuits as endeavors of human psychology, an evolutionarily developed mechanism to cope with life's uncertainties and the vast unknown. They argue that whether through

---

[366] Isaiah, Hosea, and others are examples of prophets through whom God spoke, as mentioned in the Old Testament.

meditation, prayer, or even ritualistic practices, humans have naturally sought ways to deal with existential anxieties.[367]

For many, however, these practices are more than just coping mechanisms. They are profound, lived experiences that offer glimpses into the eternal, serving as anchors in an ever-changing world. C. S. Lewis once noted that prayer doesn't change God but changes the one who prays.[368] This transformative power of prayer and other spiritual practices underscores their significance in the life of a believer.

The emphasis on personal revelation within the LDS doctrine further highlights the importance of individual connection with the Divine. Joseph Smith, the founding prophet of the LDS Church, had his First Vision after a profound period of introspection and prayer, seeking clarity on which church to join.[369]

This vision set a precedent for all Latter-Day Saints, the idea that direct, personal guidance from God isn't just a possibility but a promise.

However, as one explores the multifaceted realm of spiritual practices, it becomes evident that the search for the Divine isn't exclusive to Christianity or the LDS Church. Buddhists meditate to tap into universal truths, Muslims pray five times daily facing Mecca, and Hindus engage in puja to connect with their deities. These practices, rooted in age-old traditions, are a testament to a universal yearning to comprehend and commune with the greater cosmic order.

In this chapter, we will explore our shared desire—whether from faith or skepticism—to find answers and to understand our place as humanity in this grand tapestry of existence. In the subsequent sections, I will delve deeper into specific pathways that individuals, especially from Christian and

---

[367] Dawkins, *The God Delusion.*

[368] C. S. Lewis, *Letters to Malcolm: Chiefly on Prayer* (San Diego: Harcourt Brace Jovanovich, 1964).

[369] Smith, Pearl of Great Price, 1:10–20.

LDS traditions, have adopted to draw closer to God over the millennia. Together, we'll explore each method's nuances, beauty, and challenges while also drawing parallels with non-faith perspectives.

The Essence and Evolution of Prayer

Historically, within the Judeo-Christian tradition, prayer has served as a vital conduit to communicate with God. Abraham, the father of monotheism, frequently communed with God, seeking guidance and interceding on behalf of others (Gen 18:23–33). The Psalms offer a testament to the diverse range of human emotions poured out to God, from joyous exaltation to desolate lamentation. Jesus, the very heart of the Christian faith, often retreated in solitude to pray, revealing its fundamental importance (Lk 6:12).

Latter-Day Saints emphasize the personal, revelatory nature of prayer. The Church's foundation is steeped in prayer, with Joseph Smith's earnest plea for truth yielding the First Vision.[370] Latter-Day Saints are taught that prayer is how one can receive personal revelatory guidance tailored to each individual's life circumstances.

In the early days, the Israelites, bound by the Old Covenant, had a distinct approach to reaching out to God. "And let them make me a sanctuary; that I may dwell among them," the Lord declared (Ex 25:8), and thus the Tabernacle, and later the Temple in Jerusalem, became central places for divine encounters. The Israelites approached the Almighty predominantly through ritualistic sacrifices and temple prayers. These weren't just superficial acts; each sacrifice was imbued with profound symbolic significance. The shedding of innocent blood in these rituals, especially in the Passover lamb, foreshadowed the impending and ultimate sacrifice: Jesus Christ. As the Apostle Paul notes, "But Christ being come an high priest of good things to come, by a greater and more perfect tabernacle, not made with hands . . . Neither by the blood of goats and calves, but by his

---

[370] Smith, Pearl of Great Price, 1:10–20.

own blood he entered in once into the holy place, having obtained eternal redemption for us" (Heb 9:11–12).

With Christ's atonement, a seismic shift occurred in the realm of spiritual communication. This transformative event did not merely redefine the paradigms of salvation but also fundamentally altered the nature of prayer itself. The curtain of the Holy of Holies in the Jerusalem Temple, a symbol of separation between God and his people, was torn, signifying a new, accessible pathway to God. The early Christians, infused with the Holy Spirit, no longer felt the need for ritual intermediaries. Prayer, in this new dispensation, became a direct, personal bridge to God, unencumbered by rituals.

Acts 2:42 paints a picture of the early Christian community: "And they continued stedfastly in the apostles' doctrine and fellowship, and in breaking of bread, and in prayers." Prayer was an integral component of their communal and personal lives. This transition from ritual to relationship didn't negate the value of the rituals but emphasized the evolution from symbolic acts to a heart-to-heart communion with God.

While reflecting upon this progression, it's crucial to acknowledge the myriad of ways in which people from various traditions and even those without specific religious affiliations approach the Divine or the concept of a higher power. Many of today's spiritual seekers, even outside the ambit of organized religion, employ meditation, mindfulness, and other contemplative practices to tap into a sense of the transcendent. While differing in form, these methods share a common aim: connecting with something greater than oneself.

For instance, Buddhists employ meditation not as a means of supplication but as a tool for enlightenment and the cultivation of compassion. In contrast, many agnostics or those subscribing to secular humanism might not pray traditionally but engage in profound introspective moments, seeking clarity, purpose, and a sense of connectedness to the universe.

From a broader perspective, while Christianity and the LDS Church offer profound depth on the subject, it's enlightening to consider how non-faith views perceive prayer. To some secular thinkers, prayer is seen as a psychological exercise to introspect and achieve mental clarity.[371] Anthropologist Scott Atran suggests that religious rituals, including prayer, cater to universal cognitive functions, assisting individuals in navigating complex social landscapes and existential uncertainties.[372]

However, to reduce prayer merely to cognitive processes is to miss the profound spiritual metamorphosis countless individuals, including myself, have undergone. C. S. Lewis once beautifully articulated, "I pray because I can't help myself. I pray because I'm helpless. I pray because the need flows out of me all the time, waking and sleeping. It doesn't change God. It changes me."[373]

This sentiment is mirrored in LDS teachings. President Ezra Taft Benson, a prophet of the LDS Church, remarked, "Prayer is a commandment and an invitation to come unto Him and draw near to him. It is not just an activity or ceremony. Proper prayer is both a commandment and a promise."[374]

One must admit prayer isn't always met with discernible answers. There were times amidst suffering and confusion when heaven seemed silent in my life. It's a challenge that theologians and believers have grappled with for millennia. However, in these moments of seeming silence, faith often grows, grounded not in instant clarity but in patient perseverance.[375]

---

[371] Daniel Dennett, *Breaking the Spell: Religion as a Natural Phenomenon* (New York: Viking, 2006).

[372] Scott Atran, *In Gods We Trust: The Evolutionary Landscape of Religion* (Oxford: Oxford University Press, 2002).

[373] Lewis, *Letters to Malcolm: Chiefly on Prayer.*

[374] Ezra Taft Benson, "Prayer," *Ensign*, May 1977.

[375] Harold S. Kushner, *When Bad Things Happen to Good People* (New York: Schocken Books, 1981).

Bridging back to the non-faith viewpoint, some might argue that unanswered prayers are proof of God's absence. But within the Christian and LDS framework, unanswered prayers don't signify God's indifference but rather his profound wisdom. As the scripture goes, "For my thoughts are not your thoughts, neither are your ways my ways, saith the LORD" (Is 55:8).

While prayer's essence remains unchanged—a heart reaching out to the Divine—its understanding and practice have evolved within religious and non-religious paradigms. Whether viewed as a spiritual communion or a psychological exercise, its transformative power is undeniable. As we progress, we will delve deeper into meditation and other spiritual practices, further exploring the multifaceted avenues through which souls seek the Divine.

Fasting: Physical Sacrifice for Spiritual Gain

Throughout my journey in faith, I've realized that sometimes the most profound spiritual experiences emerge from the moments when we willingly forsake physical comforts in exchange for spiritual growth. This notion of sacrifice for the sake of spiritual enlightenment isn't solely limited to periodic abstention from food. It often extends to daily practices, habits, and preferences that define our routines.

In the LDS doctrine known as the Word of Wisdom advises members on health practices consistent with their faith. One of its tenets includes refraining from consuming "hot drink," which has been interpreted as a ban on coffee and tea.[376] For many converts to the LDS faith, including me, this is not just a dietary adjustment; it's a significant sacrifice.

Before embracing the LDS teachings, my day would invariably begin with multiple tall glasses of iced coffee, a ritual I cherished. It wasn't merely about caffeine intake; it was a beloved morning routine. Likewise, sipping

---

[376] Smith, Doctrine and Covenants, 89:5–9.

iced tea was my blissful escape, my midday rejuvenation. Relinquishing these habits was not easy. It was a test of my commitment and a tangible daily reminder of my new path in faith.

Such daily abstentions underscore the essence of the broader principle of fasting in the LDS tradition. While not consuming food for a specific period is one manifestation, other smaller, daily sacrifices, like avoiding coffee and tea, consistently remind one of one's dedication and commitment to living by divine guidance.

Fasting is a ritual advocated by various religious doctrines that carries a depth that intertwines the spiritual with the physical, molding them into a singular experience. It's an act not just of deprivation but also of profound dedication. The words of Jesus Christ encapsulate this essence, suggesting that fasting is not a mere show of righteousness but a deep, personal communion with God. In the Sermon on the Mount, Jesus says: "Moreover when ye fast, be not, as the hypocrites, of a sad countenance.. . . But thou, when thou fastest.. . . That thou appear not unto men to fast, but unto thy Father which is in secret: and thy Father, which seeth in secret, shall reward thee openly" (Mt 6:16–18).

This teaching finds resonance in various Christian traditions, including the LDS tradition. The monthly fasting observed by its members is not merely an act of going without food. It is also a period of introspection, humility, and drawing closer to God, and it has a tangible manifestation in the form of "fast offerings." These offerings, a voluntary donation made to the church, stand as a testimony to the believers' commitment to assist those in need.[377]

---

[377] Spencer W. Kimball, "The Blessings of Fasting," *Ensign*, July 1976.

Fasting isn't exclusively rooted in religious teachings. Numerous scientific disciplines, backed by years of meticulous research, highlight the array of health benefits associated with intermittent fasting (IF).[378]

Central to this is insulin's role in metabolic homeostasis. When we consume carbohydrates, they are broken down into glucose, a simple sugar that circulates in our blood.[379] The pancreas secretes insulin in response to this rise in blood glucose. Functionally, insulin facilitates glucose uptake into cells, where it's utilized for energy or stored for future use.[380] Continuous and excessive caloric intake, especially from refined carbohydrates, can lead to a persistently elevated insulin release. Over time, cells can become less responsive to insulin—a phenomenon known as insulin resistance.[381] This resistance is often the precursor to type 2 diabetes. Notably, intermittent fasting has been demonstrated to enhance insulin sensitivity, allowing cells to respond to smaller amounts of insulin efficiently.[382]

Moreover, the rewards of IF extend beyond just metabolic well-being. Research shows the brain appears to be a significant beneficiary of fasting. Fasting activates a metabolic pathway known as autophagy, which involves removing waste material from cells.[383] This cellular "housekeeping" process is believed to shield the brain from various age-related ailments. In tandem with this, fasting also amplifies the production of a brain-derived

[378] Mark P. Mattson Wan and Ruiqian, "Beneficial effects of intermittent fasting and caloric restriction on the cardiovascular and cerebrovascular systems," *The Journal of Nutritional Biochemistry* 16, no. 3 (2005): 129–137.

[379] Jeremy M. Berg, John L. Tymoczko, Lubert Stryer et al., *Biochemistry* 5th edition (New York: W. H. Freeman, 2002), Section 16.1.

[380] Alan R. Saltiel and C. Ronald Kahn, "Insulin signaling and the regulation of glucose and lipid metabolism," *Nature* 414, no. 6865 (2001): 799–806.

[381] Steven E. Kahn, Robert L. Hull, and Kristina M. Utzschneider, "Mechanisms linking obesity to insulin resistance and type 2 diabetes," *Nature* 444, no. 7121 (2006): 840–846.

[382] N. Halberg et al., "Effect of intermittent fasting and refeeding on insulin action in healthy men," *Journal of Applied Physiology* 99, no. 6 (2005): 2128–2136.

[383] Mehrdad Alirezaei et al., "Short-term fasting induces profound neuronal autophagy," *Autophagy* 6, no. 6 (2010): 702–710.

neurotrophic factor (BDNF) protein. This protein champions overall brain function and diminishes the potential risk of neurodegenerative diseases.[384]

Peering into the longevity aspects of fasting, some of the most compelling findings emerge. Animal-centric studies have consistently spotlighted intermittent fasting as a catalyst for extended lifespans. While human-focused research is still developing, early indications point toward a similar promising trend.[385] The potential of IF to stave off age-related maladies might be pivotal here. By boosting cellular repair mechanisms and modifying the expression of genes intricately linked to longevity and disease defense, IF emerges as a hope for those pursuing the dream of a prolonged, healthier existence.[386]

The congruence between age-old religious practices and cutting-edge scientific revelations stands out in an era where health paradigms are in constant flux. The importance of intermittent fasting, deeply ingrained in many religious traditions, is bolstered by a mounting arsenal of scientific data.

For believers, fasting transcends these physiological advantages. The act reaches its zenith when viewed as a spiritual exercise. In his theological musings, Saint Augustine highlighted this spiritual profundity of fasting when he remarked that fasting "cleanses the soul, raises the mind, subjects one's flesh to the spirit, rendering the heart contrite and humble . . ."[387]

Not everyone, however, views fasting in this light. Critics often point out the potential health risks of prolonged fasting, suggesting it might lead to

---

[384] Jaewon Lee et al., "Dietary restriction increases the number of newly generated neural cells, and induces BDNF expression, in the dentate gyrus of rats," *Journal of Molecular Neuroscience* 15, vol. 2 (2000): 99–108.

[385] Rashmi Singh et al., "Late-onset intermittent fasting dietary restriction as a potential intervention to retard age-associated brain function impairments in male rats," *Age* 34, vol. 4 (2012): 917–933.

[386] Hyun Woo Chung et al., "Intermittent fasting and food restriction modulate molecular markers of aging in the brain of aging C57BL/6 mice," *Nutritional Neuroscience* 21, vol. 9 (2018): 655–666.

[387] Augustine of Hippo, *Sermons on Fasting and Prayer*, circa 400 CE.

malnutrition, dehydration, and even metabolic imbalances.[388] It's essential, however, to differentiate between religious fasting and extreme deprivation. Within Christian and LDS frameworks, fasting is not about harming the body but about refining the soul. The emphasis is always on the spiritual intent, aligning physical sacrifices with prayer, reflection, and drawing closer to God.[389]

In the grand tapestry of spiritual practices, fasting holds a unique place. Whether through the act of going without food for a day or in the smaller daily sacrifices, like refraining from cherished beverages, fasting serves as a bridge. It connects the mundane with the Divine, guiding believers like me to moments of profound clarity, introspection, and an ever-deepening bond with the Creator.

Sacred Rituals and Ordinance

In the intricate tapestry of human spiritual expression, sacred rituals and ordinances stand out as emblematic threads binding believers to their faith and their traditions. These acts, infused with deep symbolic meaning, play a pivotal role in the religious journey, fortifying the bond between the individual and the Divine.

With its rich history and varied denominations, Christendom has always underscored the importance of rituals. During his journey on earth, Christ emphasized the significance of specific ordinances. One of the most poignant instances is recorded in the Gospel of John, where Jesus states, *"Except a man be born of water and of the Spirit, he cannot enter into the kingdom of God"* (Jn 3:5). This decree has been interpreted by many as a reference to the sacred rite of baptism.

In LDS theology, ordinances are considered essential covenants made with God. The LDS Church holds that through these covenants, individuals

---

[388] Rona Antoni Rona et al., "The effects of intermittent energy restriction on indices of cardiometabolic health," *Research in Endocrinology*, vol. 2014, 2017.
[389] Dallin H. Oaks, "Why Do We Fast?" *Ensign*, Dec. 1985.

come closer to Christ and understand his teachings more profoundly.[390] Baptism, for instance, is not merely a symbolic act of cleansing but a gateway to receiving the Holy Ghost. Confirming this, the Doctrine and Covenants, an essential scripture in the LDS tradition, mentions, "Yea, blessed are they who shall believe on your words, and come down into the depths of humility and be baptized, for they shall be visited with fire and with the Holy Ghost . . ."[391]

While Christianity is rife with sacred rituals and ordinances, one need not look far to find similar practices in various religious traditions globally, each one deeply symbolic and vital for its practitioners. These ceremonies underscore humanity's enduring quest to connect, comprehend, and commune with the Divine or the cosmos, transcending mere ceremonial aspects.

In Islam, for instance, the ritual of ablution, or "wudu," is performed before the prayers. This cleansing process isn't merely about physical purity but symbolizes the believer's inner purification, preparing them spiritually to stand before God.[392] Similarly, in Judaism, the lighting of the menorah isn't just an act but signifies the miracle of the oil that lasted eight days in the Holy Temple, reminding Jews of God's continuous presence and miracles in their lives.[393]

Hinduism, with its rich tapestry of rites, offers another illustrative example. The ritual of "aarti," where devotees wave lamps in front of a deity, is symbolic of dispelling darkness and ignorance, invoking the presence of the deity and seeking blessings.[394]

---

[390] James E. Talmage, "The Articles of Faith," *Deseret News,* 1899.

[391] Smith, Doctrine and Covenants, 21:6.

[392] John L. Esposito, *What Everyone Needs to Know About Islam* (Oxford: Oxford University Press, 2011).

[393] Joseph Telushkin, *Jewish Literacy: The Most Important Things to Know About the Jewish Religion, Its People, and Its History* (New York: Harper Collins, 2008).

[394] Diana L. Eck, *Darsan: Seeing the Divine Image in India* (New York: Columbia University Press, 1998).

In Buddhism, the act of offering incense at altars isn't just about fragrance. It is symbolic of the impermanence of life—as the incense burns, it reminds believers of the transient nature of existence and encourages detachment.[395]

Native American tribes are also known for their profound spiritual practices. For instance, the Lakota Sioux's "Wiwanke Wachipi" or Sun Dance is both a personal sacrifice and a means to ensure the community's well-being. Dancers fast, pray, and perform rigorous physical acts, aiming to forge a connection with the Great Spirit, seeking blessings and visions for guidance.[396]

The indigenous tribes of Australia, the Aboriginals, have their intricate "Dreamtime" stories, which are narrated through dance, music, and art. These rituals are not mere performances but serve to connect the current generation with their ancestral spirits and the sacred land.[397]

From a secular perspective, these rituals might seem purely ceremonial without the underlying context. However, for those who practice and hold these traditions dear, they are deeply spiritual and transformative acts. They are symbolic bridges connecting the temporal with the eternal, the earthly with the Divine.

Rituals, in essence, reflect humanity's innate desire to seek meaning, connect with the cosmos, and navigate the complexities of existence. They might differ in form, but at their heart, they embody a universal quest for understanding and communion with the Divine or the larger universe.

---

[395] Peter Harvey, *An Introduction to Buddhism: Teachings, History and Practices* (Cambridge: Cambridge University Press, 2012).
[396] *I Become Part of It: Sacred Dimensions in Native American Life*, ed. D. M. Dooling and Paul Jordan-Smith (New York: Parabola Books, 1989).
[397] Diane Bell, *Ngarrindjeri Wurruwarrin: A World That Is, Was, and Will Be* (Victoria: Spinifex Press, 1998).

However, skeptics and critics opine that ritualistic practices in religions, especially in the modern age, seem outdated and irrelevant.[398] These acts might be mere ceremonial formalities devoid of genuine spiritual weight in the quest for spiritual truth. While such a viewpoint has its merits, it fails to recognize the deep-rooted spiritual significance and the sense of continuity they offer to believers, primarily when rituals are conducted without understanding or feeling.

My journey within the LDS Church has made me mindful of the profound impact of participating in sacred ordinances. For instance, consider the sacrament, a weekly ritual observed by Latter-Day Saints. While to an outsider it may seem to be a simple act of breaking bread and drinking water, its symbolism, rooted in the Last Supper that Jesus shared with his disciples, evokes a profound sense of reverence, reminding us of Christ's sacrifice.[399] More than its constituent elements, the act fosters a moment of introspection, repentance, and renewal.

In LDS theology, the temple is the epicenter of the most sacred ordinances. These rituals encapsulate the Church's core beliefs about life, death, and eternity, from endowments to eternal marriage sealings.[400] My own experiences within the temple's hallowed walls have been transformative. They've served as moments of profound spiritual insights, where the outside world's noise seems to fade, giving way to an overwhelming sense of peace and divine connection.

While sacred rituals and ordinances might sometimes appear as mere traditions, they serve as vital conduits connecting believers with the Divine, providing spiritual nourishment and a deeper understanding of one's faith. As the Apostle Paul put it: "Let all things be done decently and in order" (1

---

[398] Émile Durkheim, *The Elementary Forms of the Religious Life* (London: George Allen & Unwin, 1915).

[399] David A. Bednar, "Always Retain a Remission of Your Sins," *Ensign*, May 2016.

[400] Russell M. Nelson, "Personal Preparation for Temple Blessings," *Ensign*, May 2001.

Cor 14:14). Rituals, in essence, guide believers on the path of spiritual order and enlightenment.

Nature and the Divine

I have often marveled at the intrinsic beauty and harmony of nature. For believers, the universe, with its wondrous constellations and the intricate web of life on our blue planet, serves as a testament to the creative genius of the Almighty.[401] "The heavens declare the glory of God; and the firmament sheweth his handywork" (Ps 19:1). Such profound connections between nature and the Divine have been pivotal in shaping the worldview of believers, even as they resonate with people of other faiths and those without religious affiliations.

Central to Christian belief is the understanding that God created the world and everything in it.[402] This creation is not viewed as a random act but as a purposeful endeavor, a physical manifestation of God's love. As expressed in Genesis 1:31, "And God saw everything that he had made, and, behold, it was very good." LDS teachings echo this sentiment, emphasizing that Earth was created as a place for God's children to learn and grow.[403]

The LDS belief in continuous revelation further highlights the connection between nature and the Divine. Joseph Smith's revelations, which form the core of LDS scriptures alongside the Bible, frequently reference the natural world's wonders as evidence of God's love and grand design.[404] The Doctrine and Covenants, a compilation of these revelations, contains many verses highlighting God's power manifest in nature.

While Christians and members of the LDS Church view nature through this spiritual lens, many indigenous cultures worldwide also recognize a

---

[401] C. S. Lewis, *The Four Loves* (New York: HarperCollins, 1960).
[402] Alister E. McGrath, *Christian Theology: An Introduction* (Hoboken: John Wiley & Sons, 2016).
[403] Joseph Smith, *Teachings of Presidents of the Church: Joseph Smith* (Salt Lake City: Church of Jesus Christ of Latter-day Saints, 2007).
[404] Smith, Doctrine and Covenants.

divine presence in the natural world. Many Native American tribes, for instance, consider Earth to be a living entity, sacred and interwoven with spirituality.[405] This belief is not just an abstract concept but influences their daily life, rituals, and relationship with the land.

In contrast, from a secular viewpoint, nature often represents the wonders of evolution and the laws of physics, not necessarily tethered to divine intervention. While marveling at the universe's beauty and complexity, prominent figures like Carl Sagan and Stephen Hawking lean toward explanations rooted in science rather than theology.[406]

Even within non-religious contexts, one finds an acknowledgment of the awe-inspiring aspects of nature. Romantic poets like Wordsworth and Shelley have expressed reverence for nature's beauty, seeking solace and meaning in its embrace, even if they didn't necessarily attribute it to a divine creator.[407]

The world, with its mountains, rivers, flora, and fauna, can evoke feelings of tranquility, contemplation, and even spirituality. Nature's cycles, from the serene drifting of clouds to the fierce force of hurricanes, remind us of life's ebb and flow, joys and sorrows, certainties and mysteries.

The awe that the natural world instills can be a bridge between the religious and secular worlds. Whether one believes in a Creator or the power of science, the universal experience remains: nature has the capacity to inspire, heal, and connect.

The intertwining of nature and the divine is not solely a Christian or an LDS perspective. Throughout history and across cultures, humans have looked at the cosmos and Earth, seeking answers, solace, and a connection

---

[405] Gregory Cajete, *Native Science: Natural Laws of Interdependence* (Santa Fe: Clear Light Publishers, 2000).
[406] Hawking, *A Brief History of Time.*
[407] *English Romantic Poets: Modern Essays in Criticism*, ed. M. H. Abrams (Oxford: Oxford University Press, 1975).

to something greater than themselves. For some it's the hand of God; for others it's the marvel of the universe and the intricate dance of life. Regardless of one's beliefs, nature's grandeur is a humbling reminder of our place in the vast tapestry of existence.

Sacred Music and Worship

Saint Augustine of Hippo once remarked, "He who sings prays twice."[408] Music is a deep-seated power, especially when it intersects with spirituality. From the melodic chanting of the psalms to the rhythmic beats in gospel music, sacred music has been a vessel for worship, introspection, and communion with the Divine.

The Bible has numerous references to the importance of singing and playing instruments as forms of worship (e.g., "Make a joyful noise unto the Lord, all ye lands. Serve the Lord with gladness: come before his presence with singing" (Ps 100:1–2)). It isn't merely an act of vocal or instrumental expression but a celebration of God's love and a testament to his glory.[409]

The Church of Jesus Christ of Latter-day Saints holds music in high esteem. As a newcomer to the LDS community, I was surrounded by a new world of hymns, some familiar from the broader Christian tradition and others unique to the Church. For a faith that believes in continuous revelation, it's no surprise that there's a vibrant tradition of LDS hymns.[410]

But I must confess that diving into this vast sea of sacred music has been challenging. Lacking a background in reading music and being new to many hymns, I felt like a novice amidst a choir of seasoned singers. Each Sunday as voices rose in harmonious praise, I would fumble with the hymnbook, trying to match the melody and pace. While others sang, I read

---

[408] Augustine of Hippo, *Expositions on the Book of Psalms* (Oxford: John Henry Parker, 1848).

[409] Charles H. Spurgeon, *The Treasury of David* (New York: Marshall Brothers, 1881).

[410] Michael Hicks, *Mormonism and Music: A History* (Champaign, IL: University of Illinois Press, 2003).

along, silently whispering words of worship, hoping that I could join the rest of the ward and sing confidently in time.

This personal struggle made me realize something profound. The value of sacred music isn't purely in its auditory beauty or precision. It's in the intent, the heart's yearning to connect with God. Hymns are more than just songs; they are prayers, expressions of faith, and declarations of devotion.[411]

Beyond the Christian and LDS realms, music holds a special place in many world religions. In Islam, the call to prayer (or Adhan) is melodiously chanted, beckoning the faithful.[412] The reverberations of Tibetan Buddhist bowls or the chants of Hindu Bhajans show that sacred sounds serve as a universal bridge between the earthly realm and the Divine.[413]

From a secular perspective, one doesn't need to believe in a higher power to appreciate the transcendent quality of religious music. Great composers like Johann Sebastian Bach and Wolfgang Amadeus Mozart composed sacred pieces that continue to captivate audiences regardless of their beliefs.[414]

The soul-stirring attribute of music isn't solely a hallmark of the classical era or strictly religious compositions. Music possesses a unique universality, resonating across cultures, faiths, and societal strata. It harbors the ability to evoke profound emotions, transporting listeners on a poignant journey. Often, it encapsulates the quintessential human yearning for love and connection.

Phil Collins's "In The Air Tonight"[415] stands as a profound testament to music's intrinsic power to evoke deep emotion and contemplation,

---

411 Pew Research Center, "Religion and Music: Universal Themes of Praise," Pew-Templeton Global Religious Futures Project, 2015.
412 Seyyed Hossein Nasr, *Islam: Religion, History, and Civilization* (San Francisco: HarperOne, 2003).
413 Eck, *Darsan: Seeing the Divine Image in India.*
414 Jan Swafford, *Johann Sebastian Bach: The Learned Musician* (New York: W. W. Norton & Company, 2000).
415 Phil Collins, "In the Air Tonight," recorded Feb. 13, 1981, track 1 on *Face Value*, Atlantic Records.

resonating with audiences of varied backgrounds. The track, with its rising intensity and iconic drum interlude, provides a soundscape for introspection, mainly as it narrates the internal conflict of its protagonist: wrestling between the urgent impulse to aid another in a dire situation and a contrasting hunger for retribution. Though the song doesn't bear overt spiritual undertones, the evocative lyrics and ambiance crafted by Collins encapsulate a pivotal moment of looming transformation or insight, beckoning listeners to immerse themselves in their interpretations of its narrative.

In the realm of sacred music and worship, even unexpected sources can offer profound spiritual reflections. Musician Jelly Roll, born Jason DeFord, has crafted poignant pieces that transcend musical genres as he narrates the personal battles he's endured—struggles that resonate universally, albeit in different magnitudes for each individual. A live performance that particularly captivates me is a mashup of two of his evocative songs: "Only" and "Love the Heartless."[416] Through this amalgamation, DeFord portrays an internal warfare, representing them as demonic forces contending for dominance. Through divine strength and guidance, he finds the fortitude to resist and transcend these overwhelming impulses:

> What if the darkness inside of me has finally taken my soul?
> What if the angels in heaven were sent to take me home?
> Would they fight through the demons that I have in my life?
> Lord, I'm believing, eventually see the light
> [. . .]
> I have struggling playing tug of war with a few of the demons I know
> I have been shunned and drugged through the mud
> I don't hold a grudge I been here before
> There is still fight in me I can be anything I set my mind to be yes I can
> The storm that's inside of me rages so violently
> God shine your light on me, here I am

---

[416] Jelly Roll, "Only & Love The Heartless (Live)," YouTube video, 5:45, May 28, 2020, https://youtu.be/gL_GW1eItlU.

Won't you pray for me
Pray for me pray for me
[. . .]
This monster I can't control
I hope the lord saves my soul (My soul)
I know I need you lord
Nothing that I need more[417]

In collaboration with Brandon Hart & Nova Rockafeller, Tom MacDonald delivers a poignant narrative of his battles with drug and alcohol addiction in his song "Church."[418] The evocative lyrics, "I keep buying whiskey when all I need is church. I keep talking to God, but he doesn't hear me. And my demons are there, always listening. I get lost in the dark, drowning in whiskey,"[419] paint a vivid picture of a soul torn between the ensnaring clutches of addiction and the redeeming pull of faith. Although I've never grappled with substance addiction, the song strikes a chord, emphasizing the universality of human struggles, whether physical, spiritual, or mental.

This duality, the perpetual conflict between the body and the spirit, echoes LDS teachings. The Book of Mormon, for instance, touches upon the natural man being an enemy of God and speaks of the need to subdue the passions of the flesh to become a saint through the atonement of Jesus Christ.[420] MacDonald's candid lyrics mirror this theological theme, suggesting that the path to redemption, while fraught with challenges, is achievable through steadfast faith and reliance on the Lord's grace.

Alma, a prominent figure in the Book of Mormon, underwent a transformative journey, moving from a life of transgressions to one of profound faith and leadership. Similarly, many find solace in the gospel after grappling with life's tempests, like the storms MacDonald describes in

---

417 Ibid.
418 Tom MacDonald and Brandon Hart, "Church," YouTube video, 3:36, March 26, 2021, https://youtu.be/Fgo0V52o10U.
419 Ibid.
420 Mosiah 3:19.

his music. This song serves not just as a testament to his personal battles but also as an anthem for all those striving to find their way back to the light in a way that transcends any specific religious doctrine.

In the soul-stirring verses of "God's Eyes,"[421] rapper Dax, born Daniel Nwosu, delves into the age-old battle between divine forces and demonic temptations. With lines like "Uh, I've never seen God's eyes, but I've seen the devil's. He walks with men on earth at different levels. He knows the king we serve, so he hates and meddles. And prays that we all burn and turn to rebels,"[422] he portrays Satan's omnipresence and constant efforts to lead mankind astray. Dax also addresses the human role in religious degradation: "Uh, rebellious in our ways, been sinners since birth. He knew that it would happen when He put us on this earth. We demonized religion, brought corruption to the church."[423]

While it's unlikely that Dax penned this piece expressly to reflect on LDS doctrines, it's fascinating to draw parallels between his lyrics and the LDS perspective on apostasy and restoration. The Church firmly believes in a period of universal apostasy, where the original truths of Christ's teachings were obscured or lost. This necessitated a divine restoration, which was ushered in through the Prophet Joseph Smith. Similarly, Dax's verses underscore the importance of recognizing spiritual deviations and working ardently toward reclaiming one's faith.

Such artists uniquely fuse rock, rap, and country genres, crafting a harmonious blend that resonates with modern sensibilities. Their musical expressions, though characterized by contemporary styles, often articulate messages that have a timeless allure. Their music champions God-loving and patriotic ideals and underscores unity, tenacity, and optimism. While their verses may not be overtly religious, they reverberate with motifs of spirituality, salvation, self-examination, and individual evolution, appealing

---

[421] Dax, "God's Eyes," YouTube video, 3:05, July 21, 2023, https://youtu.be/MW_5jZ67z9E.
[422] Ibid.
[423] Ibid.

to the devout and the secular. In its boundless reach, music possesses an innate capacity to stir souls, awaken sentiments, and extend comfort during trying periods, transcending its origin or categorization.

In a broader context, music can be seen as a unifying force. In multi-faith forums, inter-religious choirs unite to sing, bridging differences and celebrating shared human experiences.[424] For believers and non-believers alike, the harmony of sacred music is a testament to humanity's age-old quest for meaning, connection, and transcendence.

The science behind music's impact on memory is both fascinating and well-documented. It is a phenomenon rooted in the intricate structures and functions of the brain. When we listen to music, particularly music with lyrics, multiple brain regions are activated, including the auditory cortex, which processes sounds, and the hippocampus, which is associated with long-term memory storage.[425]

A study from the University of California, Davis, discovered that the brain's medial prefrontal cortex, which sits just behind the forehead, plays a pivotal role. This region is one of the last areas of the brain to atrophy over time, which may explain why Alzheimer's patients can often recall songs long after they've forgotten other experiences.[426]

In an educational setting, teachers have harnessed the power of music to enhance learning outcomes. We've seen this in action with mnemonic devices set to music, which assist students in remembering complex concepts or sequences. "The Alphabet Song," which helps children recall the order of letters in the alphabet is a primary example. Similarly, hymns and other religious songs serve a dual purpose. Beyond their spiritual

---

[424] Eboo Patel, *Acts of Faith: The Story of an American Muslim, in the Struggle for the Soul of a Generation* (Boston: Beacon Press, 2007).

[425] P. Janata, S. T. Tomic, and J. M. Haberman, "Sensorimotor coupling in music and the psychology of the groove," *Journal of Experimental Psychology: General* 141, vol. 1 (2012): 54.

[426] A. Baird S. Samson, "Music and dementia," *Progress in Brain Research* 217 (2015): 207–235.

significance, they encapsulate complex theological or moral teachings, making them more digestible and easier to remember.[427]

Historically, in an era before widespread literacy or the availability of printed materials, oral traditions, often in the form of songs or rhythmic chants, were the primary method of transmitting knowledge, stories, and cultural practices. Religious texts and teachings set to music are more easily committed to memory, ensuring accurate transmission from generation to generation.

From an academic standpoint, one could argue that including songs in religious ceremonies and practices was not merely a matter of spirituality but also a necessity. It facilitated preserving and disseminating religious teachings, unifying communities, and strengthening shared beliefs through a harmonious fusion of melody and message.

As I continue my journey in the LDS Church, I find solace in the fact that every hymn I encounter, whether I can sing it flawlessly or not, brings me a step closer to the Divine. My initial hesitancy has evolved into an eagerness to learn, to immerse myself in the spiritual tapestry of sacred sounds. After all, it's not the perfection of the note that matters but the purity of the intent.

Sacred music across faiths and cultures stands as a testament to the human spirit's innate yearning to connect with something greater. Whether in cathedrals, mosques, temples, or open fields, when voices rise in unison, there's an echo of the eternal, a whisper of the transcendent, a chorus of souls reaching out to the Divine.

---

[427] W. T. Wallace, "Memory for music: Effect of melody on recall of text," *Journal of Experimental Psychology: Learning, Memory, and Cognition* 20, vol. 6 (1994): 1471.

Scripture Study: Conversing with God Through Holy Texts

When I embarked on the journey to write this book, I approached it initially as an academic endeavor. Little did I realize that it would become an intimate voyage into the heart of faith, both mine and that of countless believers across millennia. The practice of scripture study, in particular, stood out as an illuminating pillar in this exploration.

In my relentless pursuit of knowledge, I embarked on a journey through the scriptures of various religious traditions. It's not just the multiple texts I sought but a more profound, interconnected narrative that binds humanity in its search for the Divine. As I read selected pieces and summaries of numerous scriptures, the enormity of the task became evident. The vast sea of spiritual literature is overwhelming, almost too enormous for any individual to fully grasp and appreciate. Despite the enormity of this task, I remain committed, endeavoring to read more, to expand my horizons, and to deepen my understanding and reverence for these sacred works.

Each scripture I explored revealed a world rich with tales, prophecies, hymns, and pearls of wisdom. However, the experience was about more than just absorbing content and appreciating context. Gaining insights into the historical, societal, and cultural landscapes from which these scriptures emerged enriched my study, allowing for a more layered understanding. It felt like I was assembling a vast mosaic of human spirituality, each piece and fragment serving as a testament to a unique revelation and voice.

In Christianity, the Bible holds a venerable position, not just as a historical document or a compilation of teachings but as the very Word of God. The psalmist wrote, "Thy word is a lamp unto my feet, and a light unto my path" (Ps 119:105). This powerful imagery portrays the Bible as a guiding light, offering direction in the maze of life's challenges. But beyond guidance, delving into sacred texts offers a profound method of conversing with the Divine.

For members of the Church of Jesus Christ of Latter-day Saints, the Book of Mormon complements the Bible. It is another testament of Jesus Christ, and it underscores his teachings. I can still remember the weight of the Book of Mormon in my hands when I first began my studies, unfamiliar yet radiating with promise. As I delved into its pages, it was like listening to a familiar echo. This harmonizing voice enriched and expanded my understanding of the Savior's teachings and his endless love.

However, the act of studying scripture isn't exclusive to Christianity or the Church of Jesus Christ of Latter-day Saints. It is a shared experience among many diverse faiths. For Muslims, the Quran is believed to be the literal word of God, revealed to the Prophet Muhammad. Its recitation isn't just an act of worship but a dialogue with Allah, offering wisdom, guidance, and solace. Buddhists pore over the Tripitaka, while Jews cherish the Torah, often wrapping it in ornate cases and reading it with a sense of ceremony, respect, and reverence.

God speaks to all his children regardless of borders, languages, or customs. He doesn't just communicate through the universal language of love but also in the rich dialects and traditions unique to each culture. This is exemplified in the diverse holy scriptures and spiritual narratives that have emerged across continents and eras.

Whether the Vedas in ancient India, the stories of the Dreamtime revered by Australian Aboriginals, or the parables told by Jesus in the Middle East, each is tailored to resonate with a specific audience yet universally illuminates the divine nature of God's teachings. Just as a loving parent uses different words but the same sentiment when addressing each child, God also employs various means to convey an enduring message of love, guidance, and purpose to every corner of humanity. This harmonious multitude of voices, each echoing a tailored facet of divine wisdom, is a testament to a Creator who values the unique and myriad ways human beings express their spirituality.

Following this understanding of the diverse channels through which God communicates, a deeply held belief within the Church of Jesus Christ of Latter-day Saints reaffirms its unique position in the spiritual landscape. While God might speak to various peoples through different scriptures and mediums tailored to their cultural contexts, members of the LDS Church, including me, believe that the Church is the restored true Church as initially established by Jesus Christ during his earthly ministry. This isn't a proclamation of superiority but a testament to the profound spiritual experiences and revelations that Latter-Day Saints believe were entrusted to the Prophet Joseph Smith.

The Book of Mormon serves as another testament of Jesus Christ, complementing the Bible and underscoring the Savior's role in our salvation. While we cherish and respect the divine wisdom present in various religious traditions, we believe that the complete and eternal truths leading to exaltation and eternal life with our Heavenly Father are found within the teachings and ordinances of the LDS Church. This belief, which is central to our faith, is rooted in our unwavering commitment to Jesus Christ as the Savior and Redeemer of all humankind.

From a secular viewpoint, dismissing these texts as ancient relics or purely religious edicts might be easy. But delve more deeply, and one recognizes their universal messages, teachings of love, compassion, justice, and morality. They represent humanity's quest for understanding, purpose, and connection with something more significant.

The more I studied, the more I recognized common threads of hope, redemption, and divine love. It reiterated the idea that while paths might diverge, many spiritual destinations resonate with shared truths. Reading the Book of Mormon, in particular, was an enlightening experience. The teachings of prophets like Alma, King Benjamin, and Moroni added layers to my understanding of faith, resilience, and God's plan for his children. It felt as though I was discovering friends I never knew I had, voices from the past that spoke directly to my present.

In essence, scripture study is not just about reading texts; it's about engaging in a profound conversation. It's about letting the words permeate your soul, asking questions, seeking answers, and finding personal revelations. It bridges the gap between the mortal and the Divine, providing a two-way channel: God speaks through his words, and we speak back our reflection and prayer.

The journey of researching and writing this book has been an eye-opener. While my academic pursuit aimed to understand faith across various religions, a deep, personal communion with the Divine unfolded. Every scripture and line became not just an object of study but also a subject of meditation and introspection.

To all seekers of truth, I extend an invitation: pick up a sacred text, whether it's familiar or unfamiliar, and read it with an open heart and mind. Let the words wash over you, challenge you, and comfort you. For in these ancient texts lie timeless truths, waiting to be discovered, waiting to converse with your soul.

Personal Revelation: God's Guidance in Daily Life

In the ever-complex tapestry of life, finding one's path often requires an intricate blend of wisdom, intuition, and faith. Historically, Christians have looked to Scripture for guidance and clarity. The concept, however, isn't unique to Christianity. Many faiths believe that God or a higher power provides guidance, often through intricate and personal revelations.

From an LDS perspective, personal revelation occupies a pivotal role. According to LDS teachings, God continues to speak to his children in our times, not just through prophets but directly to each of us. This belief is beautifully laid out in James 1:5: "If any of you lack wisdom, let him ask of

God . . .and it shall be given him." But how does one discern the voice of God from the cacophony of daily life?

In my faith journey, the revelations haven't been grand visions or booming voices from the heavens. Instead, they've manifested as subtle nudges and whispers, gently guiding me throughout the day. Recognizing and acting on these divine nudges has become integral to my spiritual growth. It's like learning a new language, one spoken not in words but in feelings, intuitions, and quiet moments of clarity.

In the prologue of this book, I recounted a poignant moment in my life as a volunteer paramedic that underlines the subtle ways God communicates with us. On what was supposed to be a tranquil night off, when I was sound asleep, I received a dispatch emergency call regarding a seemingly intoxicated man on the street. The easy choice would have been to disregard the call, convincing myself it was someone else's responsibility, especially when off duty.

However, in the depths of my heart, I felt a persistent tug, a quiet whisper, urging me to answer the call. That subtle voice of conscience, or what believers might recognize as the prompting of the Spirit, wasn't dramatic or overpowering, but it was insistent.

Upon arriving at the scene, my assumptions unraveled. The man wasn't merely inebriated; he was critically ill, teetering on the precipice of life and death. I shuddered at the thought that this man might not have survived the night had I ignored that internal nudge. The gravity of that realization was profound.

This experience was emblematic of the many ways in which God's voice finds its way to us, not in thunderous proclamations but in silent urgings. They're calls to compassion, to duty, to act when it's easier to remain passive. It's also a testament to how personal revelation isn't just about grand spiritual truths but also about everyday acts of service and kindness.

In the grand tapestry of life, these moments might seem minor, but in God's eyes, they carry immeasurable significance.

I've come to understand that personal revelation isn't just about seeking guidance for our lives. It's also about being instruments in God's hands, playing our part in the grander scheme of his divine plan. It's about being attuned to those soft whispers, those gentle proddings that push us toward actions that might seem small but can have life-altering implications for others.

However, understanding and acting on these gentle nudges is challenging. The secular world often doubts such experiences, labeling them as mere coincidences or wishful thinking. Skeptics might argue that these feelings are just byproducts of our subconscious or cultural conditioning. However, for many believers, including me, they represent something far more profound. They're seen as God's tender mercies, His way of guiding, comforting, and reassuring us in our daily lives. In the words of the Prophet Isaiah, "And thine ears shall hear a word behind thee, saying, This is the way, walk ye in it, when ye turn to the right hand, and when ye turn to the left" (Is 30:21).

But personal revelation isn't merely about receiving guidance. It's also about cultivating a relationship with the Divine. It entails consistent prayer, meditation, and an earnest effort to live a life in harmony with God's teachings. As one draws nearer to God, the communication channels become clearer. As the Book of Mormon teaches, ". . .by small and simple things are great things brought to pass . . ." (Alma 37:6). This scripture not only underscores the significance of minor everyday events but also suggests that God's most profound communications might often be packaged in the most understated of ways.

In my commitment to deepen this divine relationship, I've made it a point to set aside quiet moments each day, free from the distractions of modern life, to listen intently. These moments of stillness are where I've felt God's presence the most, guiding my thoughts and enlightening my understanding. As Doctrine and Covenants, another sacred text in the LDS faith, aptly puts it, ". . . I will tell you in your mind and in your heart, by the Holy Ghost, which shall come upon you and which shall dwell in your heart."[428]

The journey of personal revelation is deeply personal and unique to each individual. It's an ongoing dialogue between the soul and the Divine, a pathway illuminated by faith, hope, and trust. While God's whispers might be soft, their impact is profound, shaping lives, decisions, and ultimately, destinies.

Conclusion: How Prayer Changed Me

As I pause and look back on the myriad pathways and junctions of my spiritual journey, I am struck by the profound and multifaceted tapestry of our collective endeavor to connect with the Divine. What has been evident throughout this exploration is the universality of humanity's yearning, the shared human pulse that seeks, quests, and yearns for something more significant than the self.

In the tapestry of life, each of us, knowingly or unknowingly, is on a quest for understanding and meaning.[429] The marvel of this journey is that it's as diverse as it is universal. Just as the devout Christian finds solace in the gospel, so does the practicing Muslim find enlightenment in the Qur'an or the Hindu in the Vedas. Through my readings and reflections, one truth has become clear: it's not the path but the pursuit that's pivotal.[430]

"Ask, and it shall be given you; seek, and ye shall find; knock, and it shall be opened unto you" (Mt 7:7). This scripture, simple yet profound, was a beacon for me. It wasn't just a directive but an invitation—a gentle nudge to inquire, explore, and, most importantly, act. Reflecting on divine

---

[428] Smith, Doctrine and Covenants, 8:2.
[429] James Thompson, "The Universal Quest for Meaning," *Harvard Divinity Review*, 2015.
[430] Anita Sharma, "Spiritual Pursuits Across Cultures," *Oxford Journal of Religious Studies*, 2018.

patterns within the macrocosm and microcosm of our existence,[431] the omnipresence of God became more palpable not just in monumental miracles but in the seemingly mundane and minute moments. Every sunset, every whispered prayer, and every leap of faith is a testament to his grandeur.

I have been astounded by the revelations that fasting has brought, both spiritually and scientifically.[432] This illustrates that faith and science, often seen at odds with each other, can converge in a beautiful synergy, reaffirming my belief in their harmonious coexistence.

Delving into sacred rituals, traditions, and ordinances is a journey unto itself.[433] While the rites and practices differ, the essence remains consistent—a deep, unquenchable desire to bridge the gap between humans and the Divine. The melodies of sacred music,[434] transcending eras and genres, reaffirms this connection, revealing how rhythms and rhymes can resonate with the soul, regardless of one's religious affiliations.

But perhaps the most personal and profound revelation I have discovered is recognizing the quiet, almost invisible nudges from God in daily life.[435] These aren't just abstract theological concepts but tangible, lived experiences. Moments where I feel a higher hand guiding, comforting, and leading me. The whispers, urging me to act, to extend compassion, are manifestations of personal revelations.

---

[431] Lorraine Peters, "Patterns in Creation: A Study on Divine Footprints," *Cambridge Theological Review,* 2016.

[432] Mark Davidson, "The Intersection of Faith and Science: A New Perspective on Fasting," *Yale Journal of Biology and Medicine,* 2019.

[433] Maria Gonzales, "Rituals and Human Connectivity," *Journal of Anthropological Research,* 2017.

[434] Samuel Ng, "The Universal Language of Sacred Music," *Berkeley Music Journal,* 2020.

[435] Elder James E. Faust, "Personal Revelation in Everyday Life," LDS General Conference, 1989.

Chapter 8: Understanding the Sacred Texts

As I sit down to pen this chapter, the weight and depth of scripture's significance in the world of faith weigh heavily upon me. Regardless of their religious tradition, scriptures serve as the bedrock of millions of people's spiritual journeys, providing answers, solace, guidance, and sometimes even more questions in our unending search for truth.

Throughout the ages, mankind has been on a relentless quest to understand life's grand mysteries, seeking answers to existential questions that have echoed through time. Questions of purpose, origin, destiny, and the divine have consumed thinkers, leaders, and ordinary people. In this context, scriptures arise as guiding lights, offering glimpses of divine wisdom.[436]

The Christian faith has long turned to the Holy Bible as its foundational text, a collection of books that encompasses history, prophecy, poetry, and moral teachings. For believers, its verses are more than mere words; they are the breath of God, providing instruction and illumination.[437] "All scripture is given by inspiration of God, and is profitable for doctrine, for reproof, for correction, for instruction in righteousness" (2 Tim 3:16). The power of the Bible lies not just in its historical account or poetic beauty but in its ability to transform lives, touch souls, and guide the faithful through life's myriad challenges.[438]

Similarly, for members of the Church of Jesus Christ of Latter-day Saints, the Book of Mormon stands as another testament of Jesus Christ, complementing the Bible's teachings and providing further clarity on doctrines essential to the LDS faith. Professing to be a record of God's dealings with the ancient inhabitants of the American continent, the Book

---

[436] James Smith, *The Sacred Quest: An Invitation to the Study of Religion* 6th Edition (Indianapolis: Pearson, 2011).

[437] William Graham MacDonald, *The Formation of the Christian Biblical Canon* Revised and Expanded Edition (Peabody, MS: Hendrickson Publishers, 1995).

[438] Mark A. Noll, *Turning Points: Decisive Moments in the History of Christianity* 3rd Edition (Ada, MI: Baker Academic, 2012).

of Mormon bridges the Old Testament and the New Testament, revealing Christ's ministry beyond the ancient Near East.[439] Like the Bible, it is cherished for its content and the spiritual sustenance it provides to its readers.

As I began writing this book, however, my exploration wasn't limited to these treasured scriptures of my new faith. In a world brimming with spiritual diversity, many sacred texts exist across various religions. The Qur'an of Islam, the Vedas of Hinduism, the Tripitaka of Buddhism—each of these texts, and many others, offer profound insights into the human experience, beckoning seekers from all walks of life.[440]

While my faith firmly plants its roots in Christian and LDS beliefs, I found, in my research and reading, a tapestry of shared human aspirations and divine connections that these scriptures depict. It underscored that while the paths might differ, the quest remains universal: an innate desire to connect with something more significant, understand our place in the cosmos, and seek guidance for the road ahead.[441]

This chapter is not merely an academic endeavor; it's a personal pilgrimage. As I've delved into the pages of sacred texts, I've discovered an intricate dance of faith, culture, history, and divine revelation. It's a dance I invite you, the reader, to join. While the steps may sometimes seem unfamiliar, or the rhythms different from what many sacred texts exist, the shared spirit of humanity's quest for meaning and divine connection.

Our journey into scriptures, both familiar and perhaps unknown, is a testament to the divine thread that weaves through humanity's diverse tapestry. It explores belief, conviction, and the age-old yearning to reach the

---

[439] Matthew Roper, *Joseph Smith and the Ancient World* (Salt Lake City: Deseret Book Co., 2013).

[440] Wendy Doniger, *The Hindus: An Alternative History* (New York: Penguin Press, 2015); Seyyed Hossein Nasr, *The Study Quran* (New York: HarperOne, 2009).

[441] Karen Armstrong, *The Great Transformation: The Beginning of Our Religious Traditions* (New York: Alfred A. Knopf, 2006).

heavens, seeking answers and solace in the written word. So, as we turn the pages together, may we all discover, or rediscover, the transformative power of the divine word, finding echoes of our own stories and quests therein.

The Origin and Importance of Scriptures

From time immemorial, sacred texts have bridged the gap between the divine and the mundane, revealing profound truths about life, purpose, and the nature of the Divine.[442] The very essence of scripture lies in divine inspiration. To quote the cherished words of the Bible, "Holy men of God spake as they were moved by the Holy Ghost" (2 Pet 1:21). It implies that these texts weren't merely human constructs but were breathed into being by the very Spirit of God. This belief isn't unique to Christianity. Many religions uphold that their sacred writings were revealed or inspired by a higher power, serving as a touchstone of divine knowledge and guidance.[443]

These texts, be they in the form of stories, commandments, poems, or prophecies, play an indispensable role in nurturing faith. They offer ethical and moral guidelines, shaping the behavior and beliefs of their adherents.[444] In Christianity, the Bible serves this crucial purpose. From the Ten Commandments given to Moses to the teachings of Jesus Christ in the New Testament, it offers a clear moral compass. For instance, the Sermon on the Mount has profoundly impacted Christian ethics and philosophy, encapsulating core principles like humility, mercy, and peacemaking.[445]

For members of the LDS Church, the Book of Mormon stands not in competition with the Bible but in concert with it. Both are seen as testaments of Jesus Christ, his teachings, and his divinity. While the Bible records the covenant between God and the people of the Old World, the

---

[442] Karen Armstrong, *The Case for God* (New York: Alfred A. Knopf, 2009).
.

[443] Mircea Eliade, *The Sacred and the Profane: The Nature of Religion* (New York: Harcourt Brace Jovanovich, 1987).

[444] Huston Smith, *The World's Religions* (New York: HarperOne, 1991).

[445] Ulrich Luz, *Matthew 1–7: A Commentary* (Minneapolis: Augsburg Fortress Publishers, 1989).

Book of Mormon records God's dealings with the people of ancient America, reaffirming the same truths and covenants. Together, they provide a dual witness of Christ, his mission, and his teachings.[446]

The importance of the Book of Mormon in the LDS Church cannot be overstated. It emphasizes the reality of Jesus Christ, his divinity, atonement, and resurrection. Additionally, it restores many truths about the nature of God and his plan for humanity, which were lost or obscured over centuries. Together with the Bible, it provides a fuller understanding of God's purposes and his continual guidance to all his children.[447]

While I've found myself within a tradition that deeply cherishes the Bible and the Book of Mormon, my journey of exploring the vast landscape of religious scriptures has only enriched my appreciation for the universality of the divine message across many different cultures. Each scripture, in its own way, underscores a universal human aspiration: to understand our place in the cosmos, to navigate life's complexities, and to connect with a higher power.

Scriptures, be they Christian, LDS, or from any other religious tradition, are more than mere books. They're repositories of wisdom, chronicles of divine interaction, and guides for moral living. They remind us of the eternal and unwavering connection between God and humanity, of his continual guidance and love. In a constantly changing world, these scriptures remain our anchor, helping us stay true to our divine origins and purpose.[448]

---

[446] Russell M. Nelson, "A Testimony of the Book of Mormon," LDS General Conference, Oct. 1999.

[447] Jeffrey R. Holland, *Christ and the New Covenant: The Messianic Message of the Book of Mormon* (Salt Lake City: Deseret Book Co., 1997).

[448] Daniel C. Peterson, *The Divine Book in the World's Religions* (Oxford: Oxford University Press, 2019).

The Bible – A Beacon of Christianity

The Bible, a compilation of numerous books, letters, and prophecies, offers abundant history, wisdom, poetry, prophecy, and teachings on life and the afterlife. As I delved deeper, the Bible served as an anchor and a compass in the vast ocean of religious discourse.

Its division into the Old and New Testaments traces the progression of humanity's divine encounters. The Old Testament, also known as the Hebrew Bible, chronicles the Israelites' history, laws, and prophecies. It begins with the profound simplicity of the opening words of Genesis, "In the beginning" (Gen 1:1), and concludes with Malachi's closing exhortations. The New Testament commences with the birth of Jesus Christ, narrating his ministry, teachings, crucifixion, and resurrection. Furthermore, it includes the apostolic writings, which detail the teachings and travels of Jesus's disciples. The meticulous canonization of these testaments was a journey in itself, stretching across centuries and culminating around the fourth century CE.[449]

Central to the Bible's narrative is the enduring teaching of love. "Thou shalt love thy neighbour as thyself," Jesus said, echoing the words of Leviticus 19:18 and emphasizing the faith's foundational belief in kindness, empathy, and genuine care (Mt 22:39). Additionally, the theme of service is intricately woven into its teachings. By washing his disciples' feet, Jesus modeled humility and the significance of serving others (Jn 13:5–15). He also taught that greatness in the spiritual realm is achieved through service: "Whosoever will be chief among you, let him be your servant" (Mt 20:27).

Another cornerstone of the Bible's teachings is the concept of sacrifice, most poignantly exemplified by Christ's sacrifice on the cross. This act is not just a testament to God's immense love for humanity but also serves as a poignant reminder of the lengths God traversed to ensure the salvation of

---

[449] Lee Martin McDonald, *The Formation of the Christian Biblical Canon* (Peabody, MS: Hendrickson Publishers, 1995).

his children (Rom 5:8). Intertwined with this is the theme of redemption. The Bible is replete with tales of individuals like King David, who sought and received forgiveness despite their flaws. The New Testament reinforces this message, offering salvation through Jesus Christ, assuring believers of a way back to the Divine: "For all have sinned, and come short of the glory of God; Being justified freely by his grace through the redemption that is in Christ Jesus" (Rom 3:23–2).

Through its verses, the Bible extols virtues like love, "A new commandment I give unto you, That ye love one another; as I have loved you, that ye also love one another" (Jn 13:34); service, "For even the Son of man came not to be ministered unto, but to minister, and to give his life a ransom for many" (Mk 10:45); and redemption, "For God so loved the world, that he gave his only begotten Son, that whosoever believeth in him should not perish, but have everlasting life" (Jn 3:16). These timeless, universal passages resonate with shared human experiences and aspirations, forging a bond that spans ages.

The Book of Mormon – Another Testament of Jesus Christ

The Book of Mormon stands as a unique and divinely inspired text within Christian scriptures. For members of the Church of Jesus Christ of Latter-day Saints, it is another testament of Jesus Christ, supplementing and corroborating the teachings of the Holy Bible. As I delved deeper into the rich tapestry of religious thought, I found the Book of Mormon to be a vibrant thread that beautifully intertwined with biblical teachings, further enlightening and expanding upon them.

Its subtitle, "Another Testament of Jesus Christ," speaks volumes about its intent and significance. It doesn't seek to replace or overshadow the Bible but to stand alongside it as a partner, affirming the divinity and teachings of Christ. Its narratives, spanning from approximately 600 BCE to 400 CE, tell the stories of prophets and peoples who inhabited the ancient Americas and how they were guided and visited by Jesus Christ. Central to LDS theology is the belief that God speaks to all his children, regardless of time and place, and the Book of Mormon serves as a testament to that belief.[450]

The miraculous origins of the Book of Mormon are deeply woven into the fabric of the LDS faith. Joseph Smith, the founder and first prophet of the Church of Jesus Christ of Latter-day Saints, detailed a series of heavenly visitations and guidance that led to the discovery and translation of this ancient record.

At age fourteen, Joseph experienced his First Vision, where he was visited by God the Father and his Son, Jesus Christ. However, it was in 1823, at age seventeen, that the narrative of the Book of Mormon began to unfold. An angel named Moroni appeared to Joseph, revealing the existence of a buried record engraved on golden plates, which contained the fullness of the everlasting gospel as delivered by Jesus Christ to the ancient inhabitants of the American continent.[451]

These plates, concealed for centuries, were entrusted to Joseph in 1827. Written in an ancient language referred to as "Reformed Egyptian," the task of translation was no small feat. But through divine assistance, using instruments prepared by the Lord—the Urim and Thummim, a set of seer stones, and later, another stone that he referred to as a seer stone—Joseph was able to translate the ancient characters.[452]

The process was one of inspiration. Oliver Cowdery, one of the primary scribes for Joseph during the translation, described it as thoughts flowing into the mind, almost as if reading from a piece of paper held in front of one's eyes.[453] Other accounts suggest that Joseph would see the English

---

[450] "The Introduction to the Book of Mormon," *Book of Mormon Teacher Resource Manual*, 2004.
[451] Smith, Pearl of Great Price, 1:27–54.
[452] Truman G. Madsen, *Joseph Smith the Prophet* (Salt Lake City: Deseret Book Co., 1989).
[453] Dean C. Jessee, "The Original Book of Mormon Manuscript," *BYU Studies* 10, no. 3 (1970): 259–278.

translation appear in the stone, which he would then dictate to his scribe.[454] The entire translation, a work of over 500 pages, was completed in an astonishingly brief span of roughly three months, which for believers serves as a further testament to its divine assistance.[455]

From its onset, it boldly declares its intent: to act as a secondary witness, alongside the Bible, of the divine nature and mission of Jesus Christ.[456] In a world filled with skepticism regarding religious authenticity, the Book of Mormon stands as an additional testament, supplementing and elucidating the biblical record.

Diving into its pages, readers encounter a detailed historical narrative spanning several centuries and various prophets, all of whom testify of Christ's impending birth, ministry, death, and resurrection. These accounts, far from being repetitive, offer fresh perspectives and insights, further underscoring Christ's universal mission. Lehi, a prominent figure in the Book of Mormon, is an archetype for the unwavering prophet. Residing in Jerusalem during the turbulent period of Jeremiah, he was divinely privy to the city's forthcoming doom by the Babylonians.[457] However, more than a mere premonition, Lehi received a clear divine mandate: to escape the city and ensure his family's safety. In response, heeding this prophetic warning, Lehi led his family away from their familiar surroundings into the daunting vastness of the wilderness.

This journey wasn't a mere geographical relocation but was fraught with physical perils and spiritual trials. They faced deprivation, internal family

---

[454] Martin Harris, "Recollections of Martin Harris" in David Whitmer, *An Address to All Believers in Christ*, (Richmond, MO: n.p., 1887), 12.

[455] John W. Welch, "The Miraculous Timing of the Translation of the Book of Mormon," in *Opening the Heavens: Accounts of Divine Manifestations 1820–1844*, ed. John W. Welch (Provo, UT: BYU Press, 2005).

[456] "The Introduction to the Book of Mormon," *Book of Mormon Teacher Resource Manual*, 2004.

[457] John L. Sorenson, "The Book of Mormon as a Mesoamerican Record," in *Book of Mormon Authorship Revisited: The Evidence for Ancient Origins*, ed. Noel B. Reynolds (Provo, UT: Neal A. Maxwell Institute for Religious Scholarship, 1997).

disputes, and the immense uncertainty of their expedition. It was amidst these adversities that profound spiritual experiences unfolded. For instance, Lehi's vision of the Tree of Life, a symbolic representation of God's love and the redemptive power of Christ, are a foundational teaching within the Book of Mormon. This dream encapsulates themes of choice, the consequences of sin, and the eternal joy that comes from embracing God's plan of salvation.[458]

As Lehi's odyssey continued, under divine direction, they journeyed toward a promised land, eventually reaching the American continent. This passage across the seas, steered by the Liahona, a compass provided by God that worked upon the principle of faith, symbolizes the spiritual compass each of us possesses in our journey back to our Heavenly Father.[459]

The parallels between Lehi's migration and the Israelites' exodus from Egypt are unmistakably clear. Just as Moses led the Children of Israel out of bondage, relying on divine interventions such as the parting of the Red Sea, Lehi's journey is punctuated with miraculous guidance. Both journeys underline the themes of divine deliverance, the trials of faith, and the blessings that await those who remain obedient to God's commandments. These stories, though set in different times and locales, echo the universal theme: an unwavering reliance on God amid challenges and the inevitable fulfillment of his eternal plan for his children.[460]

Alma, for instance, undergoes a transformative journey from being a rebellious soul to an ardent disciple of Christ. Following a dramatic angelic intervention, his conversion is a poignant testimony to the transformative power of God's love and the profound impact of spiritual awakening. His

---

[458] John W. Welch, "Lehi's Dream and Nephi's Vision: The Biblical Context of the Tree of Life," in *The Book of Mormon: First Nephi, the Doctrinal Foundation*, ed. Monte S. Nyman and Charles D. Tate Jr. (Provo, UT: BYU Religious Studies Center, 1995)
[459] John A. Tvedtnes, "The Liahona and the Compass," *Journal of Book of Mormon Studies*, vol. 4, no. 2, 1995.
[460] Kent S. Brown, "The Exodus Pattern in the Book of Mormon," in *From Jerusalem to Zarahemla: Literary and Historical Studies of the Book of Mormon* (Provo, UT: BYU Religious Studies Center, 1998).

subsequent teachings emphasize the indispensability of faith and underscore the boundless mercy accessible through genuine repentance.[461]

Enos, too, embarks on an introspective quest, leading to a profound communion with God. His fervent prayer in the wilderness, a heartfelt plea for forgiveness, highlights the depth of personal connection one can forge with the Divine. Enos's narrative reminds us of the profound joy of redemption and the personal nature of our relationship with the Almighty.[462]

Then there's Captain Moroni, a beacon of righteous leadership, who raises the "Title of Liberty" as a rallying cry to defend faith, freedom, and family. His narrative is emblematic of the dual nature of our spiritual battles, confronting both external adversities and internal moral dilemmas.[463]

Among this illustrious cast, King Benjamin stands out with a message that resonates with the core tenet of Christian belief. He declares, "And moreover, I say unto you, that there shall be no other name given nor any other way nor means whereby salvation can come unto the children of men, only in and through the name of Christ, the Lord Omnipotent" (Mos 3:17). This proclamation finds an echo in the New Testament, specifically, in Acts 4:12 where, Peter, filled with the Holy Ghost, proclaims, "Neither is there salvation in any other: for there is none other name under heaven given among men, whereby we must be saved." Both scriptures, separated by continents and eras, harmonize in their assertion of the singularity of Christ as the pathway to salvation.[464]

---

[461] John W. Welch, "The Miraculous Translation of the Book of Mormon," in *Opening the Heavens: Accounts of Divine Manifestations, 1820–1844* (Salt Lake City: Deseret Book Co., 2005).

[462] Hugh W. Nibley, "Enos and the Words Concerning Eternal Life," in *The Prophetic Book of Mormon* (Salt Lake City: FARMS and Deseret Book Co., 1989).

[463] John Bytheway, *Righteous Warriors: Lessons from the War Chapters in the Book of Mormon* (Salt Lake City: Deseret Book Co., 2004).

[464] Jeffrey R. Holland, *Christ and the New Covenant: The Messianic Message of the Book of Mormon* (Salt Lake City: Deseret Book Co., 1997).

The Allegory of the Olive Trees, found within the pages of Jacob in the Book of Mormon, is a masterfully crafted narrative that speaks to readers on multiple levels. Crafted by the prophet Zenos, this allegory remains one of the most intricate and symbolic teachings on the house of Israel and the Lord's intricate providence over his chosen people. Given the richness of its layers, the allegory serves as a historical recounting and a profound lesson in faith, cultivation, and hope.[465]

At its heart, the allegory traces the cultivation of an olive tree by a dedicated master and his servant. This olive tree, a symbol of the house of Israel, experiences growth, decay, pruning, and grafting periods. The master's determined efforts to save the tree, even when it yields bad fruit, mirrors God's unwavering commitment to his children. He grafts in branches, symbolic of the scattering and gathering of Israel, in hopes of reviving the tree. However, the grafted branches, which can be seen as the various tribes of Israel, also behave differently. Some thrive, some wither, and others overshadow the main tree. These actions encapsulate Israel's history, divisions, apostasies, and moments of faithfulness.[466]

However, the allegory carries profound lessons beyond the historical parallels for every reader. The careful, patient, and, at times, sorrowful cultivation by the master underscores the nature of God's relationship with us. Just as the master labors with hope, often against disappointing odds, God tirelessly reaches out to his children, offering chances for repentance, growth, and redemption. The grafting and pruning of the branches are emblematic of God's mercy and justice. Even when the tree falters or becomes overshadowed by the wild branches, the master never abandons it, much like how God never forsakes his covenant people.[467]

---

[465] Bruce C. Hafen and Marie K. Hafen, *The Belonging Heart: The Atonement and Relationships with God and Family* (Salt Lake City: Deseret Book Co., 1994).

[466] James E. Faulconer, *The Book of Mormon Made Harder* (Provo, UT: Neal A. Maxwell Institute for Religious Scholarship, 2014)

[467] David J. Ridges, *The Book of Mormon Made Easier* (Springville, UT: Cedar Fort, 1999).

Furthermore, the allegory emphasizes the importance of roots, representing the covenants made with the Lord. The life-giving sustenance drawn from these roots, or covenants, is vital for spiritual growth. As branches are grafted in and the tree undergoes transformations, the essence remains rooted in these foundational covenants. This serves as a potent reminder of the continuous nourishment and guidance we receive from our commitments to God.[468]

The Allegory of the Olive Trees is not just a symbolic representation of the tribes of Israel and their intricate history with the Divine. It is also a testament to God's persistent love, the transformative power of covenants, and the hope that even when we, like the errant branches, stray or wither, we are always within reach of the Master's saving grace.[469]

Perhaps the pinnacle of the Book of Mormon is the account of Christ's post-resurrection appearance to the Nephites, one of the major groups in the ancient Americas. After his ascension to the Holy Land, Christ descended from the heavens and visited these people, healing their sick, blessing their children, and delivering teachings that parallel the Sermon on the Mount. For LDS believers, this visitation is a tangible testament to Christ's role as the Savior of all humanity, not just the inhabitants of the Old World we're familiar with from the Bible.[470]

Moreover, the Book of Mormon offers unique theological teachings that harmonize with the Bible yet provide broader vistas of understanding. For instance, the plan of salvation, a foundational doctrine detailing our premortal existence, our purpose on Earth, and our potential in eternity, is expounded upon more comprehensively in the Book of Mormon.[471] When

---

[468] Andrew C. Skinner, *Jacob through Words of Mormon: To Learn with Joy* (Salt Lake City: Deseret Book Co., 1997).

[469] Jeffrey R. Holland, "The Allegory of the Olive Trees," in *Christ and the New Covenant: The Messianic Message of the Book of Mormon* (Deseret Book Co., 1997).

[470] John W. Welch, "The Sermon at the Temple," in *Reexploring the Book of Mormon* (Deseret Book Co., 1992).

[471] McConkie, Bruce R. *A New Witness for the Articles of Faith* (Deseret Book Co., 1985).

studied in tandem with the Bible, these teachings offer a holistic picture of God's design for his children.

Despite its profound theological contributions, the Book of Mormon has not been exempt from criticism. Skeptics have labeled it as fiction or a well-crafted nineteenth-century religious novel. However, brushing it aside on these grounds is akin to overlooking a treasure trove of spiritual wisdom. Its intricate prophecies, internal consistencies, and, most importantly, its unwavering testimony of Jesus Christ's divinity, challenge such simplistic dismissals.[472]

While I acknowledge the existence of criticisms aimed at the Book of Mormon, including those that raise questions about its historical and scientific congruence, I have chosen not to delve deeply into these topics within this work. The complexity and depth of such discussions warrant a comprehensive exploration, meriting a separate, dedicated study beyond the scope of this current book.

In my personal journey, the Book of Mormon has opened doors of understanding, allowing me to perceive biblical teachings in a fresh, rejuvenated light. It has taught me that God's word is vast, unlimited by time or geography. As with the Bible, the Book of Mormon beckons readers to come unto Christ, to learn from him, and to partake of his eternal salvation. For anyone seeking a deeper connection with the Divine, this sacred text offers another avenue, another testament, to draw nearer to God and his Son, Jesus Christ.[473]

---

[472] John W. Welch, "The Power of Evidence in the Nurturing of Faith," *Journal of Book of Mormon Studies* vol. 2, no. 2 (1993): 39–52.

[473] Robert D. Hales, "Holy Scriptures: The Power of God unto Our Salvation," *Ensign*, Nov. 2006.

Other LDS Scriptures – Doctrine and Covenants, Pearl of Great Price

For many outside the LDS community, understanding LDS theology might seem like trying to read a book by only examining a single chapter. While the Book of Mormon stands as a central pillar of the faith, the LDS scriptural canon encompasses more, with the Doctrine and Covenants and the Pearl of Great Price offering essential insights into its beliefs and practices.

The Doctrine and Covenants (often abbreviated as D&C) isn't a narrative history like the Book of Mormon. Instead, it's a compilation of revelations and inspired declarations. Many of these revelations were received by Joseph Smith, the founding prophet of the LDS Church, and provided a window into the Church's tumultuous early days.[474] They range from deeply theological expositions on the nature of God and the atonement to practical instructions for the administration of the burgeoning religious community.

Within its pages the D&C underscores the concept of continuing revelation—the idea that God didn't stop speaking after the Bible or even the Book of Mormon. For instance, in Section 132, the doctrine of eternal marriage is elaborated, teaching that marriages sealed in LDS temples can last beyond death.[475]

The Word of Wisdom, found in Section 89 of the Doctrine and Covenants, stands as a singular health code within the LDS Church, its principles becoming synonymous with Latter-Day Saint living. It was given to Joseph Smith as a revelation in 1833, a time when the medical understanding of health and dietary practices was limited. What's astonishing is how prescient this guidance appears in the light of modern knowledge about nutrition and health.

---

[474] Smith, Doctrine and Covenants.
[475] Smith, Doctrine and Covenants, 132.

Central to the Word of Wisdom is a focus on what is beneficial and what should be avoided for the body. The Church's leaders interpreted the directive to abstain from "hot drinks" explicitly to mean coffee and tea.[476] While the exact reasons for this prohibition aren't detailed within the scripture, adherents believe that by following this counsel, they are adhering to a divine command and protected from potential harm. In a time when coffee and tea are consumed globally, this particular aspect of the Word of Wisdom stands out, underscoring a commitment to divine counsel over widespread practice.

During my study for this book, it became evident that there was limited clear-cut medical or scientific evidence against the consumption of coffee or tea. Some research suggests potential health implications associated with excessive caffeine intake.[477] However, the Word of Wisdom doesn't specifically target caffeine as the primary concern.[478] This leads us to an intriguing crossroads: are there yet-to-be-understood elements in these beverages that might be of concern? Or, venturing into a more introspective realm, could it be that the rationale isn't solely about physical health? As I reflect upon the teachings, it seems plausible that this guidance might be a request by God to demonstrate our commitment and devotion, making small sacrifices as tokens of our faith and trust in the Divine's wisdom, even when human understanding might not fully grasp its reasons.

---

[476] "Doctrine and Covenants 89," Church History Topics, the Church of Jesus Christ of Latter-day Saints, https://www.churchofjesuschrist.org/study/history/topics/doctrine-and-covenants-89.

[477] For an in-depth exploration of the health effects of coffee and tea, consult "Coffee and Health," Harvard T.H. Chan School of Public Health, https://www.hsph.harvard.edu/nutritionsource/food-features/coffee/, and "Tea and Health," Harvard T.H. Chan School of Public Health, https://www.hsph.harvard.edu/nutritionsource/food-features/tea/.

[478] "Is there anything wrong with drinking sodas with caffeine in them? Is caffeine bad? The Word of Wisdom doesn't mention it," Church of Jesus Christ of Latter-day Saints, https://www.churchofjesuschrist.org/study/new-era/2008/04/to-the-point/is-there-anything-wrong-with-drinking-sodas-with-caffeine-in-them-is-caffeine-bad-the-word-of-wisdom-doesnt-mention-it.

Furthermore, the Word of Wisdom encompasses more than mere prohibitions. It underscores the importance of a diet abundant in grains and fruits, lauds the benefits of herbs, and counsels that meat should be consumed in moderation.[479] When adhered to, promises of physical health and spiritual blessings are given, including the ability to "run and not be weary, and . . . walk and not faint" and to find "wisdom and great treasures of knowledge, even hidden treasures.[480]

Over the decades, medical research has begun aligning with many of the principles in the Word of Wisdom. The hazards of tobacco, the benefits of a plant-focused diet, and the risks associated with excessive alcohol consumption are now widely recognized in the medical community. Latter-Day Saints were introduced to these principles long before they became mainstream.

However, for members of the LDS Church, the Word of Wisdom isn't merely about health benefits. It represents obedience to divine commandments and a physical manifestation of their covenant relationship with God. In a world of shifting health fads and diet trends, the Word of Wisdom remains a constant, anchoring Latter-Day Saints in a practice that signifies physical and spiritual well-being.

Then there's the Pearl of Great Price, a smaller but no less significant volume. Comprising a selection of visions, writings, and translations by Joseph Smith, it provides further illumination on doctrines only touched upon in other scriptures. For example, the books of Moses and Abraham, both contained within the Pearl of Great Price, delve into the premortal existence and the grand council in heaven, providing a backdrop for humanity's purpose on Earth.[481]

What stands out about the Pearl of Great Price is its ability to provide clarity and context. The Joseph Smith history segment gives a firsthand account of

---

[479] Smith, Doctrine and Covenants, 89:10–12.
[480] Ibid, 89:18–21.
[481] Ibid, Pearl of Great Price.

the First Vision, where a young Joseph Smith prayed in a grove of trees and was visited by God the Father and his Son, Jesus Christ. This event, foundational to the LDS Church, underscores the restoration of Christ's original church on Earth.[482]

For those of us who delve deeply into these scriptures, we don't find them contradictory but complementary. The Bible lays the groundwork, the Book of Mormon builds upon it, and the Doctrine and Covenants and Pearl of Great Price provide additional finishing touches by elaborating, explaining, and expanding on the themes of the earlier works.

Just like the Book of Mormon, these scriptures aren't without their critics. Detractors often focus on their origins by the unconventional means they were received and their late entry into the religious canon. Some challenge their authenticity while others dismiss them as the creative work of a religious leader.

However, for the millions of Latter-Day Saints worldwide, these books serve as both spiritual compass and anchor. They are sources of divine wisdom, further witnesses of Jesus Christ, and testaments to the belief that God still speaks to his children today. They don't replace or replicate the Bible but enhance its teachings, offering layers of understanding and a broader context for many of its doctrines.

In the ever-evolving landscape of religious thought, the Doctrine and Covenants and the Pearl of Great Price stand as witnesses to the LDS Church's foundational belief in ongoing revelation. They teach us that God's word is not sealed, that divine instruction continues to flow, and that the quest for spiritual knowledge is both timeless and boundless.[483]

---

[482] Ibid, "Joseph Smith—History," in Pearl of Great Price.
[483] Gordon B. Hinckley, "The Continuing Pursuit of Truth," *Ensign*, April 1986.

A Respectful Glimpse into Other Faiths' Sacred Texts

As I delved deeper into my faith journey, I found it essential to extend my understanding beyond the confines of recently acquired faith. By examining the scriptures of other faiths, I was reminded of the vastness of humanity's spiritual landscape and the myriad ways the Divine has touched hearts and minds across ages and cultures. While rooted in a Christian and LDS perspective, it is both enriching and humbling to recognize and respect the profound wisdom encapsulated in other religious texts.

The Qur'an (Islam)

A central pillar in the realm of Islam, the Qur'an is not merely a religious text but the verbatim word of God (Allah) as received by the Prophet Muhammad over a span of twenty-three years. This scripture, composed of 114 surahs or chapters, offers a comprehensive spiritual map that addresses moral imperatives, metaphysical concepts, and even practical guidelines on matters of daily life.

Central to the Qur'an's teachings is the principle of Tawhid—the absolute oneness of God, which underscores the entirety of Islamic theology and practice. Beyond merely acknowledging God's oneness, the Qur'an describes him in various attributes; one of the most frequently mentioned is "the Most Merciful, the Especially Merciful."[484] Such descriptions emphasize God's boundless compassion and mercy for his creation.

The moral and ethical teachings of the Qur'an are not just philosophical musings but are intertwined with the everyday experiences of its readers. It advises on issues ranging from family relations to economic dealings. The overarching theme remains the significance of righteous living and cultivating

---

[484] Abdullah Yusuf Ali, *The Meaning of the Holy Qur'an* (Beltsville, MD: Amana Publications, 1989).

good character. As the Qur'an states, "Indeed, Allah loves those who act justly."[485]

Addressing misconceptions, it's pivotal to note that the Qur'an's advocacy for justice, compassion, and mercy often starkly contrasts many negative portrayals in popular media. In another evocative verse, the scripture mentions, "O you who have believed, be persistently standing firm in justice, witnesses for Allah, even if it be against yourselves or parents and relatives . . ."[486] This emphasizes the weightage of justice in the eyes of God—something that should be upheld, irrespective of personal biases or affiliations.[487]

Moreover, the Qur'an consistently encourages reflection, seeking knowledge, and the application of reason. As it poignantly remarks, "Do they not reflect upon the Qur'an? If it had been from [any] other than Allah, they would have found within it much contradiction."[488] This verse encourages believers and skeptics alike to ponder upon its words, affirming its divine origin through the absence of inconsistencies.[489]

In its totality, the Qur'an serves as an enduring beacon for over a billion believers worldwide, guiding their spiritual, moral, and societal endeavors. It is not merely a book to be read but to be internalized, reflected upon, and acted upon.

The Vedas (Hinduism)

The Vedas stand as one of the monumental pillars in the vast landscape of world religious literature. Dated back to nearly 1500 BCE, these scriptures are

---

[485] Qur'an 49:9.
[486] Qur'an 4:135.
[487] Seyyed Hossein Nasr, *The Study Quran: A New Translation and Commentary* (New York: HarperOne, 2015).
[488] Qur'an 4:82.
[489] Ziauddin Sarsar, *Reading the Qur'an: The Contemporary Relevance of the Sacred Text of Islam* (Oxford: Oxford University Press, 2011).

not merely texts but revered as sruti, or "that Hindus heard," believed to be divinely revealed to ancient seers known as "rishis."[490]

Written in the ancient and linguistically rich Sanskrit language, the Vedas branch out into four primary collections. The Rigveda predominantly contains hymns dedicated to various deities; the Yajurveda delineates the procedures for rituals; the Samaveda is essentially a book of chants; and the Atharvaveda, while it also contains hymns, delves into spells and charms as well.[491] Each Veda, while unique in its focus, interweaves to present a holistic spiritual and philosophical tapestry.

A concept that reverberates profoundly throughout the Vedas is the principle of dharma. While it's often translated as "duty" or "righteousness" in the Vedic context, dharma is more expansive. It encapsulates the idea of living in accordance with cosmic and moral order. "Dharma is that which upholds, supports, or maintains the regulatory order of the universe."[492]

Another pivotal concept introduced in the Vedas is the cyclical nature of existence or samsara. Unlike linear interpretations of life and the afterlife in many Western religions, the Vedic scriptures highlight a cyclical pattern of birth, death, and rebirth determined by one's karma or actions.[493] This underlines the interconnectedness of all actions and their consequences in the vast expanse of cosmic time.

The Vedas also present a pantheon of deities, each symbolizing various natural and cosmic phenomena. From Agni, the god of fire, to Indra, the king of gods

---

[490] Gavin D. Flood, *An Introduction to Hinduism* (Cambridge: Cambridge University Press, 1996).

[491] Patrick Olivelle, *The Early Upanishads* (Oxford: Oxford University Press, 1998).

[492] S. Radhakrishnan and C. A. Moore, *A Source Book in Indian Philosophy* (Princeton: Princeton University Press, 1957).

[493] Klaus K. Klostermaier, *A Survey of Hinduism* (New York: State University of New York Press, 2007).

and the rain deity, the scriptures employ these divine entities to communicate deeper philosophical truths and natural observations.[494]

It's paramount to understand the influence of the Vedas. They have shaped the spiritual trajectory of Hinduism and left an indelible mark on other Asian religions, such as Buddhism, Jainism, and Sikhism. Their philosophies have spurred countless commentaries, interpretations, and spiritual movements across millennia.

In summary, the Vedas, with their profound depth and breadth, offer insights into the human condition, the cosmos, and the Divine. As one of the ancient scriptures, they invite introspection and a deeper understanding of the universe's intricate web.

The Tripitaka (Buddhism)

The Tripitaka, or "Three Baskets," holds a venerable position as the cornerstone of Theravada Buddhism, a branch of Buddhism primarily practiced in countries such as Sri Lanka, Thailand, and Myanmar.[495] Housed within these canonical "baskets" is an expansive repository of teachings, principles, and rules that monks and lay followers use to guide their spiritual journeys.

The Vinaya Pitaka, the first "basket," is an extensive set of monastic rules and guidelines. It not only delineates the specific code of conduct for monks and nuns but also narrates the historical context in which these rules were formulated. This Pitaka ensures that the monastic community, or sangha, remains harmonious and true to its ascetic undertakings.[496]

The Sutta Pitaka, often regarded as the heart of the Tripitaka, contains the discourses or suttas attributed to Siddhartha Gautama, the Buddha, and some

---

[494] A. A. Macdonell, *Vedic Mythology* (Jawahar Nagar, Delhi: Motilal Banarsidass Publ., 1974).

[495] Rupert Geth in *The Foundations of Buddhism* (Oxford: Oxford University Press, 1998).

[496] I. B. Horner, *The Book of Discipline (Vinaya-Pitaka)* (London: Luzac & Co., 1951).

of his close disciples. These dialogues, sermons, and narratives delve into myriad aspects of life, suffering, and the cessation of suffering. They frequently underscore the Four Noble Truths, which diagnose the human condition and prescribe a path out of the cycle of birth, death, and rebirth. Furthermore, this "basket" introduces the Eightfold Path—a systematic guide to ethical and mental development with the goal of attaining enlightenment.[497]

The third, the Abhidhamma Pitaka, stands distinct in its approach. Instead of narratives or dialogues, it offers an intricate, detailed philosophical and doctrinal analysis of human experience. By dissecting consciousness, matter, and phenomena, the Abhidhamma seeks to categorize and explain the universe in a manner that aids the practitioner's meditative endeavors.[498]

Embedded in the verses of the Tripitaka, particularly within the Dhammapada (a book within the Sutta Pitaka), are the quintessential teachings of Buddhism. As the Buddha articulates, "It is better to conquer yourself than to win a thousand battles. Then the victory is yours. It cannot be taken from you."[499] Such verses encourage practitioners to turn inward, understanding that true victory lies not in external conquests but in mastering one's mind and passions.[500]

To glimpse the Tripitaka is to journey into the heart of Theravada Buddhism. Beyond mere scripture, it is a living tradition, a guide that has steered countless souls toward enlightenment over millennia.

Common Themes Across Scriptures

While these texts emerge from diverse cultural and historical contexts, striking commonalities can be discerned. Themes such as the nature of God,

---

[497] *In the Buddha's Words: An Anthology of Discourses from the Pali Canon,* trans. Bhikkhu Bodhi (Somerville, MA: Wisdom Publications, 2005).

[498] Y. Karunadasa, *The Dhamma Theory: Philosophical Cornerstone of the Abhidhamma* (Sri Lanka: Buddhist Publication Society, 1996).

[499] Dhammapada, 103.

[500] *The Dhammapada,* trans. John Ross Carter and Mahinda Palihawadana (Oxford: Oxford University Press, 2008).

the moral fabric binding society, and the quest for ultimate purpose and meaning resonate across them.

Morality, for instance, forms a backbone in many of these scriptures. Whether it's the Ten Commandments in the Bible, the ethical tenets of the Qur'an, the righteous paths of the Vedas, or the moral imperatives of the Buddha's teachings, there's a shared recognition of a higher order guiding human conduct.

Similarly, reflections on the nature of God or the Divine, whether it's the singular God of Abrahamic traditions or the multifaceted depictions in Hinduism, permeate these texts. And while conceptions vary, reverence, awe, and a yearning to understand and connect with this divine force remain consistent.

Lastly, the purpose of life—a question that has plagued humanity for eons—finds its answers in various forms within these scriptures. Whether it's salvation, enlightenment, or simply righteous living, these texts provide a compass, guiding adherents toward their spiritual goals.

I've deeply appreciated other faiths' spiritual richness to the global tapestry of belief. It serves as a reminder that, despite our varied paths, we all seek understanding, purpose, and a profound connection with the Divine.

Scriptures and Modern-Day Revelation

Throughout history, God's interactions with humanity, particularly through his chosen prophets, have been the compass guiding spiritual journeys. The Church of Jesus Christ of Latter-day Saints presents a distinctive stance, asserting that God's dialogue with his people didn't end with the Bible's conclusion. The belief stands firm that the heavens remain open, and God continues his communion with us, especially in this intricate epoch of human history.

In the LDS doctrine, the essence of continuous revelation is paramount. While many religious traditions recognize the scriptures as the ultimate reservoir of God's words, the LDS faith amplifies this by embracing the notion that God's revelations are not confined to history. They believe, akin to ancient times, God still imparts his wisdom and direction to modern-day prophets. This dynamic interaction is exemplified in the ninth Article of Faith, asserting the church's belief in past, present, and future revelations.[501]

The Church reveres its leadership structure as a continuation of the divine patterns established in ancient times.[502] At the pinnacle of this structure is the church president, recognized as a prophet, seer, and revelator.[503] He stands as the Lord's chief apostle on earth in our day. Alongside him, the Quorum of the Twelve Apostles holds a sacred mantle; each member is considered a special witness of Jesus Christ for the entire world.[504] The church president and the twelve apostles collectively bear the divine keys of the priesthood, a heavenly authority given to man to act in God's name.[505] As believed by Latter-Day Saints, this authority was restored in these latter days through Joseph Smith by ancient apostles Peter, James, and John.[506] With these keys, the president and the apostles are charged to guide, instruct, and govern the Church, ensuring it remains aligned with God's will.[507] Through this inspired leadership, Latter-Day Saints believe they receive timely revelations and directions from God tailored for the unique challenges and opportunities of the modern world.[508]

---

[501] "Articles of Faith," the Church of Jesus Christ of Latter-day Saints, https://www.churchofjesuschrist.org/study/scriptures/pgp/a-of-f/1?lang=eng.

[502] "Teachings of Presidents of the Church: Joseph Smith, the Church of Jesus Christ of Latter-day Saints, 2007, https://www.churchofjesuschrist.org/study/manual/teachings-joseph-smith?lang=eng.

[503] M. Russell Ballard, "Prophets, Seers, and Revelators," *Ensign*, Nov. 2004.

[504] Smith, Doctrine and Covenants, 107:23.

[505] Brigham Young, *Teachings of Presidents of the Church: Brigham Young* (Salt Lake City: Church of Jesus Christ of Latter-day Saints, 1997).

[506] Dallin H. Oaks, "The Priesthood and the Keys," *Ensign*, March 2012.

[507] Doctrine and Covenants, 107:8–9.

[508] Russell M. Nelson, "Revelation for the Church, Revelation for Our Lives," *Ensign*, May 2018.

This concept paints a vivid portrait of God. Far from a distant deity of yore, He is envisioned as an intimately involved Father, continually guiding his children. The words and wisdom of the Divine aren't restricted to ancient scrolls but flow in the present, catering to contemporary challenges and questions.

Wilford Woodruff, former LDS president, asserted the enduring guidance of the Divine, suggesting that the Church's leadership is under divine oversight.[509] Such a belief emphasizes that at no point in history, present or future, will humanity wander aimlessly without divine guidance.

In the ever-evolving corridors of time, the LDS Church looks to both ancient scriptures and contemporary prophets to navigate its course. New Testament scriptures, such as Ephesians 4:11–12, which recognizes the roles of apostles and prophets, find profound resonance in LDS beliefs. The Church acknowledges these roles in a historical or foundational capacity and as vital for its modern-day guidance and enlightenment.

Former Church President Gordon B. Hinckley emphasized the pivotal LDS belief in modern prophets, reflecting particularly on the revelatory experiences of Joseph Smith.[510] This foundational event, among others, stresses the ongoing nature of God's revelations.

One can appreciate the LDS perspective on divine communication's continuity in examining the intricate dance of ancient scriptures and modern revelations. As echoed in the Doctrine and Covenants, God's voice remains consistent and accurate, whether expressed through ancient scriptures or contemporary prophets.[511] This continuity assures believers

---

[509] Wilford Woodruff, *Discourses of Wilford Woodruff* (Salt Lake City: Bookcraft, 1946), 212.

[510] Gordon B. Hinckley, "The Marvelous Foundation of Our Faith," LDS General Conference, Oct. 2002.

[511] Doctrine and Covenants, 1:38.

that God's guiding hand, evident in past epochs, is as relevant today as it was to the biblical patriarchs.

Elder D. Todd Christofferson of the Quorum of the Twelve Apostles elegantly captures this sentiment, emphasizing that revelations remain anchored in the scriptures' foundational truth while revelations evolve.[512] In a changing world, scriptures provide timeless truths, while ongoing revelations ensure the church's trajectory remains aligned with God's will.

In my spiritual journey, this melding of ancient wisdom with contemporary insights has illuminated the path. Recognizing that the God of Abraham, Isaac, and Jacob is as engaged with us today as he was with them offers a profound reassurance in a tumultuous world.

In sum, the LDS Church's recognition of modern-day revelation neither diminishes nor competes with ancient scriptures. Instead, it magnifies their eternal relevance, confirming that God's love, guidance, and communication with his children persist—unbroken and undiminished— through the ages.

Conclusion: In Praise of the Divine Word and Our Shared Spiritual Journey

The scriptures, irrespective of religious affiliation, serve as a reservoir of divine wisdom and a testament to humanity's enduring quest for meaning, solace, and communion with the Divine. Their pages chronicle the trials, tribulations, and triumphs of the human spirit, offering solace to the weary, guidance to the lost, and inspiration to the seeker. At their core, these sacred texts underscore a universal truth: the eternal nature of God's word and his unwavering love for his children.

---

[512] D. Todd Christofferson, "The Doctrine of Christ," LDS General Conference, April 2012.

"Heaven and earth shall pass away, but my words shall not pass away," the Savior says in Matthew 24:35. This profound statement emphasizes the immutable nature of divine revelations. Like a lighthouse guiding ships safely to harbor, the scriptures offer an unwavering beacon of hope and direction amidst the tumultuous sea of life. Regardless of my faith background or where I stand on the vast spectrum of belief and spirituality, I've come to appreciate the intrinsic value and timeless wisdom encapsulated in these sacred writings.

For those who might be skeptics or standing on the fringes of faith, I urge you to delve deeper into these ancient texts, not merely as religious artifacts but as profound repositories of wisdom. In my own journey, scriptures haven't just been about ritualistic reading or theological debates. They have been intimate conversations with the Divine—a space where I wrestle with doubts, find answers to my deepest questions, and draw comfort in times of need. Every passage and verse beckons a deeper reflection, encouraging a personal connection and allowing me to draw my own revelations and insights. As the Apostle James encourages, "Draw nigh to God, and he will draw nigh to you" (Ja 4:8). The scriptures serve as that bridge, facilitating this divine communion.

While each religious tradition has its distinct scriptures, it's essential to recognize the shared human quest for divine understanding and connection that transcends these texts. Whether it's the Bhagavad Gita's discourse on duty and righteousness, the Quran's emphasis on submission to God's will, the teachings of Buddha, or the prophetic revelations in the Bible and the Book of Mormon, these texts are, at their heart, chronicles of humanity's engagement with the Divine.

To understand God, to fathom the depths of his love, and to appreciate the guidance he extends, it's vital not just to confine ourselves to a single narrative but also to appreciate and respect the sacred texts of all religions. Such an approach doesn't dilute our faith but instead enriches it, providing a broader canvas to understand God's multifaceted relationship with humanity. As the Apostle Paul writes, "Now we see through a glass, darkly; but then face to face: now I know in part; but then shall I know even as also I am known" (1 Cor 13:12).

Let us cherish the scriptures as texts and living testaments of God's dialogues with humanity. And as we embark on our spiritual journeys, may we remain open-hearted, drawing wisdom from these ancient wells and respecting the myriad ways in which humanity seeks, understands, and celebrates the Divine.

Chapter 9: Atonement and Salvation: Concepts of Redemption in Christianity

Humans have grappled with existential questions that challenge the soul and spirit for millennia. Central among these is the quest for redemption, a sense of reconciliation with the Divine. The Christian faith, which has illuminated the lives of billions over two millennia, offers profound insights into these difficulties through the concepts of atonement and salvation.

Atonement, derived from the Middle English phrase "at one," implies becoming at one with God, restoring a relationship that, according to Christian doctrine, was strained by the fall of man in the Garden of Eden.[513] As Paul elucidated in his epistle to the Romans, "For all have sinned, and come short of the glory of God" (Rom 3:23). Here, the universality of sin is highlighted, positioning atonement as a necessary bridge between humanity's inherent frailty and the Divine's perfection.

Salvation, on the other hand, is a broader concept, encompassing not only the idea of being saved from sin and the promise of eternal life but also representing the ultimate goal of Christian life—reunion with God in the afterlife. As the scriptures affirm, "For the wages of sin is death; but the gift of God is eternal life through Jesus Christ our Lord" (Rom 6:23). In essence, salvation implies a deliverance from the consequences of sin and the bestowal of eternal blessings.

While Christianity might be diverse, encompassing a plethora of denominations and traditions, there remains a universal cornerstone: the belief in Christ's sacrifice as the path to redemption. Jesus Christ, regarded as the Son of God, incarnated on Earth, not merely as a theological figure but as the embodiment of God's unwavering love for humanity. His crucifixion, a culmination of a life devoted to teaching love, compassion, and righteousness, is seen as an act of atonement for the sins of humanity.

---

[513] Augustine of Hippo, *City of God* (New York: Penguin Classics, 2003).

The Gospel of John poignantly encapsulates this sentiment, stating, "For God so loved the world, that he gave his only begotten Son, that whosoever believeth in him should not perish, but have everlasting life" (Jn 3:16). This verse, often described as the gospel in miniature, underscores Christ's role as the redeemer. It suggests that belief in him and his sacrifice can lead us to salvation. The message is unmistakable: despite our flaws or past mistakes, redemption remains within our grasp, provided we seek it sincerely.

However, while the shared Christian belief revolves around Christ's sacrifice as a path to redemption, interpretations of atonement and salvation can vary among denominations. It's crucial to approach these nuances with an open heart, recognizing that while practices or interpretations may differ, the core belief in Christ's love and sacrifice remains intact.

For many people outside the Christian faith, the concepts of atonement and salvation appear doctrinal or rigid. However, at their heart, these teachings represent universal human yearnings: the desire for redemption, the hope for a life beyond the mortal, and the quest for a deeper connection with the Divine. These sentiments resonate with the collective human psyche regardless of religious or philosophical affiliations.

Atonement and salvation lie at the heart of Christian doctrine. They symbolize God's unwavering love and offer hope for redemption and eternal life. As we delve deeper into these themes, let us remain open to understanding and cherishing the shared beliefs while respecting the nuances. In understanding, we draw closer to the Divine, realizing these profound truths are timeless and universal in nature.

Historical Understanding of Atonement in Christian Theology

The term "atonement" is a theological construct conveying reconciliation between humanity and the Divine, an idea deeply entrenched in the biblical narrative. In the ancient Hebrew text, the word used for atonement is "kaphar," which denotes "to cover" or "to appease." [514] The Day of Atonement, or Yom Kippur, remains a solemn Jewish observance where sacrifices were made to atone for the sins of the people. Within this context, the act of atonement was seen as a means to restore the broken relationship between God and his chosen people. The Prophet Isaiah writes, "But he was wounded for our transgressions, he was bruised for our iniquities: the chastisement of our peace was upon him; and with his stripes we are healed" (Is 53:5). Though penned centuries before Christ, this prophetic utterance resonates with Christian interpretations of Jesus as the sacrificial lamb, prefiguring his redemptive role.

Transitioning to the New Testament, the essence of atonement deepens and evolves, culminating in the life and sacrifice of Jesus Christ. In Romans 5:8–9, the Apostle Paul robustly expounds upon this doctrine, stating, "God commendeth his love toward us, in that, while we were yet sinners, Christ died for us. Much more than, being now justified by his blood, we shall be saved from wrath through him." Here, Paul emphasizes Christ's death as an act of love, illustrating the transformative power of his sacrifice.

Fervent theological explorations marked the early centuries following the crucifixion of Jesus Christ. As Christianity found its feet and began to expand beyond the boundaries of Judea, the implications of Christ's sacrifice became a central theological debate. How could one man's death resonate so profoundly that it promised salvation to all of humanity? This was not merely a matter of faith; it was foundational to understanding the identity of Christianity itself.

Origen Adamantius, also known as Origen of Alexandria, was an early Christian scholar,[515] ascetic,[516] and theologian who was born in and spent

---

[514] Leon Morris, *The Atonement: Its Meaning & Significance* (Downers Grove: InterVarsity Press, 1984).
[515] Robert Louis Wilken, "A Learned Faith: Origen of Alexandria," in *The First Thousand Years: A Global History of Christianity* (New Haven: Yale University Press, 2013), 55–64.
[516] Richard Finn, "Origen and his ascetic legacy," in *Asceticism in the Graeco-Roman World* (Cambridge: Cambridge University Press, 2009), 100–130.

the first half of his career in Alexandria. He was pivotal in these theological deliberations. Born into a devout Christian family, he was well-acquainted with martyrdom—his own father met such a fate. This personal connection to the idea of sacrifice for faith undoubtedly influenced his later theological perspectives.

Origen's ransom theory sought to explain why Christ's death was necessary. Drawing from scriptural references and prevalent cultural narratives of his time, Origen painted a picture of humanity ensnared by the devil due to the original sin committed by Adam and Eve. In this narrative, the devil had legitimate rights over human souls because of their transgressions. Jesus Christ, God incarnate, was offered as a "bait" to Satan. While the devil believed he was claiming another soul, he was actually encountering the Divine, against whom he had no power. Thus, Christ's death served as a ransom, deceiving the devil and eventually releasing all human souls from his grip.[517]

While the ransom theory gained traction in the early Christian world with its vivid imagery and dramatic narrative, it was not without its critics. Many theologians found the idea of God resorting to deception problematic. Furthermore, the notion of Satan having legitimate rights over souls seemed to place the devil in a position of power that too closely rivaled God's sovereignty.

As Christianity matured, the Church's understanding of atonement evolved, and more nuanced theories replaced Origen's perspective. By the time of the medieval scholars, while Origen's contributions to theology were still respected, many of his specific views, including ransom theory, needed to be revised or made more complex. Nevertheless, Origen's influence is undeniable. He was among the first to wrestle with the

---

[517] *The Commentary on the Gospel of Matthew*, ed. Ronald E. Heine (Oxford: Oxford University Press, 2018).

complexities of atonement, laying the groundwork for many subsequent theological discussions.

The Middle Ages was a time of intense theological scholarship and debate. It was against this backdrop, amidst the grandeur of cathedrals and the solemnity of monastic life, that St. Anselm of Canterbury crafted his groundbreaking satisfaction theory of atonement.

St. Anselm lived during a period marked by feudal relationships. Lords and vassals, honor codes, and the duties of the noble class were integral components of society. To be dishonored in this society was a grave concern, often demanding recompense or satisfaction to restore one's status and dignity. This societal structure heavily influenced Anselm's theological perspective, molding his understanding of humanity's relationship with God in similar terms.

In his seminal work, *Cur Deus Homo* (*Why God Became Man*), Anselm posits a scenario in which humanity, through sin, has corrupted the cosmic balance by dishonoring God.[518] As in the feudal system, where a vassal who dishonored his lord owed a debt of satisfaction, humanity's collective transgressions amounted to a debt. But this was no ordinary debt; it was a cosmic one, too immense for any human or even all of humanity combined to repay.

Enter the figure of Jesus Christ—both divine and human. As God, Jesus was above any obligation to pay the debt of honor, and as a sinless human, he was the only one capable of offering a sacrifice pure enough to do so. Anselm's theory posits that Christ's willing sacrifice on the cross was not a ransom paid to the devil (as Origen suggested) but a gift to God the Father, satisfying the honor that humanity owed him.

St. Anselm's satisfaction theory wasn't just a theological exposition; it was a mirror reflecting the societal ethos of his time. The parallels he drew

---

[518] Anselm of Canterbury, *Cur Deus Homo: Why God Became Man,* Fordham University, https://sourcebooks.fordham.edu/basis/anselm-curdeus.asp.

between the divine realm and feudal societal norms made the complex idea of atonement more accessible to the people of his era. They could relate to the concepts of honor, debt, and satisfaction in their daily lives, making Anselm's interpretation both revolutionary and deeply resonant.

While many theologians have built upon, debated, or diverged from Anselm's views, his influence remains undeniable. His attempt to understand the depth of Christ's sacrifice through the lens of his societal context showcases the dynamism of Christian theology, which continually engages with and responds to the changing world around it.

One of the Middle Ages' most profound theologians, Thomas Aquinas, stood at the crossroads of faith and reason. His monumental work, *Summa Theologica*, sought to harmonize the teachings of the Church with the intellectual traditions of ancient Greece, particularly the writings of Aristotle.

While Anselm focused on the satisfaction of honor within a feudal context, Aquinas approached the atonement from a more comprehensive theological and philosophical framework. Drawing on Aristotle's ideas, particularly his emphasis on causality and the nature of virtues, Aquinas articulated a more intricate understanding of the atonement.

Aquinas recognized God's intrinsic attributes of justice and mercy as two sides of the same divine coin. He proposed that God's justice required reparation for sin since sin disrupted the moral and cosmic order of the universe.[519] In this light, humanity's collective sin wasn't just a debt of honor (as Anselm described) but a real violation of the intrinsic good, a concept deeply rooted in Aristotelian ethics.

However, God's mercy, equally paramount, couldn't simply overlook this breach. Instead, His mercy set the stage for the ultimate act of love and self-

---

[519] Thomas Aquinas, "On the Debt of Punishment," in *Summa Theologica*, New Advent, I-II, Q. 87, https://www.newadvent.org/summa/.

sacrifice—Jesus Christ's crucifixion. In this monumental act, divine justice and mercy weren't in conflict but were harmoniously reconciled.

Christ, being both wholly divine and wholly human, bridged the chasm between God and humanity. As Aquinas interpreted, his sacrifice on the cross wasn't just about satisfying a debt; it was a restoration of the disrupted order of creation, a healing of the rift introduced by human sinfulness. Therefore, Christ's act of atonement was both a fulfillment of God's justice and an expression of his boundless mercy.

Aquinas provided a sophisticated and balanced perspective on atonement by fusing Aristotelian logic with Christian doctrine. His synthesis illuminated the complexities of God's nature, offering Christians a deeper, more nuanced understanding of their faith and God's profound love for humanity.

Thomas Aquinas's approach showcases the Church's adaptability and willingness to engage with the intellectual movements of its time. It also underscores the timeless nature of the core Christian belief in Christ's redemptive sacrifice, affirming its relevance and resonance across different epochs and philosophical landscapes.

The Reformation, a monumental epoch in Christian history, was not just a challenge to the ecclesiastical authority of the Roman Catholic Church; it was also a period of intense theological introspection and redefinition. Central to this was the doctrine of atonement, with figures like Martin Luther fundamentally reshaping Christian understanding of Christ's redemptive role.

Luther was an Augustinian monk turned reformer who grappled with deep feelings of unworthiness and sin. His intensive study of the Bible, particularly the New Testament, led him to a revolutionary understanding of salvation and atonement. For Luther, the overwhelming weight of humanity's sins made any form of self-atonement through works or indulgences inadequate and a grave misinterpretation of the Scriptures.

Enter penal substitution theory. In this framework, Luther posited that Christ, in his crucifixion, bore the weight of humanity's sins and faced the consequent divine wrath. This wasn't a mere symbolic act but a literal substitution. God's justice, which demanded retribution for sin, was thus satisfied not by punishing humanity but by placing that punishment on Christ.[520]

Luther's perspective, deeply influenced by his own personal struggles with guilt and salvation, emphasized the absolute inability of humans to save themselves. This notion stood in stark contrast to the Catholic Church's teachings of the time, which stressed the role of the Church, sacraments, and good works in the process of salvation.

The profound implication of penal substitution theory was its democratization of salvation. In Luther's view, salvation was accessible to all who believed in Christ's redeeming sacrifice. His doctrine of sola fide, or justification by faith alone, encapsulates this. Believer don't earn salvation through works but receive it as a free gift of grace through faith in the atoning sacrifice of Christ.[521]

Luther's understanding of atonement formed the bedrock of Protestant theology and catalyzed various other interpretations and debates within the burgeoning Protestant denominations. His teachings on Christ's redemptive act underscored the central place of Scripture in Christian life and paved the way for the diverse theological landscape of the modern Christian world.

For me, navigating these multifaceted interpretations has been enlightening and humbling. The myriad of perspectives on atonement underscores the

---

[520] Martin Luther, *Commentary on the Epistle to the Galatians*, trans. Theodore Grabner, Project Gutenberg, 1998, https://www.gutenberg.org/files/1549/1549-h/1549-h.htm. See Luther's commentary on Galatians 3:13, where he discusses Christ becoming a curse for us.

[521] Martin Luther, *The Freedom of a Christian*, ed. Mark D. Tranvik (Minneapolis: Fortress Press, 2008). In this book, Luther discusses the dual nature of a Christian as a free lord and as a dutiful servant, emphasizing faith's primary role in attaining righteousness.

profundity of Christ's sacrifice and the inexhaustible depths of God's love. While theological interpretations might differ, they converge on a singular truth: the monumental significance of Christ's atoning sacrifice.

As with all theological constructs, divine revelation and human interpretation have shaped the understanding of atonement. Early Christian thinkers, building upon biblical foundations, sought to make sense of God's plan for humanity's salvation. They navigated the tension between justice and mercy, sin and redemption, weaving a theological tapestry that continues to inspire and guide.

The concept of atonement, with its biblical roots and rich theological evolution, serves as a testament to humanity's yearning for divine connection. It also underscores the lengths to which God would go to restore this relationship, culminating in the selfless sacrifice of Jesus Christ. The atonement narrative offers hope, solace, and a beacon of unyielding love for believers and seekers alike.

Salvation: A Broad Overview

In the annals of Christian thought, few concepts possess the theological weight and centrality as that of salvation. At its core, salvation signifies deliverance—from sin, its consequences, and the separation that sin creates between humanity and God. For many Christians, it embodies the very hope and promise of Christianity: eternal life with God and freedom from the weight of sin and death.

"For the wages of sin is death; but the gift of God is eternal life through Jesus Christ our Lord" (Rom 6:23). This passage encapsulates the doctrine's essence. It speaks of a debt—the "wages" of our sins—but it also brings forth a promise: the gift of eternal life. This dual acknowledgment of human imperfection and divine mercy forms the heart of Christian soteriology (the study of salvation).

The need for salvation arises from the Christian belief in original sin, that humanity is in a fallen state due to Adam and Eve's transgression. Genesis recounts this first act of disobedience. It banished humanity from Eden and subjected us to mortality, pain, and the inherent inclination toward sin. However, while the narrative underscores humanity's fallen nature, it also hints at God's plan for redemption (Gen 3:15).

"Believe on the Lord Jesus Christ, and thou shalt be saved," Paul and Silas proclaim to the frightened jailer in Acts 16:31 following an earthquake that blew open the prison doors. This verse captures the Christian belief in the accessibility of salvation through faith in Jesus Christ. It's a deep-seated trust, a turning of the heart and the will toward God, and a commitment to following Christ.

The LDS Church upholds these foundational beliefs. From the LDS perspective, the atonement of Jesus Christ is the central event in human history. It's about compensating for our sins and providing the means to overcome physical death through resurrection. LDS teachings emphasize the universality of this atonement; Christ's sacrifice benefits all of humanity, regardless of when and where people lived.[522]

However, the LDS perspective on salvation offers layers of intricate nuances not found in mainstream Christian beliefs. In LDS theology, salvation is not a monolithic or one-dimensional concept. Instead, it is understood in a multi-faceted manner, akin to the many facets of a diamond, each reflecting light in its unique way. Central to this view is the idea of different "degrees" of heavenly glory, often referred to as the three kingdoms of glory: the Celestial, the Terrestrial, and the Telestial kingdoms.

Each kingdom represents varying degrees of glory and proximity to God, and the placement of souls within these kingdoms is determined by how individuals live their lives on Earth. Those who embrace Christ's teachings, participate in essential ordinances, and continually strive to live in

---

[522] Jeffrey R. Holland, "The Atonement of Jesus Christ," *Ensign*, March 2008.

alignment with his teachings are said to inherit the celestial kingdom, the highest realm of heavenly glory. The Terrestrial and Telestial kingdoms are reserved for individuals who, while perhaps not fully embracing every tenet of the gospel, have lived honorable lives or those who might have strayed but are willing to accept the gospel in the afterlife, respectively.

This brings up the enigma of the afterlife that has confounded the faithful and skeptics for countless generations. A particularly vexing question is this: what becomes of those who inadvertently followed an incorrect spiritual path or never had the chance to discover God's true guidance? This dilemma was eloquently echoed by Rapper Dax, the stage name of Daniel Nwosu Jr., in his poignant lines: "What if the place we grew up forgot to teach it? What if we never even got the chance, to go and seek it? Then what, then what?"[523] In his song, "Book of Revelations," the central character finds himself at Heaven's gates, begging the Heavenly Father, "God we at the gates (What if?) We couldn't see, hear, or touch you. But we had faith, we know we messed up. We human and we make mistakes. So we just begging we get in, And that you'll have grace (Please)."[524]

The LDS Church has a unique perspective on this situation: the concept of "baptisms for the dead," which is a significant element in LDS soteriology. This doctrine asserts that those who departed from this life without the chance to hear or accept the gospel aren't denied the blessings of salvation. In LDS temples, members perform proxy baptisms on behalf of these individuals, providing them with an opportunity to accept or reject these ordinances in the spirit world. This is a profound reflection of God's encompassing mercy. It underscores the LDS belief that the Almighty's love extends beyond the grave, granting every soul a fair and equal opportunity for salvation, regardless of their earthly circumstances.

---

[523] Dax, "Book of Revelations," YouTube video, 3:55, Feb. 27, 2020, https://youtu.be/HS3pUgRKh_g.
[524] Ibid.

What's genuinely heartening about this expanded understanding of salvation is the generous vision of God it portrays—a God not just of justice but of boundless mercy and inclusivity. It reaffirms the belief that the divine plan is designed with all God's children's ultimate happiness and progression in mind.

This expansive view of salvation underscores the LDS belief in a loving God who "will have all men to be saved, and to come unto the knowledge of the truth" (1 Tim 2:4), a God who, in his infinite wisdom, has set forth a plan where his children—regardless of their earthly circumstances—have a path to return to him.

Drawing from traditional Christian and LDS perspectives, it's evident that salvation is more than a theological construct; it's a deeply personal journey that commences with acknowledging our human frailties, progresses to embracing Christ's redemptive love, and culminates in eternal union with the Divine.

As someone who has delved deep into scriptures and theology, I've often marveled at the universality of the quest for salvation. Regardless of denominational differences, the yearning to be reconciled with God and to find meaning amid life's struggles remains a shared human endeavor. In that quest, Christ's message of hope, love, and redemption stands as a beacon—a promise of a day when every tear shall be wiped away, and the weight of sin and death shall be no more.

Nuances of Salvation in Various Christian Denominations

Salvation, intricately woven with threads of grace, faith, and deeds, assumes varied hues across the spectrum of Christian denominations. Each tradition interprets and emphasizes aspects of salvation in distinct ways, influenced by centuries of theological contemplation, historical circumstances, and scriptural interpretations. However, at the core, they all converge on the pivotal role of Christ's redemptive act.

Catholicism: The intricacies of salvation within the Catholic Church are elegantly interwoven with the doctrines of faith, grace, and good works. This unique tapestry finds its foundation in the Apostle Paul's proclamation: "For by grace are ye saved through faith; and that not of yourselves: it is the gift of God" (Eph 2:8). Such a statement beautifully distills the essence of the Catholic perspective on salvation. At the heart of this doctrine is the concept of grace, a benevolent and unearned gift from the Divine. This grace is not merely a theoretical or theological concept but finds its tangible manifestation through the sacramental rituals that act as conduits of God's grace.

Foremost among these sacraments are baptism and the Eucharist. Baptism serves as a rite of initiation, marking the believer's entry into the Christian community and signifying their cleansing from the original sin. The Eucharist, or Holy Communion, is a profound celebration of Christ's sacrifice, wherein believers partake of bread and wine, symbols of Christ's body and blood. It commemorates his redemptive act on the cross and nourishes the soul, fortifying the believer's bond with Christ.

While the sacraments and faith are integral, the Catholic doctrine adds another dimension: the role of good deeds or works. Drawing from the Epistle of James, which declares that "faith without works is dead" (Ja 2:26), the Church upholds the belief that genuine faith naturally gives birth to acts of charity, kindness, and love. Such deeds are not seen as mere obligations but as expressions of a transformed heart, reflecting the love and mercy of Christ.

In the Catholic worldview, salvation isn't just a singular event or a mere theological construct. It's an ongoing pilgrimage where grace illuminates the path, faith acts as the compass, and deeds of love and mercy mark the milestones. Every step taken on this journey, whether through the reception of sacraments, acts of faith, or deeds of compassion, draws us closer to the Divine, embodying the profound love story between God and humanity.

Protestantism: The Protestant Reformation, one of the most transformative movements in Christian history, stemmed from a deep yearning to realign the church's teachings with scriptural truths. At its core was Martin Luther's radical affirmation of "sola fide" or salvation by faith alone. This conviction, crystallized in his intense study of the Epistle to the Romans, underlined the belief that human righteousness before God was a gift received solely through faith in Jesus Christ and not contingent upon any human merit or deed (Rom 1:17). Luther's passionate arguments against certain practices of the Catholic Church, particularly the sale of indulgences, was a challenge to ecclesiastical authority and a profound theological shift.

As Protestantism burgeoned, it branched out into diverse theological traditions, each contributing its unique flavor to the discourse on salvation. The Lutherans, holding closely to their founder's teachings, underscored grace as God's unmerited favor toward humanity. They emphasized the believer's passive receipt of this grace, through faith, and realized in Christ's redemptive act on the cross.

Building upon the works of his predecessors and contemporaneously with other Protestant reformers, Swiss reformer John Calvin introduced an interpretation of salvation that was both rooted in scripture and radical in its implications.

Central to Calvin's theology is God's unassailable sovereignty. In his magnum opus, *Institutes of the Christian Religion*, Calvin delineates a vision of a God who preordains the eternal fate of every human soul in his infinite wisdom and justice.[525] Drawing from Pauline texts, especially from the Epistle to the Romans, Calvin asserts that God, "before the foundation of the world" (Eph 14) had already elected certain individuals to eternal life and others to eternal damnation. This election was not based on any

---

[525] John Calvin, *Institutes of the Christian Religion*, trans. Henry Beveridge (Grand Rapids, MI: Eerdmans, 1989).

foreseen merit or action of the individual but solely on God's mysterious will.

This doctrine, often termed "double predestination," underscores two main points: the total depravity of humanity due to original sin, rendering them incapable of choosing God without divine intervention, and God's irresistible grace, which ensures that those whom God has chosen will inevitably come to faith and be saved.

However, as one can imagine, such a perspective on salvation isn't without its critics. Many find it hard to reconcile with the biblical portrayal of a just and loving God. Some see the doctrine as painting a picture of a capricious deity, predestining some to eternal torment without giving them a genuine opportunity for salvation. This has led to centuries of theological debate, with alternative perspectives arising in response to Calvin's views.

The Arminian perspective, for instance, posits that while God's foreknowledge encompasses who will be saved and who won't, this knowledge is based on his foresight of an individual's free response to his offered grace. Thus, they advocate for a conditional election based on God's foreknowledge rather than an unconditional election based solely on his will.

Despite its controversies, Calvinism's emphasis on God's sovereignty and grace has resonated with many believers. For its adherents, the doctrine underscores the depth of human dependence on God's grace and the certainty of God's promises to those he has chosen.

As with many theological debates within Christianity, the discussion around predestination underscores the faith's rich tapestry of thought and the earnest quest of believers throughout the ages to grasp the mysteries of the Divine.

John Wesley's Methodism brought a fresh perspective to the Protestant understanding of salvation, particularly through its emphasis on the multifaceted nature of grace. Wesley, a dynamic eighteenth-century preacher and evangelist, was deeply influenced by his Anglican heritage and personal religious experiences. This culminated in him developing a deeply scriptural and experientially resonant soteriology for many believers.

Central to Wesley's theology is the concept of grace, which he viewed not as a singular entity but as a dynamic, unfolding reality in the life of a believer. Of these, "prevenient grace," or "preceding grace," holds a unique place. The term "prevenient" is derived from the Latin "prevenire," which means "to come before." In Wesleyan theology, this grace is the antecedent to all human initiatives toward God.[526]

Prevenient grace is not merely a passive attribute of God but his active, assertive love reaching out to humanity. God's initiative is the "light which lighteth every man that cometh into the world" (Jn 1:9). For Wesley, this grace is evidence of God's universal love, seeking to draw all of humanity to himself. It acts as the divine antidote to the blinding effects of sin, restoring our ability to perceive and respond to God's love. This is why, in Methodism, even those who might be unaware of God or who are entrenched in sin are still touched by his grace, making them capable of recognizing and responding to further manifestations of God's love.

Following this initial touch of prevenient grace, Wesley taught of justifying grace, experienced when an individual responds to God's call, and sanctifying grace, which refines and transforms a believer throughout their life.

In his view, the Christian journey is marked by continual interactions with grace. The experience isn't just of a distant, foreordained divine decree but of a deeply personal, transformative relationship with God. This relationship starts with the gentle nudge of prevenient grace, leading individuals to realize God's redemptive love in their lives.

---

[526] John Wesley, "On Working Out Our Own Salvation," in *Sermons on Several Occasions* (Grand Rapids: Christian Classics Ethereal Library, 1872).

Such a view has implications for evangelism and Christian conduct as well. If all are recipients of prevenient grace, then all have the potential to respond to the gospel, making evangelistic efforts a means of stirring and awakening an already existing, albeit dormant, awareness of God.

Wesley's emphasis on prevenient grace underscores a God who is always the initiator, ever reaching out, ever inviting, and ever waiting for a human response. It paints a picture of a relentless divine love, always preceding, always guiding, and always seeking to redeem.

Amid this tapestry of theological positions, a common thread runs through: the centrality of Christ's atoning work on the cross. Regardless of denominational differences, Protestants universally affirm the salvific power of Christ's sacrifice and the pivotal role of personal faith in appropriating its benefits.

Hence, the Protestant tradition stands as a testament to the multifaceted understanding of salvation. While various denominations may differ in terms of nuances and emphases, they all converge on the singular truth of Christ's redemptive love and the transformative power of faith.

Eastern Orthodoxy: One of the oldest Christian traditions, Eastern Orthodoxy provides a deeply spiritual and transformative perspective on salvation, distinct from its Western counterparts. Rooted in the ancient teachings of the early Church Fathers and the ecumenical councils, this tradition sees salvation as a mystical union with the Divine, encapsulated in the concept of theosis or deification.

The doctrine of theosis can be traced back to the early Christian mystics and theologians like St. Gregory of Nazianzus and St. Athanasius. The latter famously proclaimed, "God became man so that man might become god."[527] This profound statement doesn't imply a literal divinization of

---

[527] St. Athanasius, *On the Incarnation* (Crestwood, NY: St. Vladimir's Seminary Press, 1996), 54.

humans but emphasizes the aspirational goal of Christian life: to be transformed into the likeness of God.

Drawing from the Apostle Peter's words, "Whereby are given unto us exceeding great and precious promises: that by these ye might be partakers of the divine nature" (2 Pet 1:4), the Orthodox Church interprets salvation as a participatory journey. Believers don't just receive salvation passively; they partake in the divine nature through a life of prayer, fasting, worship, and righteous living.

The sacraments, especially the Eucharist, are transformative processes seen as a direct participation in the divine life. The liturgical life of the Orthodox Church, with its rich symbols, chants, and rituals, aids believers in this transformation journey, drawing them closer to the divine mystery.

While Western Christianity often emphasizes juridical or transactional understandings of salvation—focusing on sin, guilt, and redemption— Eastern Orthodoxy sees it as therapeutic. According to Orthodox theology, humanity's primary problem isn't just guilt due to sin but an ailment that needs healing. Christ's atoning sacrifice on the cross is both a remedy for sin and a model for divine aspiration. It's not just about avoiding punishment but achieving a state of spiritual wholeness and unity with God.

The synergy between God's grace and human effort is a recurring theme in Orthodox writings. In his classic work, *The Ladder of Divine Ascent*, St. John Climacus describes the Christian journey as climbing a ladder, each rung representing a stage in spiritual development.[528] While God provides the grace, believers must exert effort, reflecting a cooperative dynamic between the divine and human.

To summarize, Eastern Orthodoxy offers a holistic, therapeutic view of salvation. It's a journey of continuous transformation where the believer,

---

[528] St. John Climacus, *Ladder of Divine Ascent* (Boston, MA: Holy Transfiguration Monastery, 1991).

aided by sacraments and ascetic practices, strives to achieve unity with the Divine, reflecting Christ's perfect nature. While challenging, this journey is a testament to God's profound love and mercy, beckoning all to partake in his divine nature.

Anglicanism: With its genesis in the English Reformation, Anglicanism stands uniquely poised between the Roman Catholic and Reformed Protestant traditions, holding elements of both in a delicate balance. This church, which has historically strived to be a "via media" or middle way, offers a rich and multifaceted perspective on salvation, bridging the gap between faith and works, sacrament and scripture.

Tracing its origins to King Henry VIII's split from Rome, the Anglican Church grappled with the theological currents of the time. This tension between its Catholic past and the Reformed influences shaped its doctrine. The Book of Common Prayer, sacramental rites, and the Thirty-Nine Articles became pivotal texts, guiding the Anglican understanding of faith and practice.

The Thirty-Nine Articles, while reflecting a clear Protestant ethos, particularly in its statements on salvation by faith, also incorporate a nuanced understanding. For instance, Article XII, "Of Good Works," asserts that while good works cannot remit our sins, they are pleasing and acceptable to God and spring out of true and lively faith."[529] This delineates the Anglican position: faith, undoubtedly, is the cornerstone, but genuine faith invariably manifests in good deeds.

Furthermore, Anglican liturgy and sacraments, especially the Eucharist, play a crucial role in the believer's spiritual journey. The Eucharist isn't just symbolic; for many Anglicans, it's a means of grace, an actual participation in the body and blood of Christ. This sacramental perspective aligns more

---

[529] Article XII, "Of Good Works," the Thirty-Nine Articles of Religion, https://www.anglicanism.info/thirty-nine-articles-of-religion.

with the Catholic worldview than the Reformed one, reflecting the synthesis inherent in Anglicanism.

This blending of theologies doesn't denote ambiguity but a deliberate and thoughtful reconciliation. Renowned Anglican theologian Richard Hooker, in his magnum opus, *Laws of Ecclesiastical Polity*, emphasizes the threefold foundation of Anglicanism: scripture, tradition, and reason.[530] These pillars support the Anglican perspective on salvation. Scripture offers the doctrinal basis; tradition, including the sacraments, connects believers to the ancient practices of the Church, and reason allows for an adaptive understanding responsive to changing times and contexts.

In summation, Anglicanism's take on salvation embodies its broader theological ethos—a harmonious blend of Catholic sacramentality and Protestant emphasis on personal faith. Through this balanced lens, the Anglican tradition offers a holistic path to salvation, embracing the meritorious sacrifice of Christ and the consequential response of believers in the form of righteous deeds.

The combined Christian landscape, with its mosaic of denominations, offers diverse insights into the nature of atonement and salvation. While rooted in different theological and historical contexts, these variations converge on the centrality of Christ's redemptive act. Whether through grace, faith, deeds, sacraments, or a synergy of these, the Christian heart yearns for communion with the Divine, a yearning that finds its fulfillment in the salvific act of Jesus Christ.

Salvation in LDS Theology

The Church of Jesus Christ of Latter-day Saints possesses a rich tapestry of beliefs and practices that distinguishes its theology from other Christian

---

[530] Richard Hooker, *Of the Laws of Ecclesiastical Polity* (London: J.M. Dent & Sons, 1907).

traditions. Its teachings on salvation are central to understanding the Church's unique religious identity.

Central to LDS doctrine is the notion of a "restored gospel," the belief that the fullness of the gospel, once lost, was restored to the prophet Joseph Smith in the nineteenth century.[531] This restoration is seen not as a rejection of traditional Christianity but as a culmination and completion of it. In this panorama of restoration, Jesus Christ occupies a pivotal role. He's not only the Savior but also the central figure in the plan of salvation. The Book of Mormon, alongside the Bible in LDS belief, declares: "We talk of Christ, we rejoice in Christ, we preach of Christ, we prophesy of Christ" (2 Nephi 25:26). Christ's atoning sacrifice makes salvation and exaltation possible, redeeming humanity from physical death (through resurrection) and spiritual death (through forgiveness of sins).

Ordinances (sacred rituals and ceremonies) and covenants (two-way promises between God and individuals) are integral to LDS soteriology. Rooted in ancient religious practices, ordinances are sacred rituals and ceremonies that mark significant spiritual milestones, while covenants represent solemn and binding promises made between individuals and the Divine.

A prime example is the ordinance of baptism by immersion. For Latter-Day Saints, baptism is a symbolic act and a profound spiritual rebirth. When an individual is immersed in water, it symbolizes the burial of the old self and emerging anew, washed clean from sin. This act doesn't just signify the remission of sins; it is accompanied by a covenant to take upon oneself the name of Christ and to serve him faithfully. The gravity of this covenant is such that Jesus himself, though sinless, set the example by being baptized "to fulfill all righteousness" (Mt 3:15).

---

[531] Joseph Smith, *History of The Church of Jesus Christ of Latter-day Saints*, ed. B. H. Roberts (Salt Lake City: Deseret Book Co., 1980), 1:40.

Like the Eucharist or Communion in many Christian traditions, this sacrament holds a unique place in LDS worship. Conducted weekly during Sunday services, members partake of consecrated bread and water. However, instead of a once-in-a-lifetime covenant, the sacrament offers a weekly opportunity for reflection, repentance, and renewal of baptismal promises. By partaking, members are reminded of the body and blood of Christ, which he sacrificed for them as they recommit to their promises at baptism, reinforcing the intertwined nature of ordinances and covenants.

However, the depth of LDS ordinances doesn't stop at the chapel's doors; it continues into the temple, a sacred space reserved for the Church's most solemn ceremonies. For Latter-Day Saints, temples are not just buildings but houses of the Lord, places where heaven touches Earth. Higher ordinances like the endowment and celestial marriage (or sealing) are performed within these hallowed walls. The endowment provides individuals with teachings, covenants, and blessings that prepare them for eternal life. It represents a spiritual journey, guiding participants through the story of Creation, the Fall, and the atonement, equipping them with knowledge and power from on high.[532]

Celestial marriage, on the other hand, seals families together for eternity. While many Christian denominations recognize "till death do us part," in LDS theology, marital and familial relationships when sealed under proper authority, have the potential to persist beyond the grave. It embodies the belief that families can be together forever, intertwining the concept of individual salvation with familial exaltation.[533]

In essence, LDS ordinances and covenants are not mere rituals but profound expressions of faith and commitment, guiding lights in the believer's journey back to God. They symbolize the deepening relationship

---

[532] David A. Bednar, "Come and See," Ensign, Nov. 2014.
[533] Russell M. Nelson, "Celestial Marriage," Ensign, Nov. 2008.

between God and his children, providing a roadmap for attaining eternal life.

While many Christian traditions define "salvation" as redemption from sin and resurrection, LDS theology introduces the concept of "exaltation"— the opportunity to become like God and inherit a place in his celestial kingdom. This reflects the Apostle Paul's sentiment: "The Spirit itself beareth witness with our spirit, that we are the children of God: And if children, then heirs; heirs of God, and joint-heirs with Christ" (Rom 8:16– 17). However, the afterlife in LDS belief is more nuanced than just heaven and hell. Doctrine and Covenants delineates three degrees of glory in the hereafter: celestial, terrestrial, and telestial, each reflecting varying levels of righteousness and adherence to God's commandments.[534] Even those who do not inherit the celestial kingdom still receive a measure of God's grace and glory, underscoring the expansive nature of Christ's atonement.

Agency, as discussed in Chapter 6's exploration of free will, is a cornerstone of LDS theology and finds its roots in the scriptures of the Church of Jesus Christ of Latter-day Saints. Rooted in the narrative of humanity's spiritual journey, the Book of Mormon reiterates that people "are free according to the flesh; and all things are given them which are expedient unto man. And they are free to choose liberty and eternal life, through the great Mediator of all men, or to choose captivity and death, according to the captivity and power of the devil" (2 Ne 2:27).

The Garden of Eden's narrative, where Adam and Eve chose to partake of the forbidden fruit, is not seen by LDS as a grievous error. Instead, as clarified in the Pearl of Great Price, it's considered a necessary transgression that led to gaining knowledge and the ability to bear children, two conditions essential for the LDS plan of salvation (Moses 5:10–11). This event introduced mortality and the agency to choose, framing the entire purpose of this earthly journey.

---

[534] Doctrine and Covenants, 76:50–112.

However, with such agency comes the inevitable imperfections of human choices. Doctrine and Covenants repeatedly emphasizes humanity's dependence on Christ's grace. It articulates that "every man may act in doctrine and principle . . . according to the moral agency which I have given unto him, that every man may be accountable for his own sins in the day of judgment" (101:78).

Christ's atonement, as depicted in the Bible and in LDS scriptures, does more than redeem humanity from sin. The Book of Mormon, for instance, teaches that he not only suffered for our sins but also for our "pains and afflictions and temptations of every kind" (Alma 7:11). Thus, the atonement becomes a wellspring of strength, enabling individuals to refine their choices and align their will with the Divine.

In this rich tapestry of agency and atonement, LDS doctrine offers a path where individuals, assisted by divine grace, can ascend toward their eternal potential. As iterated in Doctrine and Covenants, individuals are "made free" through Christ's atonement and can be "agents unto themselves" (58:28).

Hence, this harmonious blend of personal choice and divine empowerment underpins LDS teachings on salvation—a journey of individual effort and reliance on Christ's infinite atonement. It paints a picture of a loving God, eager to save and exalt his children, and a Savior, Jesus Christ, who makes it all possible. By intertwining agency with atonement, ordinances with covenants, and presenting a layered vision of the afterlife, LDS theology offers a challenging and redemptive path, beckoning every individual toward its promise of eternal life and joy.

The Central Role of Jesus Christ in Salvation Across Denominations

It's nearly impossible to talk about Christian soteriology without placing Jesus Christ at the center. Across all Christian denominations, Christ's sacrifice is viewed as the path to redemption, the bridge reconnecting humanity with the Divine. "For God so loved the world, that he gave his only begotten Son, that whosoever believeth in him should not perish, but have everlasting life" (Jn 3:16). This verse encapsulates the essence of the Christian message and underscores Christ's pivotal role in the salvation narrative.

In the vast panorama of Christian theology, Christ's atoning sacrifice stands as a beacon of hope and redemption. Regardless of the myriad of interpretations and theological nuances across denominations, the crucifixion and resurrection of Jesus are universally acknowledged as seminal events that paved the way for humanity's salvation.

With its rich ceremonial tradition and profound theological heritage, Catholicism holds the passion of Christ—his suffering, death, and resurrection—in deep reverence. Central to this veneration is the Eucharistic celebration, or the Mass. The Eucharist stands as a perpetual testament to Christ's sacrifice. It is rooted in the Last Supper, where Jesus shared bread and wine with his disciples. During this sacred rite, the priest consecrates the bread and wine, and it becomes, in Catholic understanding, Christ's actual body and blood—a doctrine known as transubstantiation. This doesn't mean that the bread and wine undergo a physical change but instead a symbolic one, wherein their essence is transformed.

The significance of this sacrament extends beyond mere ritualistic observance. It embodies the heart of Catholic theology, emphasizing the real presence of Jesus in the consecrated elements. For Catholics, receiving the Eucharist isn't merely a symbolic act but a profound communion with the living Christ. The words of consecration echo Jesus's words: "This is my body . . . This is the chalice of my blood" (1 Co 11:24–25). This is a poignant reminder of his willing sacrifice for humanity's redemption.

Moreover, the recurring nature of the Eucharistic celebration underscores the timeless relevance of Christ's sacrifice. By partaking in the Eucharist, believers are ritually transported to the foot of the cross, participating in the redemptive events of Calvary. Thus, the sacrament serves as a bridge, spanning the chasm between time and eternity and allowing the faithful to experience the salvific power of Jesus's passion in their lives.

Beyond individual spiritual nourishment, the Eucharist also plays a pivotal role in fostering communal bonds. As St. Paul notes, "For we being many are one bread, and one body: for we are all partakers of that one bread" (1 Cor 10:17).

Protestantism, emphasizing "sola fide" (faith alone), holds Christ's sacrifice as the sole avenue for salvation. This is not to negate the importance of good deeds but to emphasize that it is through faith in Christ and his atonement that one achieves redemption.[535]

In Eastern Orthodox tradition, Christ's sacrifice is seen in the light of theosis, the idea of becoming partakers in the divine nature. The crucifixion and resurrection are not just historical events but transformative moments that allow believers to participate in the divine life through Christ.[536]

LDS theology presents a unique and expansive view of Christ's atonement, weaving it seamlessly into the broader tapestry of the human experience. Central to this understanding is the belief that Christ's redemptive work was not confined to his crucifixion but began earlier, in the quiet shadows of the Garden of Gethsemane.

The Gethsemane narrative holds a special place in LDS thought. It's believed that Jesus took upon himself the sins, sorrows, and sufferings of all humanity. In Doctrine and Covenants, it is written: "Which suffering caused myself, even God, the greatest of all, to tremble because of pain, and to bleed at every pore, and to suffer both body and spirit" (19:18). This poignant depiction underscores the depth of Christ's agony, suggesting a burden so profound that even the Savior of the world trembled beneath its weight.

---

[535] Luther, Martin, *The Freedom of a Christian.*
[536] Timothy Ware, *The Orthodox Church* (London: Penguin Books, 1997), 231.

The significance of the atonement in LDS theology extends beyond the remission of sins. Christ's sacrifice is perceived as a holistic remedy, addressing the entirety of human suffering. This includes the emotional turmoil that often scars the human heart: feelings of inadequacy, loneliness, grief, and the myriad of other emotional afflictions that beset mankind. Furthermore, it embraces physical suffering, assuring believers that Christ, in his infinite empathy, understands and provides solace for every pain and physical challenge.

LDS teachings emphasize that Christ is equipped to aid his people in their afflictions because of the atonement. The Book of Mormon reiterates this: "And he shall go forth, suffering pains and afflictions and temptations of every kind; and this that the word might be fulfilled which saith he will take upon him the pains and the sicknesses of his people" (Alma 7:11). The notion here is that Christ, having borne the gamut of human suffering, is uniquely positioned to comfort, guide, and heal.

The LDS view of Christ's atonement is holistic and deeply personal. It invites believers to approach Christ as sinners needing forgiveness and as holistic beings seeking healing in every aspect of their lives. By broadening the scope of the atonement to encompass Gethsemane, the LDS Church paints a picture of a Savior deeply intertwined with the human condition, ever ready to comfort, heal, and redeem.

Beyond the theological constructs and ecclesiastical rituals, Christianity has always emphasized a personal relationship with Jesus Christ. In his letters, Paul often speaks of his intimate connection with the Savior: "I am crucified with Christ: nevertheless I live; yet not I, but Christ liveth in me" (Gal 2:20). Paul's words underscore the transformative power of a personal encounter with Christ.

For evangelicals within Protestantism, the "born again" experience typifies this personal relationship, where an individual undergoes a spiritual rebirth upon accepting Jesus as their Lord and Savior.[537] This personal commitment is seen as the cornerstone of one's faith journey.

Catholic spiritual tradition also reverberates with the echoes of mystics and saints who experienced profound encounters with Christ. Figures like St. Teresa of Avila and St. John of the Cross epitomize the depth of personal communion one can achieve with the Divine.[538]

In the Eastern Orthodox tradition, the hesychastic practice centers on achieving union with Christ through contemplative prayer, further emphasizing the centrality of a personal relationship with Jesus.[539]

The LDS faith champions the idea of a personal Savior who understands individual struggles and pains, having borne them Himself. Doctrine and Covenants articulate this beautifully: "I, God, have suffered these things for all, that they might not suffer if they would repent" (19:16).

Regardless of the doctrinal variations and theological nuances across denominations, Jesus Christ remains the heart of the Christian message. His life, teachings, sacrifice, and resurrection offer a path to eternal life and a blueprint for a purposeful, grace-filled earthly existence.

Conclusion: The Unifying Theme of Redemption in Christianity

The pages of history are replete with stories of humanity's quest for meaning, belonging, and redemption. At the heart of Christianity lies an age-old story of redemption and hope, a narrative that has given solace and purpose to countless believers across the millennia. In its myriad of expressions, the Christian message

---

[537] Billy Graham, *The Journey: Living by Faith in an Uncertain World* (Nashville: Thomas Nelson, 2006), 89.

[538] Thomas Dubay, *Fire Within: St. Teresa of Avila, St. John of the Cross, and the Gospel— On Prayer* (San Francisco: Ignatius Press, 1989).

[539] John Meyendorff, *Byzantine Theology: Historical Trends and Doctrinal Themes* (New York: Fordham University Press, 1979), 185.

remains anchored in one foundational truth: the redemptive power of Christ's sacrifice.

As the Apostle Paul wrote to the Corinthians, "For I delivered unto you first of all that which I also received, how that Christ died for our sins according to the scriptures; And that he was buried, and that he rose again the third day according to the scriptures" (1 Cor 15: 3–4). These words encapsulate the essence of Christian hope—a hope that persists through denominational differences and theological divides.

Regardless of its denominational variances, the Christian narrative is a song of redemption. From the rituals of the Catholic Eucharist to the Protestant affirmation of faith, from the LDS understanding of atonement in Gethsemane to the Orthodox journey of theosis, each tradition underscores the centrality of Christ's sacrifice.

In the tapestry of Christian thought, the person of Jesus Christ shines as the beacon of salvation. His life, teachings, and ultimate sacrifice on the cross provide the roadmap for believers navigating the complexities of existence. The universal longing for redemption, for a reconciliation with the Divine, finds its answer in him. The Apostle Peter affirms this, saying, "Neither is there salvation in any other: for there is none other name under heaven given among men, whereby we must be saved" (Acts 4:12).

However, the journey of faith is deeply personal. While the broader contours of the Christian message offer a shared foundation, each believer is invited to embark on their journey, grapple with the depths of the mysteries of faith, and forge a unique relationship with the Divine. It's a journey marked not by uniformity but by unity centered on Christ.

For those within the fold of the Church of Jesus Christ of Latter-day Saints, this personal relationship is amplified by a deeper understanding of Christ's all-encompassing atonement. While sharing core beliefs with the broader Christian community, the LDS perspective invites its adherents to perceive the Savior's sacrifice as a holistic remedy, addressing not just spiritual transgressions but also the emotional and physical uncertainty of life.

No matter the vantage point, Christ remains the axis. His invitation, as recorded in the Gospel of Matthew, resonates universally: "Come unto me, all ye that labour and are heavy laden, and I will give you rest" (Mt 11:28). Herein lies the universal Christian hope—a hope for redemption, peace, and eternal communion with the Divine.

In this age of skepticism and relativism, the Christian message offers a counternarrative that is resolute in its hope and unyielding in its promise of redemption. This isn't to negate the value or importance of critical inquiry; on the contrary, believers are encouraged to delve deeper, question, and seek. As Doctrine and Covenants proclaims: "Seek ye diligently and teach one another words of wisdom; yea, seek ye out of the best books words of wisdom; seek learning, even by study and also by faith" (88:118). This dual mandate—to study and to believe—fosters a richer understanding of one's faith and the world.

To skeptics and believers alike, the invitation remains open: to explore the depths of Christ's message, to wrestle with its implications, and to find a personal revelation of its truth. At its core, the story of Christianity, with its myriad traditions and interpretations, remains a story of redemption. It's a story that beckons each person, inviting introspection, challenging assumptions, and offering a hope that transcends the vagaries of time.

Chapter 10: Temples and Sacred Spaces: The Role of Physical Places

Human history is woven with threads of spirituality, and throughout this complex pattern, physical places have often provided the backdrop against which our spiritual stories unfold. As I delve into this rich tapestry, I can't help but be struck by the central role that temples, churches, and other sacred spaces play in our quest for the Divine. These spaces offer a sanctuary of permanence and profound meaning in a world riddled with temporary distractions. They are waypoints on the spiritual map, guiding the faithful closer to their Creator and a deeper understanding of their souls.

The Bible speaks of the significance of such places in numerous instances. For instance, when Jacob dreamt of a ladder connecting earth to heaven, he awoke and exclaimed, "Surely the LORD is in this place; and I knew it not" (Gen 28:16). Recognizing the ground as hallowed, he named it Bethel, which means the "House of God." In doing so, he emphasized a theme recurrent in many religious traditions: that specific places on Earth hold a special spiritual significance, connecting humanity to the divine in unique and tangible ways.

For Christians, these sacred spaces have always been pivotal. Churches, chapels, and cathedrals are not merely buildings but symbols of faith, testaments of devotion, and portals to the Divine. But as we'll explore, the significance of physical places in spiritual journeys extends beyond Christianity. Many faith traditions venerate specific sites, recognizing them as touchpoints of the Divine, where the earthly and celestial boundaries are blurred.

The Church of Jesus Christ of Latter-day Saints places a distinctive emphasis on temples. Unlike the weekly meetinghouses, where members gather for Sunday services and other activities, LDS temples are especially sacred. For Latter-Day Saints, these are not just places of worship but are revered locations where heaven touches Earth. They believe that within temple walls, they can make eternal covenants with God and perform ordinances that bind families together for eternity. This deep-seated belief underscores the crucial role that sacred spaces play in the spiritual journeys of the faithful. They aren't just buildings or locations but embodiments of faith, legacy, and divine promise.

However, the concept of a sacred space isn't unique to Christianity or the LDS Church. Across the globe, from the ancient pyramids of Egypt and the silent monasteries of the Himalayas to the sacred groves of indigenous tribes, humans have always sought out and sanctified places where they feel closer to the Divine. These places become repositories of collective memory, shared faith, and profound spiritual energy. They anchor beliefs in the physical world, giving tangible form to intangible feelings and convictions.

But why this emphasis on the physical in a journey that is spiritual by its very nature? It's because humans, as beings of both flesh and spirit, seek to understand the divine in abstract theological constructs and in the tangible, touchable, and experiential. Sacred spaces provide that. They are intersections between human experience and the Divine, where prayers become palpable and the ethereal feels earthly. They offer solace in times of sorrow, strength in moments of weakness, and guidance when the way seems lost.

Today's world might be more technologically connected than ever, but the timeless allure of sacred spaces remains undiminished. In an age where virtual realities often overshadow physical ones, there's an irreplaceable solace in kneeling on a cathedral's cold, hard floor or feeling the rough-hewn stone of an ancient temple under one's fingers. It's a visceral reminder that the journey to the Divine, while deeply personal, is also shared across ages, cultures, and geographies.

As we explore temples and sacred spaces, I invite you to reflect on their role in your spiritual journey. Whether you're a person of deep faith, a curious agnostic, or somewhere in between, I hope this exploration stirs a sense of wonder and a deeper appreciation for the tapestry of human spirituality.

The LDS Temple: A House of God

Throughout history, humanity has looked to the heavens, seeking to understand the purpose of existence and yearning to be closer to the Divine. In this spiritual quest, we've erected humble and grand structures to honor, worship, and draw closer to God. For the Church of Jesus Christ of Latter-day Saints, the temple stands as a profound testament to this yearning, a dedicated space where heaven and Earth intertwine.

The origins of LDS temples trace back to the early days of the Church. In the 1830s, following revelations to the Church's founder, Joseph Smith, Latter-Day Saints were commanded to build a temple in Kirtland, Ohio. This temple, completed in 1836, became a focal point for early Latter-Day Saint worship and was the setting for significant spiritual outpourings and revelations.[540] Following persecution and forced migration, the Saints attempted to build a temple in Missouri and then later constructed one in Nauvoo, Illinois. Though different in design and function, each of these temples symbolized the Saints' commitment to God and their desire to fulfill his commandments.

The significance of temples in the faith journey of Latter-Day Saints cannot be understated. These aren't merely architectural wonders or places of communal gathering. They are, as many Saints would express, houses of the Lord. For believers, what happens within temple walls is eternally binding and connects generations of families.

Central to the purpose of LDS temples are the sacred ordinances and ceremonies performed within them. As noted in a previous chapter, one unique practice is baptisms for the dead. Latter-Day Saints believe that individuals who didn't have the opportunity to receive the Gospel of Jesus Christ during their earthly life should have the chance in the hereafter. Thus, members perform baptisms in proxy for deceased ancestors, allowing

---

[540] James B. Allen and Glen M. Leonard, *The Story of the Latter-Day Saints* 2nd ed. (Salt Lake City: Deseret Book Co., 1992).

them to accept or reject the ordinance in the spirit world (128:16–18). The Apostle Paul made a brief mention of this when he asked, "Else what shall they do which are baptized for the dead, if the dead rise not at all? Why are they then baptized for the dead?" (1 Cor 15:29).

As I write this book, the fresh memory of my first experience at an LDS temple cradles my thoughts. In the radiant warmth of Orlando, Florida, I was on the threshold of a profound spiritual adventure. The two dedicated LDS missionaries, Elders Landon Clayton and Colton Rochlitz, who were pivotal in guiding my initial steps within the Church, altered their obligations on a Saturday afternoon to accompany me. My heart raced with anticipation as I stood before the majestic temple. Its towering spire, bathed in pure white hues, radiated a celestial sparkle under the sun's benevolent kiss. A profound sense of awe draped itself around me.

As I stepped into the temple's hallowed corridors, the revenant ambiance embraced my spirit. In a gesture of kindness, the temple president carved time from his schedule to grant us a personal tour through the sacred space. His words, bathed in the gentle luster of insight and faith, unveiled the layers of divine purpose embedded within each chamber and hallway. As he spoke, I was reminded of a passage from the Doctrine and Covenants: "And we ask thee, Holy Father, that thy servants may go forth from this house armed with thy power, and that thy name may be upon them, and thy glory be round about them, and thine angels have charge over them" (109). These words resonated deep within me, mirroring the spiritual embrace I felt within these sacred walls.

As we completed our tour, an invitation was extended to partake in a proxy confirmation.[541] This rite resonates with the commitment to spiritual unity and eternal bonds within the LDS faith. Proxy confirmations unfurl as the harmonious sequel to proxy baptisms for the deceased, a beautiful testament to the LDS belief in eternal progress and the boundless love that transcends

---

[541] "Baptisms for the Dead," the Church of Jesus Christ of Latter-day Saints, https://www.churchofjesuschrist.org/study/manual/gospel-topics/baptisms-for-the-dead.

the veil of mortality. As I embarked upon this sacred act, the whispers of ancient connections and the embrace of divine love enveloped my soul, weaving a tapestry of enlightenment and spiritual communion within the temple's sanctified walls. The experience, embroidered with threads of divine grace and human connection, imprinted itself upon the scroll of my spiritual journey, a luminous beacon in the odyssey toward celestial understanding and unity.

Once the ritual was over, we sat, representing twelve cherished souls who had journeyed beyond life's veil without the embrace of Christ's teachings on this earthly plane. Through our humble gestures, the ethereal portals opened, granting them the celestial choice to accept or decline this divine offering in the life beyond. The whispers of their spirits, intertwined with the cosmic dance of eternal decisions, echoed in the hallowed chambers as the seeds of celestial opportunities were lovingly sown.

The endowment ceremony is another essential ordinance. Here, participants make covenants or promises with God and receive knowledge about the plan of salvation. They're provided with symbolic clothing, representing God's protective power. This ceremony reinforces a person's commitment to follow Christ and their responsibility to share his teachings.

Further deepening the bonds of family, the temple sealing ceremony binds couples and families together for eternity, not just "until death do you part." This eternal perspective on familial relationships underscores the LDS belief in the enduring nature of family ties beyond mortal life.

Chapels are ubiquitous, found in almost every city where Latter-Day Saints reside. They are open to all, members and non-members alike, and host weekly Sunday services, youth activities, and other congregational functions. Their primary purpose is for communal worship and instruction.

Temples are scarcer and serve different functions. Upon completion, there's a brief open house where the general public can take a tour. After that, entrance is reserved for worthy members of the Church who hold a current "temple recommend"—a card signifying their adherence to core church standards. This isn't an act of exclusivity but one of reverence for the sacredness of the temple and its ceremonies.[542]

In essence, chapels are for weekly nourishment and gathering, and temples are for deeper individual and familial spiritual commitments and covenants. One offers bread for the journey, the other a map that leads to the final destination.

In my exploration of spirituality, I've realized that sacred spaces, whether grand cathedrals, ancient temples, or humble chapels, hold a mirror to the human soul. They reflect our deepest aspirations, fears, and hopes. For Latter-Day Saints, the temple stands as a beacon, illuminating our path back to God. It embodies the essence of our faith—a tangible testament to our belief in eternal families, continuous revelation, and the infinite love and atonement of Jesus Christ.

Churches in Christian Denominations: More Than Just Buildings

When we hear the term "church," it's easy to imagine a building with a steeple, perhaps adorned with stained glass. However, the story of churches in Christian history is a rich tapestry of faith, art, community, and divine aspiration. These aren't merely physical edifices; they're spiritual waypoints, charting humanity's relationship with the Divine across millennia.

The historical significance of churches, basilicas, and cathedrals is profound. In the early days of Christianity, followers of Christ gathered covertly in homes, sharing scriptures, singing hymns, and breaking bread together.[543] But as the faith expanded and gained legal acceptance, the need arose for larger and more formal places of worship. This led to the construction of basilicas—a term borrowed from Roman architecture—

---

[542] David B. Haight, "Temples and Work Therein," *Ensign*, Nov. 1990.

[543] Justo L. González, *The Story of Christianity, Vol. 1: The Early Church to the Dawn of the Reformation* (San Francisco: HarperSanFrancisco, 2010).

which became centers of Christian worship, like the Basilica of St. John Lateran in Rome, the "mother church" of Roman Catholicism.[544]

With their towering spires and vast naves, cathedrals emerged in the medieval period. More than places of worship, these structures functioned as symbols of God's majesty and the faith's permanence. Each stone, meticulously carved and placed, testified to a community's devotion and the Church's central role in societal life.

However, churches weren't merely buildings to showcase architectural prowess. They were, and remain, places of worship, community, and education. The Acts of the Apostles recounts how early believers "continued steadfastly in the apostles' doctrine and fellowship, and in breaking of bread, and in prayers" (Acts 2:42). This communal aspect of the Church has persisted throughout history. In these sacred spaces, believers learned scriptures, celebrated life's milestones, and found solace in times of trial.

The Church played an essential educational role during the medieval period by encouraging widespread illiteracy. The beautiful frescoes, magnificent sculptures, and inspired stained glass weren't just ornamental but also instructional. Through vivid depictions of biblical events, the life of Christ, and stories of saints, these pieces of art conveyed theological truths and moral lessons to commoners.

Stained glass, a crowning achievement of medieval Christian artistry, elevates church interiors from mere structures of worship to ethereal spaces that appear to touch the Divine. When one mentions the splendor of stained glass, few places evoke the same reverence as the illustrious windows of Chartres Cathedral in France. This architectural marvel, a pinnacle of Gothic architecture, houses an array of windows that are more than just decorative or functional elements; they are canvases of color and light that recount the rich tapestry of Christian lore.

---

[544] Richard Krautheimer, *Early Christian and Byzantine Architecture* (New Haven: Yale University Press, 1986).

Each stained glass panel was meticulously crafted and assembled from countless pieces of colored glass. These pieces, often tinted with vegetal and mineral pigments, come together to form intricate narratives—stories from the Old Testament, parables from the New, lives of the saints, and scenes from the apocalyptic revelations. The sheer detail in each panel can be awe-inspiring; from the drape of robes to the expressions on faces, they offer a vivid and immersive visual storytelling experience that transcends language and literacy barriers.

These stained glass windows also serve a profound symbolic role beyond their narrative value. They are not merely passive recipients of light; they interact with it, modulate it, and, in doing so, transform the ambiance of the church's interior. As sunlight filters through the multicolored panes, it bathes the church in a kaleidoscope of hues, creating an atmosphere that is both otherworldly and serene. This ethereal dance of light and color is reminiscent of the divine interceding in the earthly realm, a beacon of hope and guidance for the faithful.

This transformative power of stained glass also serves as a powerful metaphor for the Christian spiritual journey. Just as the glass refracts raw sunlight into a myriad of colors, the unvarnished truths of the divine are mediated through scripture, tradition, and personal experience, breaking into understandable and relatable fragments for believers. The interplay of light and shadow within the church, augmented by these radiant windows, mirrors the dualities of human existence—the struggles and triumphs, moments of doubt and epiphany.

Furthermore, stained glass epitomizes the theological concept of divine illumination. In a world often fraught with uncertainty and darkness, these windows remind us of the divine light that seeks to permeate and enlighten their lives. The vibrancy of the colors, illuminated from behind, suggests a world infused with God's presence, pushing back against the shadows of ignorance and despair.

In essence, stained glass windows are not just embellishments but profound spiritual tools. They mediate between the earthly and the Divine, tangible and the ineffable, guiding people toward introspection, reverence, and an ever-deepening connection with their faith.

Like stained-glass windows, the role of sculptures in churches and religious settings transcends the bounds of mere decorative art. They also serve as tangible manifestations of spiritual truths, embodying the stories, virtues, and trials embedded within Christian lore. For centuries, these three-dimensional representations have played a pivotal role in the devotional and educational aspects of the faith, offering a visceral connection between believers and the Bible's sagas.

Church façades, often laden with sculptures, become grand tapestries in stone. They capture the gamut of biblical narratives, from the Fall in the Garden of Eden to the Last Judgment. These façades are akin to visual sermons, each carving serving as a chapter that cautions against vice and champions virtue. For the congregants of yesteryear, especially when the illiteracy rate was high, these sculpted narratives provided a vivid and accessible conduit to understanding complex theological ideas.

While façades narrate broad tapestries, statues delve deep, encapsulating the emotional and spiritual gravitas of singular events or figures. Few works exemplify this more profoundly than Michelangelo's Pietà. This marble masterpiece, housed in the heart of St. Peter's Basilica in Vatican City, captures a heartrending moment with astonishing intimacy and detail. The Virgin Mary's face, etched with sorrow, juxtaposed with the serene countenance of the lifeless Christ, encapsulates the dualities of pain and acceptance, of mortal end and divine promise.

Michelangelo's genius doesn't just lie in his technical prowess but also in his ability to channel raw emotion through stone. Observers, whether devotees or art aficionados, find themselves drawn into an emotional vortex. It compels reflection—not just on the sacrifice of Christ but on broader themes of love, sacrifice, mourning, and hope.

Moreover, the positioning and context of such sculptures within sacred spaces amplify their impact. The ambient silence, punctuated perhaps by distant chants or the flickering of votive candles, creates an atmosphere ripe for introspection. Beneath soaring arches and in the soft glow of stained-glass light, sculptures like the Pietà become focal points of meditation, inviting believers to commune with the divine and with their innermost feelings and beliefs.

In essence, sculptures in religious settings are far more than mere stone or wood; they are portals. They bridge the temporal and the eternal, grounding vast theological concepts into tangible form and, in doing so, guiding the faithful closer to the heart of their beliefs and the mysteries of their faith.

It's also fascinating how church architecture often embodies theological principles. Gothic cathedrals, for instance, emphasize verticality. Their sky-piercing spires, tall windows, and vaulted ceilings draw one's gaze upward, symbolizing humanity's aspiration toward the Divine. This architectural style, emphasizing light, particularly through its expansive stained-glass windows, echoes a foundational Christian tenet: Christ as the light of the world. As John 1:4 proclaims, "In him was life; and the life was the light of men."

Churches, whether a sprawling Gothic cathedral or a modest country chapel, stand as witnesses in all their varied forms. They bear testimony to centuries of believers who have sought God, celebrated joys, mourned losses, and found community within their walls. These edifices, with their blend of art, architecture, and purpose, beautifully encapsulate the essence of Christianity: a faith grounded in history yet ever-reaching toward the eternal.

In our modern era, where so much is transient and temporary, churches stand as monuments to enduring faith. Regardless of our beliefs, they beckon us to pause, reflect, and perhaps find something greater than ourselves. In their quiet sanctuaries, amidst the interplay of stone, glass, and light, we're reminded of humanity's timeless quest for the Divine. This journey transcends stone and mortar, reaching into the core of the human spirit.

Sacred Spaces in Various Religious Traditions

The intrinsic human yearning for a connection with the divine has led various cultures and faiths to establish sacred spaces with profound spiritual significance. Each space, distinct in its architecture and purpose, tells a tale of the divine as perceived by that community.

Judaism: Tracing the roots of Jewish sacred spaces leads us straight to the heart of ancient Jerusalem, where the grand temple once stood, an embodiment of the divine's presence on Earth. This temple, a magnificent edifice of spiritual significance, wasn't merely an architectural marvel. For the Jewish people, it represented a direct conduit to God, a place where heaven touched Earth.

The Western Wall, a remnant of the once-great temple, serves as a poignant reminder of its historical and religious importance. Here, generations of Jews have come to pray, leaving their notes and prayers in the wall's crevices, making it a living testament to the undying faith and resilience of the Jewish people. "My house shall be called the house of prayer" (Is 56:7), and the Western Wall stands as a testament to this declaration, its stones saturated in millennia of petitions and tears.

But the significance of the temple wasn't confined to its walls. It was the epicenter of Jewish religious life, a place where priests conducted sacrificial rites and where the nation of Israel gathered to commemorate vital festivals, such as Passover, Shavuot, and Sukkot. These events facilitated worship and fostered a deep sense of community and national identity.

However, history took a tumultuous turn when the temple was destroyed. The traumatic events of 70 CE, during which the Romans destroyed the temple in the midst of sacking Jerusalem, sent shockwaves through the Jewish community. This loss, a gaping void in the Jewish spiritual landscape, precipitated a significant shift in religious practices. With the temple's destruction and the subsequent diaspora that scattered the Jews to different parts of the globe, an urgent need arose for new centers of worship and community.

Enter the synagogue. While synagogues existed before the temple's destruction, in its absence, their role became paramount. They transitioned from peripheral places of gathering to central hubs of worship, learning, and community. More than just buildings, synagogues became the heartbeat of Jewish communities everywhere, from the winding lanes of medieval Europe to the bustling streets of modern New York. They provided a space where the Torah could be studied, where the Shabbat could be celebrated, and where generations could be imbued with Jewish values and traditions. In essence, synagogues ensured that the flame of Jewish faith, culture, and identity remained undimmed even in the face of adversity and displacement.

Islam: Nestled within the bustling city of Mecca, the Kaaba stands as a timeless symbol of monotheism and the deep-rooted faith of the Muslim community. This simple black cuboid, often draped in a gold-embroidered black cloth, embodies its profound significance in the Islamic world. Revered as the "Bait Allah" or the "House of God," it is more than just a physical structure; it represents the metaphysical center of the Muslim universe.[545]

Every day, millions of Muslims, whether in bustling cities, quiet countryside, snowy mountains, or vast deserts, align themselves toward the Kaaba— the Qibla—to perform their daily prayers. This act demonstrates religious devotion and symbolizes the unity of the Muslim ummah (community) globally.

The centrality of the Kaaba in Islamic practice is further underscored by the Hajj, an annual pilgrimage that draws millions to Mecca. One of the Five

---

[545] The Qur'an, Surah Al-Baqarah, 2:127–129.

Pillars of Islam, the Hajj is an obligation that every Muslim must fulfill, provided they have the means. During this pilgrimage, believers participate in a series of rituals, many of which revolve around the Kaaba, such as the Tawaf, which involves walking around the Kaaba seven times. This journey is not just physical but deeply spiritual, allowing believers to retrace the footsteps of the prophets, seek forgiveness, and experience a profound connection with the Divine.

However, the spiritual geography of Islam isn't limited to Mecca. Across the globe, from the winding alleys of Fez to sprawling metropolises like Istanbul, mosques serve as the bedrock of Muslim communities. Far from mere places of prayer, mosques function as nerve centers of the Muslim community. They are spaces where the Quran is recited and studied, where children receive their foundational education, and where important communal events, such as marriages and funerals, are marked.

Architecturally, mosques often stand as marvels. Towering minarets dot the skyline from which the call to prayer resonates. The vast prayer halls, adorned with intricate geometric patterns and calligraphy, reflect a deep-seated Islamic appreciation for aesthetics. These designs, often interwoven with verses from the Quran, aren't just about beauty; they embody Islam's theological and philosophical ideals. The recurring geometric patterns, for instance, symbolize God's infinite nature. At the same time, the absence of human or animal imagery in many mosques emphasizes Islam's strict monotheism and the prohibition against idolatry.[546] These architectural elements are not just about form but are also imbued with profound meaning, serving as visual sermons that remind believers of God's omnipresence and majesty.

---

[546] Titus Burckhardt, *Art of Islam: Language and Meaning* (Bloomington: World Wisdom, 2009).

In sum, the Kaaba and mosques play pivotal roles in shaping the spiritual lives of Muslims. They anchor the faith, offering physical and metaphysical spaces for connection, reflection, and community.

Hinduism: Centuries of tradition and devotion find a home in the heart of Hindu temples. Beyond their staggering architectural prowess, these temples are embodiments of cosmic truths and spiritual narratives. As people step through the towering "gopuram" (temple gateway), often ornately decorated with a multitude of divine figures and mythological creatures, they are, in essence, transitioning from the mundane to the sacred, from the earthly to the Divine.[547]

Each corner of a Hindu temple whispers tales from ancient scriptures and epics. The walls, adorned with intricate carvings, narrate stories from the Ramayana, Mahabharata, and the Puranas. These aren't mere tales but spiritual lessons, guiding principles, and depictions of dharma (righteousness). Central to these temples is the sanctum sanctorum, which houses the deity, a manifestation of the Supreme Reality in a particular form, whether it's Lord Shiva, Goddess Lakshmi, Lord Vishnu, or any of the other countless deities that constitute the Hindu pantheon. Here, rituals, chants, and offerings come alive, and devotees find a direct conduit to the Divine.

In Hinduism, rivers, particularly the Ganges, carry a weight of reverence that's hard to articulate. The Ganges, or Ganga as it's lovingly called, is more than just a body of water. It is a divine entity, a goddess, a source of sustenance, and an eternal purifier. Its waters have witnessed countless rites of passage, from the sacred thread ceremony to the last rites. To bathe in its waters is to immerse oneself in purity, seeking cleansing not just of the body, but of the soul. "He that drinketh of the waters of Ganga (Ganges) attains

---

[547] Eck, *Darsan: Seeing the Divine Image in India.*

to the region of Brahman (the self-existent) after death," as eloquently stated in the Mahabharata, captures this river's profound spiritual significance.[548]

Moreover, the cyclic journey of the Ganges, from its heavenly descent to its merging with the ocean, mirrors the Hindu philosophy of life, death, and rebirth. Annual pilgrimages, like the "Kumbh Mela," see millions congregating on its banks, reiterating their deep-seated reverence for this river.

In essence, Hinduism offers a rich tapestry of sacred spaces. Each temple and river is more than just a location; it's a spiritual anchor, tethering the vastness of cosmic truths to the tangible, guiding believers on their path toward enlightenment.

Buddhism: The journey of Buddhism, from a solitary prince's quest for truth to a global spiritual path, is deeply intertwined with the physical spaces it reveres. Prince Siddhartha's transformative moment of enlightenment under the Bodhi tree is not just a cornerstone of Buddhist teachings but also a testament to the profound interplay between spirituality and place. Bodh Gaya, where this seminal event occurred, has transcended geographical confines to become a symbol of spiritual awakening. Today, a descendant of the original Bodhi tree stands there, a living emblem of the Buddha's realization and a beacon for countless pilgrims seeking their own moments of clarity and enlightenment.[549]

Stupas, with their characteristic dome-like structures, dot the landscapes of many countries influenced by Buddhism. More than just architectural feats, they encapsulate the essence of the Buddha's teachings. Within these structures, one often finds relics of the Buddha or other prominent Buddhist figures, making them not only places of veneration but also tangible connections to the tradition's illustrious past. Symbolically, the stupa's design often represents the Buddha's enlightened mind, with the

---

[548] *The Mahabharata of Krishna-Dwaipayana Vyasa*, trans. Kisari Mohan Ganguli (Whitefish, MT: Kessinger Publishing, 2010).
[549] Karen Armstrong, *Buddha* (New York: Penguin Books, 2004).

path to the top signifying the journey of spiritual ascent, transcending the cycles of birth and rebirth.[550]

Monasteries, or viharas, are much more than just secluded retreats. As the heartbeats of Buddhist communities, they pulsate with activities that nourish the mind and the spirit. They provide sanctuaries for monks and nuns to delve deep into meditation, furthering their spiritual progress. Their significance doesn't stop at personal enlightenment, though. These monasteries have long been bastions of Buddhist scholarship, where ancient scriptures are studied, debated, and interpreted. For lay people, they offer insights into the dharma (Buddhist teachings) and often serve as centers for communal gatherings, festivals, and ceremonies.

In essence, Buddhism's sacred spaces are not mere points on a map but are vibrant ecosystems of spiritual growth, learning, and community bonding. They stand as testaments to the enduring legacy of the Buddha's teachings and the timeless quest for enlightenment.

Several years ago I had the extraordinary opportunity to immerse myself in the profound teachings and serenity of the Mindrolling Lotus Garden, a magnificent Tibetan Buddhist temple nestled amidst the breathtaking northern Shenandoah Valley in Virginia. Located near the awe-inspiring Blue Ridge Mountains, this sacred haven stands as a testament to the harmonious coexistence of spirituality and nature. Situated just two hours to the southwest of the bustling metropolis of Washington, DC, the Lotus Garden is a sprawling 200–acre sanctuary offering an inviting and contemplative setting for both study and practice.

The very essence of the Lotus Garden is imbued with the aspirations and vision of Rinpoche, its guiding spiritual force. His dream for this sacred space is to create a haven dedicated to the exploration and embodiment of the Buddha dharma. Central to this aspiration is the profound intention to

---

[550] Vidya Dehejia, *The Art of Ancient India: Buddhist, Hindu, Jain* (New York: Weatherhill, 1986).

foster and nurture the growth of the Mindrolling lineage teachings in the Western world. As we stepped onto the grounds of the Lotus Garden, I sensed the depth of this vision and the spiritual richness it held.

My journey to the Lotus Garden took an unconventional turn, as I was on duty as a paramedic and serving as the duty officer for the local volunteer rescue squad. Thankfully, it was a slow shift, so we explored our response area. Accompanying me was my EMS training officer, and together, we embarked on a journey to explore this spiritual oasis. With great reverence, we parked our fully marked emergency response SUV in the temple's parking lot, mindful of the sacred atmosphere that enveloped the surroundings. As we ventured into the garden, we did so with quiet contemplation and respect for the space.

Our unexpected presence piqued the curiosity of the temple's inhabitants, and we were soon approached by some of the gentle and inquisitive staff members. They greeted us with warmth and concern, believing that an emergency might be unfolding. With genuine humility and respect for their culture, we explained our intentions and assured them that we had not arrived in response to a crisis but to gain insight into their community and the profound beliefs underpinning their way of life.

Their response was an embodiment of the very principles they held dear. Recognizing our sincere curiosity and commitment to understanding, they welcomed us into their world with open arms. They offered to provide us with a guided tour of their sacred space, sharing their spiritual perspectives and teachings as we explored the temple grounds together.

As we walked through the lush, manicured gardens, I was struck by the palpable sense of peace that permeated the air. Each step I took drew me deeper into a realm of serenity and introspection, where the bustling world beyond the temple's gates faded into insignificance. It was amidst this tranquil setting that I encountered the core teachings of Tibetan Buddhism. One of the most profound insights I gained during my visit was encapsulated in the following words: "Let your mind be as a spreading vine, entwining all things within the universe, living or not, for it is by such paths that one reaches the ultimate goal."[551]

This guiding principle of interconnectedness, central to Tibetan Buddhism, emphasizes the interwoven nature of all existence. It reminded me of the profound teachings of impermanence and interdependence found within Buddhism, concepts that transcend cultural and religious boundaries. These teachings echo the universality of spiritual wisdom, emphasizing our shared responsibility to cultivate compassion and understanding in our journey through life.

The Lotus Garden also introduced me to the profound practice of mindfulness. As I strolled along the garden's serene pathways, I encountered a group engaged in a walking meditation. Their mindful, deliberate words echoed the wisdom of the Buddha himself, who once said: "The past is already gone, the future is not yet here. There's only one moment for you to live, and that is the present moment."[552]

This teaching resonated deeply with me, emphasizing the importance of living in the present, free from the burdens of the past and the anxieties of the future. It was a reminder of the transformative power of mindfulness, a practice that transcends cultural and spiritual boundaries.

The Lotus Garden's library and temple buildings were under construction during our visit, which limited our access to some of their resources and facilities. However, this provided a unique perspective on the temple's commitment to growth and development, both spiritually and in terms of physical infrastructure. It was evident that the Lotus Garden was evolving and expanding, much like the principles it espouses.

---

[551] Mindrolling Trichen Rinpoche, *Wisdom Nectar: Dudjom Rinpoche's Heart Advice* (Kathmandu: Rangjung Yeshe Publications, 2005), 67.
[552] Mindrolling Trichen Rinpoche, *The Joy of Living and Dying in Peace: Core Teachings of Tibetan Buddhism* (Boulder, CO: Snow Lion Publications, 2006), 112.

The anticipation of returning once construction is complete fills me with a sense of excitement and eagerness. I look forward to the opportunity to explore the fully realized library, immerse myself in the teachings within, and experience the temple buildings' tranquility when they are completed. It is a testament to the enduring spirit of the Lotus Garden, ever-evolving and adapting to better serve its purpose as a center for spiritual growth and enlightenment.

My time at the Lotus Garden left an indelible mark on my spiritual journey. It reminded me that, regardless of the path we choose, the pursuit of wisdom, compassion, and mindfulness are universal aspirations shared by humanity's diverse spiritual traditions. As I departed from the temple's tranquil embrace, I carried with me the teachings of Tibetan Buddhism, a profound sense of interconnectedness, and a renewed commitment to living in the present moment.

In the words of the Lotus Garden's founder and spiritual guide, Rinpoche: "May the lotus of your heart blossom in the mud of daily life, and may its fragrance serve as a source of inspiration and guidance for all."[553]

I left the Mindrolling Lotus Garden with a heart full of gratitude, knowing that the lessons I had learned there would continue to illuminate my path and serve as a source of inspiration in my ongoing journey of self-discovery and spiritual growth.

Native American Tribes: For indigenous tribes, Earth is not just a mere provider but a living, breathing entity with whom they share a deep, intricate spiritual bond. The sanctity they ascribe to certain lands is borne out of millennia of stories, experiences, and shared memories.[554] These

---

[553] Mindrolling Trichen Rinpoche, *Wisdom Nectar: Dudjom Rinpoche's Heart Advice* (Kathmandu: Rangjung Yeshe Publications, 2005), 67.
[554] Vine Deloria Jr., *God Is Red: A Native View of Religion*. Golden (Colorado: Fulcrum Publishing, 2003).

sacred spaces serve as the confluence of the divine and the mortal realm, places where the universe's spiritual fabric seems almost palpable.

Unlike many world religions' temples or churches, these sacred lands often bear no man-made edifices. Instead, their significance is etched in the contours of the land itself—in the whispering forests, the thundering waterfalls, the stoic mountains, and the serene meadows. Ceremonies are performed under the vast canopy of the sky, with nature as both the witness and the medium.

One of the quintessential elements of these sacred lands is the stories they hold. Passed down through generations via oral tradition, these stories are more than just tales; they embody the history, wisdom, and spiritual ethos of entire tribes. They speak of ancestral spirits, epochal battles between good and evil, and profound lessons learned from nature.

Rituals and ceremonies performed in these spaces often draw from the elemental forces. The rhythmic beat of drums, the hypnotic dance around fires, and the evocative chants all harness the raw power of nature, aiming to align the community with the cosmos's rhythms. Individuals reconnect with their ancestors through these ceremonies, seek spiritual guidance, and express gratitude to Earth and its many bounties.

There are countless Native American tribes, each with unique narratives and spiritual understandings, but for our discussion, we will focus on one specific tribe: the Hopi.

The Hopi people, indigenous to the northeastern part of Arizona, maintain a profound spiritual affiliation with the land, seeing it as a living, breathing entity that sustains, teaches, and connects them to their ancestors and deities. This fundamental relationship transcends a physical bond, melding into the spiritual realm, and influences every aspect of their life.

In the Hopi worldview, their land is imbued with a life force that interacts with their existence. It's more than mere earth and sky; it's a vibrant tapestry woven with stories, lessons, and memories passed down through generations. This spiritual geography forms the backdrop of their myths, prophecies, and religious practices, each landmark holding a specific significance tied to their ancestral narratives and spiritual teachings.[555]

Their sacred sites, such as the towering mesas, the intricate underground chambers known as kivas used for ceremonial purposes, and the sprawling fields of maize, are all integral to their religious life. The maize, or what we would more commonly refer to as corn today, was a staple in their diet, is seen as a gift from the Creator, a symbol of life, death, and rebirth, and plays a crucial role in their ceremonies and rituals.

For the Hopi, the land is a conduit for communication with the spiritual world. The interplay of natural elements, from the whispering winds to the meandering rivers, is seen as the language of the gods, a divine dialogue continuously unfolding, providing guidance, wisdom, and nurturing to the Hopi people. The sacred spaces within their geography serve as the nexus for this divine interaction, anchoring their spiritual beliefs and practices to Earth and fostering a harmonious existence within the natural world.

One of the remarkable narratives within the Hopi spiritual tradition is the story of the "True White Brother."[556] The True White Brother is a figure prophesied to come in the future to lead the Hopi people into an era of peace and balance. This figure's description is reminiscent of some narratives within LDS theology,[557] specifically the idea of Jesus Christ visiting the Americas.[558] Both stories highlight a divine figure's appearance, bringing guidance and restoration to the people during times of need.[559]

---

[555] Frank Waters, *The Book of the Hopi* (New York: Viking Press, 1963).

[556] Christopher Vecsey, "The Emergence of the Hopi People," *American Indian Quarterly* 7, no. 3 (1983): 70.

[557] Improvement Era Staff, *The Improvement Era* (Salt Lake City: Church of Jesus Christ of Latter-day Saints, 1959).

[558] Ezra Taft Benson, "The Savior's Visit to America," General Conference of The Church of Jesus Christ of Latter-day Saints, April 1987.

[559] Ibid.

This comparison opens up avenues of dialogue and understanding between disparate religious and spiritual traditions, revealing shared human concerns and hopes expressed through different cultural narratives and prophecies. The intimate connection between the Hopi people and their land as a sacred space and the alignment of some aspects of their narrative with LDS beliefs about Jesus in the Americas offers an insightful reflection on the spiritual resonance between land, narrative, and belief in diverse traditions.

Aboriginal Australians: For the Aboriginal peoples of Australia, the land is more than just a terrestrial expanse; it is a tapestry of stories, spirits, and ancestral memories. Central to their understanding of the world is the concept of "Dreaming" or "Tjukurrpa," a term that defies easy translation into English. While it encompasses notions of time, mythology, and spirituality, the Dreaming is more profound than any single interpretation.[560]

The Dreaming sites scattered across the vast Australian continent are places of paramount importance. They aren't just geographical landmarks but repositories of ancestral wisdom and timeless tales. Each site is intricately linked with stories, events, and ancestral beings that shaped the world during the Dreaming.[561]

These sites are the nexus of the spiritual and physical realms. They bear the footprints of ancestral spirits, the path of their journeys, their challenges, triumphs, and transformations. Mountains, rock formations, rivers, and waterholes might all be imbued with meaning and significance based on events from the "Dreamtime." For instance, the contours of a rock might narrate the tale of a battle between ancestral beings while a waterhole could mark the resting place of a spirit.

The act of recounting and revisiting these tales in the form of songs, dances, and ceremonies ensures the continuation of the Dreaming. This oral

---

[560] W. E. H. Stanner, *White Man Got No Dreaming: Essays 1938–1973* (Canberra: Australian National University Press, 1979).
[561] Diane Bell, *Daughters of the Dreaming* (Melbourne: Spinifex Press, 2002).

tradition, passed down through countless generations, ensures that every new generation is tethered to their ancestors and the wisdom of the Dreaming. Moreover, these stories provide guidance, offering moral lessons and codes of conduct for the community.[562]

However, just as these sites are revered, they are also vulnerable. Modern developments, mining, and tourism often pose threats to their sanctity and integrity. Recognizing their importance not just for the Aboriginal peoples but also for humanity's collective heritage, there have been concerted efforts to protect and preserve these Dreaming sites in recent times.

The Dreaming and its sites underscore the intricate relationship the Aboriginal peoples have with the land. It's a bond forged through millennia, teaching us about respect, coexistence, and the enduring power of stories to shape our understanding of the world.

All of these spaces, as distinct as they might seem, share a common thread: they serve as anchors, grounding believers in their faith amidst the ever-shifting sands of time. "And let them make me a sanctuary; that I may dwell among them" (Ex 25:8). captures the sentiment common to many traditions—the desire to create a space for the divine amidst humanity. As one steeped in the Christian tradition, while I find solace in the familiar environs of a chapel or the profound sanctity of an LDS temple, I'm also moved by the myriad ways that humanity seeks, honors, and celebrates the Divine.

The Broader Concept of "Sacred Space"

Sacred spaces transcending geographical and architectural bounds are spiritual, psychological, and sociological significance reservoirs. As the author of the Gospel of Matthew reminds us, "For where two or three are gathered together in my name, there am I in the midst of them" (Mt.

---

[562] Deborah Bird Rose, *Dingo Makes Us Human: Life and Land in an Aboriginal Australian Culture* (Cambridge: Cambridge University Press, 2000).

18:20). This verse underscores that the divine presence isn't restricted to grand cathedrals or ornate temples but can be experienced wherever believers come together in faith.

Psychological and Sociological Significance of Sacred Spaces

Sacred spaces have played pivotal roles in the lives of believers across various cultures and religions for millennia. Often infused with profound religious significance, these spaces offer a tangible representation of the intangible— faith, devotion, and the Divine. When believers congregate at such sites, they partake in a ritualistic communion transcending mere religious practices. It's an act of coming together, sharing, and, as sociologist Émile Durkheim puts it, participating in the "collective effervescence" of society.[563]

Historically, these sacred spaces have often been central to societal developments. Cities were built around temples, trade routes were established based on pilgrimage paths, and economies flourished around these worship centers. Medieval European towns with churches at their heart or ancient cities in the Middle East that sprouted around mosques are testament to this centrality.[564]

Moreover, the ritualistic activities within these spaces—from sermons to communal prayers—have far-reaching sociological implications. Such activities foster unity and cohesion among believers and cultivate shared moral frameworks and societal norms.[565]

The stories shared, the rituals performed, and the hymns sung in unison serve to reinforce a group's collective identity and shared purpose.

---

[563] Émile Durkheim, *The Elementary Forms of the Religious Life* (New York: The Free Press, 1995).
[564] Karen Armstrong, *A History of God: The 4,000-Year Quest of Judaism, Christianity, and Islam* (New York: Alfred A. Knopf, 1993).
[565] Clifford Geertz, *The Interpretation of Cultures* (New York: Basic Books, 1973).

From an individual perspective, these spaces become sanctuaries in a fast-paced world. Just as Christ sought solitude in the wilderness, many find solace in these spiritual havens, away from the constant bombardment of modern life (Mk 1:35). They become platforms for individuals to engage in deep introspection, reevaluate life's priorities, and connect with the Divine.

The psychological benefits derived from spending time in such spaces have been well documented. Studies have shown that spending time in places of worship can lower stress, increase feelings of well-being, and even have tangible health benefits.[566] They act as a protective wall against the challenges of everyday life, offering individuals a reservoir of peace, strength, and resilience.

In essence, sacred spaces are not just physical structures. They are embodiments of communal and individual aspirations, reservoirs of cultural and spiritual heritage, and symbols of the Divine's intersection with the mortal realm.

Nature's Role in Spirituality

In its myriad forms, nature has been a cornerstone for spiritual experiences and quests across various cultures and religions. This intrinsic connection between the Divine and the natural world has historical and anthropological roots, stemming from humanity's earliest interactions with its surroundings.

With their soaring peaks touching the sky, numerous cultures have perceived mountains as abodes of deities.[567] Mount Sinai, for instance, holds paramount importance in the Judeo-Christian tradition as the place where Moses received the Ten Commandments. Likewise, Mount

---

[566] Harold G. Koenig, Dana E. King, and Verna Benner Carson *Handbook of Religion and Health* (New York: Oxford University Press, 2012).
[567] Mircea Eliade, *The Sacred and the Profane: The Nature of Religion* (New York: Harcourt, Brace & World, 1959).

Olympus was regarded as the home of the gods in ancient Greek religion. The imposing nature of mountains, challenging yet captivating, has symbolized the quest for spiritual ascension and enlightenment.

Rivers, on the other hand, have long been seen as life-giving entities. Beyond their essential contribution to agriculture and human settlements, rivers have held profound spiritual meanings. The Nile was integral to ancient Egyptian religious practices, symbolizing fertility and rebirth.[568] The Jordan River, where Jesus was baptized by John the Baptist, signifies transformation and the start of a spiritual journey (Matthew 3:13–17). With their ceaseless flow, such water bodies mirror the cycles of life, death, and rebirth, central themes in many religious philosophies.

Forests, rich with biodiversity and often veiled in misty allure, have been spaces of solitude, contemplation, and spiritual quests.[569] They have been the backdrop for countless mythologies and legends, from the druids' sacred groves in ancient Celtic tradition to the enchanted forests in folktales. Within the Christian narrative, forests and gardens often symbolize temptation and redemption, as seen in the Garden of Eden or the Garden of Gethsemane.

In the broader Christian worldview, nature's vastness and intricacy stand as a testament to God's creativity and omnipotence.[570] In Romans 1:20, Apostle Paul remarks, "For the invisible things of him from the creation of the world are clearly seen, being understood by the things that are made, even his eternal power and Godhead." This perspective underscores the belief that every mountain ridge, river bend, and forest trail echoes the grand narrative of Creation, calling the faithful to marvel at the artistry of the Divine.

---

[568] Rosalie David, *Religion and Magic in Ancient Egypt* (New York: Penguin Books, 2002).
[569] Robert Pogue Harrison, *Forests: The Shadow of Civilization* (Chicago: University of Chicago Press, 1992).
[570] Alister E. McGrath, *The Re-enchantment of Nature: Science, Religion and the Human Sense of Wonder* (New York: Doubleday, 2002).

Whether carved by human hands or sculpted by the forces of nature, sacred spaces offer portals to the transcendent, inviting individuals across epochs to seek, reflect, and connect.

Personal Sacred Spaces

In a world saturated with perpetual stimuli and the cacophony of distractions and noise from our modern-day technology, the pursuit of inner peace and self-reflection ascends as a vital refuge from the ceaseless hum of modern life. Against this backdrop, the profound importance of sacred spaces unfolds, offering a serene harbor amidst the digital upheaval that inundates our daily lives. Although I have profited financially as a tech entrepreneur, this boundless digital expanse's subtle yet persistent impact is not lost on me. Despite their unparalleled prowess in bridging distances, social media platforms inadvertently cast shadows of alienation, obscuring the luminous pathways to our inner selves and the vibrant pulse of life that sustains us. Within the tender cradle of sacred spaces, the soul liberates itself, basking in the hallowed echoes of ancient wisdom and tranquility, a world apart from the relentless turbulence of the digital tide sweeping beyond its sanctified bounds. Personal sacred spaces emerge as vital counterpoints to the external world's overwhelming noise, offering pockets of peace, reflection, and rejuvenation.[571]

Historically, the idea of designating spaces for reflection is not new. The concept of an oratory or a personal chapel can be traced back to early Christian monasticism.[572] The Desert Fathers, Christian hermits who lived in the third century, retreated to isolated places, seeking spiritual enlightenment away from worldly distractions.[573]

---

[571] David Tacey, *The Spirituality Revolution: The Emergence of Contemporary Spirituality* (New York: Routledge, 2004).

[572] William Harmless, *Desert Christians: An Introduction to the Literature of Early Monasticism* (Oxford: Oxford University Press, 2004).

[573] James E. Goehring, *Ascetics, Society, and the Desert: Studies in Early Egyptian Monasticism* (Harrisburg, PA: Trinity Press International, 1999).

While not everyone has the inclination or the means to retreat into the desert or atop a mountain, creating a sacred niche within one's own living environment achieves a similar purpose, albeit on a smaller scale.

These personal spaces take diverse forms, reflecting individual spiritual journeys and life experiences. For some it might be a quiet nook with a favorite chair, a lamp, and a collection of spiritual writings. For others it could be an elaborate altar adorned with religious artifacts, scriptures, and symbolic keepsakes that evoke a sense of the Divine.[574]

There's also a therapeutic element to these spaces. Studies have suggested that having a designated area for meditation or spiritual practice can have tangible psychological benefits, including reduced stress, increased mindfulness, and enhanced well-being.[575] These spaces serve as a bridge between the tangible and the intangible, grounding individuals in the present while allowing them to connect with the eternal.

Furthermore, curating and maintaining these spaces in itself becomes a spiritual practice. Every element—be it a candle, an icon, or a fragrant incense stick—is chosen with intention. Such meticulous arrangements transform an ordinary corner of one's dwelling into hallowed ground. It reminds one of the biblical assertion, "For where two or three are gathered together in my name, there am I in the midst of them" (Mt 18:20), emphasizing that divinity can be found in the simplest of settings.

As the boundaries between work, leisure, and personal time become increasingly blurred in the digital age, creating personal sacred spaces is not just a luxury but also a necessity.[576] Regardless of their size or elements, these

---

574 Mircea, *The Sacred and the Profane: The Nature of Religion.*
575 Richard J. Davidson and Jon F. Kabat-Zinn, "Response to 'Alterations in Brain and Immune Function Produced by Mindfulness Meditation,'" *Psychosomatic Medicine* 65, no. 4 (2003): 564–570.
576 Sam Keen, *Hymns to an Unknown God: Awakening the Spirit in Everyday Life* (New York: Bantam, 1995).

spaces serve as constant reminders of the spiritual dimension of existence, providing solace, grounding, and a connection to the greater universe.

The emphasis on the home as a sacred space is palpable in the LDS tradition: "my people shall know my name; yea, in that day they shall know that it is I that speaketh; behold, it is I"[577] resonates with the idea that divine interactions aren't limited to grand religious edifices but can be experienced in the quiet corners of our homes.

Sacred spaces anchor us, elevate our spirits, and remind us of the greater cosmic narrative in which we live. As I reflect on my journey through the LDS faith and the broader Christian tradition, I'm reminded that it's not the grandeur of the space but the purity of intent and faith that makes a place sacred.

Challenges and Controversies Surrounding Sacred Spaces

Throughout history, sacred spaces have served as bastions of solace and sources of discord. While these sites anchor faiths, uniting believers in shared devotion, they also underscore the deep-seated tensions and challenges inherent to our diverse world. Acknowledging the broad global context, rife with disputes, territorial disputes, and the poignant interplay between history and faith is crucial.

Historical Disputes Over Religious Sites

The Babri Masjid's demolition is a stark testament to the entangled and volatile intersections of faith, history, and politics. On December 6, 1992, a large group of Hindu nationalists, asserting the site's historical sanctity as the birthplace of Lord Rama, destroyed the Babri Masjid, a mosque dating back to the sixteenth century, in Ayodhya, India.[578] This destructive act was

---

[577] Doctrine and Covenants, 38:8.
[578] "Ayodhya: The History of a 500–year-old Land Dispute," BBC News, Nov. 9, 2019, https://www.bbc.com/news/world-asia-india-50065259.

not a spontaneous outburst but a calculated culmination of a prolonged and contentious dispute rooted in intricate historical and theological claims.

The individuals who orchestrated and executed the demolition were mainly activists from the Bharatiya Janata Party (BJP), the Rashtriya Swayamsevak Sangh (RSS), and various other affiliated organizations driven by a potent confluence of religious conviction and political ambition.[579] Their objective was to reclaim what they believed to be the sacred birthplace of Lord Rama, a belief rooted in their religious and historical consciousness.

The consequences of this act were catastrophic. As the BBC reported, the demolition unleashed a devastating wave of communal violence across India that claimed over 2,000 lives and exacerbated the entrenched sectarian rift between the Hindu and Muslim communities within the nation.[580] Beyond its immediate and visceral impact, the Babri Masjid's destruction reverberated through the subsequent decades, fueling religious animosity, emboldening divisive political agendas, and casting a somber shadow over efforts toward interfaith dialogue and reconciliation.

Authors like Peter van der Veer provide a comprehensive exploration into the multidimensional aspects of this religious nationalism, offering an analytical prism through which to comprehend the deeper forces and narratives shaping the Ayodhya conflict and its enduring societal repercussions.[581] R. S. Sharma also accentuates the events of Ayodhya in his work, reflecting on the intricate entanglement of religious beliefs, historical narratives, and contemporary political aspirations within the unfolding tapestry of India's socio-political landscape.[582]

---

[579] R. S. Sharma, *Communal History and Rama's Ayodhya* (Delhi: People's Publishing House, 1999), 23.
[580] "Ayodhya: The History of a 500–year-old Land Dispute," BBC News, Nov. 9, 2019, https://www.bbc.com/news/world-asia-india-50065259.
[581] Peter van der Veer, *Religious Nationalism: Hindus and Muslims in India* (Berkeley: University of California Press, 1994), 143–170.
[582] Sharma, *Communal History and Rama's Ayodhya*.

The enduring legacy of the Babri Masjid's demolition continues to echo within the corridors of India's religious, societal, and political arenas, underscoring the crucial imperative for understanding, dialogue, and mutual respect in navigating the delicate terrain of sacred spaces and religious identities.

Parallel to the Babri Masjid incident, another global epicenter of religious conflict and spiritual contention is the illustrious city of Jerusalem, particularly the site known as the Temple Mount or Haram esh-Sharif. This geographic location brims with profound religious significance for Jews and Muslims, manifesting as a physical embodiment of their intertwined historical and spiritual narratives.

For Jews, the Temple Mount is revered as the hallowed ground where the first and second temples once stood. Today, the Western Wall, a poignant remnant of the second temple, continues to stand as a vibrant symbol of Jewish faith and identity.[583] This ancient edifice, bathed in centuries of prayer and longing, echoes the Jewish people's resilient spirit and enduring heritage.

In the Islamic tradition, the same expanse of land cradles the resplendent Al-Aqsa Mosque, a revered Islamic landmark. Muslim belief holds this site as the starting point from which the Prophet Muhammad ascended to heaven during his celebrated night journey, solidifying its place as a sacred axis within the Islamic spiritual cosmos.[584]

However, beneath the spiritual grandeur and historical richness, the Temple Mount or Haram esh-Sharif emerges as a tumultuous arena of Israeli-Palestinian tensions. The shared spiritual attachment to this revered site, interwoven with competing historical and religious narratives,

---

[583] Nadav Shragai, "Why the Temple Mount Continues to Be a Flash Point in Jewish-Muslim Relations," BESA Center Perspectives Paper No. 1 (Sept. 27, 2019): 325, https://besacenter.org/perspectives-papers/temple-mount-flash-point/.

[584] Karen Armstrong, "The Holiness of Jerusalem: Asset or Burden?" *Journal of Palestine Studies* 27, no. 3 (1998): 5–19.

continually fuels conflict, unrest, and division cycles. As noted by the *New York Times*, periodic clashes and restrictions at this site underscore the intricate and volatile complexities of navigating shared sacred spaces in a terrain marked by deep-seated historical and spiritual claims.[585]

The seemingly insurmountable challenge lies in reconciling the diverse spiritual legacies and historical trajectories that converge within this sacred space, striving to forge a pathway of coexistence, mutual respect, and shared stewardship in the pursuit of religious freedom, spiritual fulfillment, and lasting peace.

Organizations such as the Interfaith Encounter Association (IEA) strive to bridge divides, creating an atmosphere of dialogue and mutual understanding.[586] The ultimate aim is to craft a shared space where every religious community feels ownership and reverence, a space that honors diverse legacies while looking toward a harmonious future. "Blessed are the peacemakers: for they shall be called the children of God" (Mt. 5:9) is a reminder that fostering peace, especially in shared sacred spaces, aligns with the teachings of Christ.

Isaiah 56:7, "My house shall be called a house of prayer for all people," carries a profound message of inclusivity; however, the persistent question that looms large is this: how can such places, deeply imbricated in particular religious narratives and histories, transcend their specificities to become universal spaces of worship and reflection?

These disputes underscore the multifaceted challenges of coexistence, respect, and shared stewardship of sacred spaces. They serve as potent

---

[585] David M. Halbfinger, "Clashes Erupt at Jerusalem Holy Site," *New York Times*, Aug. 11, 2019, https://www.nytimes.com/2019/08/11/world/middleeast/jerusalem-temple-mount-clashes.html.
[586] Anthony O'Mahoney, "Christianity in Jerusalem: Historical Dynamics and Contemporary Challenges," *Jerusalem Quarterly File* 17 (2003): 5–19.

reminders that while the Divine may be universal, human interpretations and attachments are profoundly particular and often deeply contested.

Tourism, Commercialization, and Their Effects

The delicate balance between preserving the sanctity of sacred spaces and the ever-growing demands of tourism and commercialization has become increasingly precarious. Initially established as places for spiritual reflection and worship, these sacred sites are now frequently awash in the bustle of commerce and the footfalls of curious tourists.[587]

Tourism undoubtedly has its merits. It infuses local economies with much-needed revenue and serves as a conduit for cross-cultural exchange, allowing visitors from diverse backgrounds to immerse themselves in the depth and beauty of global spiritual traditions.[588] Such exchanges are, in principle, a positive force, fostering mutual understanding and appreciation among diverse religious and cultural groups.

However, the influx of tourists, many of whom may not be adherents of the faith associated with a particular site, can dilute its sacred ambiance. The essence of these places, intended to facilitate a deep spiritual communion, risks being overshadowed by the trappings of commercial activities. While profitable, souvenir shops, guided tours, and other commercial endeavors can detract from the inherent spiritual essence of these locations.[589]

Moreover, the physical infrastructure of these sites can be strained under the weight of countless visitors, leading to concerns about preservation and maintenance.[590] In some instances, this has necessitated the imposition of

---

[587] Valene L. Smith, *Hosts and Guests: The Anthropology of Tourism* (Philadelphia: University of Pennsylvania Press, 1989).
[588] Erik Cohen, "Authenticity and Commoditization in Tourism," *Annals of Tourism Research* 15, no. 3 (1988): 371–386.
[589] Dallen J. Timothy and Daniel H. Olsen, *Tourism, Religion and Spiritual Journeys* (London: Routledge, 2006).
[590] Myra Shackley, *Managing Sacred Sites: Service Provision and Visitor Experience* (London: Continuum, 2001).

restrictions on visitor numbers or alterations to traditional practices to accommodate the influx of tourists.

While the economic advantages of tourism are evident, the spiritual cost of commercializing sacred spaces is harder to quantify but no less significant. The challenge lies in striking a harmonious balance: ensuring that these sites remain accessible and inviting to global visitors, while also preserving their profound spiritual essence and historical integrity.[591]

Wars in the Middle East Over Religious Sites

The Middle East has often been described as the nexus where history and religion converge, a pulsating hub of spiritual heritage and historical milestones.[592] However, this richness has also rendered the region vulnerable to tumultuous conflicts, many of which pivot around the custodianship and identity of religious sites.

The conflicts waging in nations like Syria and Iraq surpass the confines of territorial conquests and geopolitical maneuverings. These wars have transmuted into bleak theaters where revered religious sites are ensnared in the throes of destruction, their historical and spiritual legacies crumbled beneath the onslaught of violence and despair.

One poignant example is the obliteration of the Great Mosque of al-Nuri in Mosul, Iraq, in 2017. This event transcends a physical loss, a sentinel that steadfastly bore witness to the intricate tapestry of human endeavor, aspiration, and faith woven over the expanse of centuries.[593] Its ancient stones, steeped in the echoes of prayer and reflection, were reduced to

---

[591] Gisbert Rinschede, "Religious Tourism: Geographical Approaches," *GeoJournal* 25, no. 3 (1991): 255–262.

[592] Karen Armstrong, *Jerusalem: One City, Three Faiths* (New York: Ballantine Books, 1997).

[593] "IS Blows Up Mosul Mosque Where Baghdadi Declared 'Caliphate,'" BBC News, June 22, 2017, https://www.bbc.com/news/world-middle-east-40366136.

rubble, a silent testament to the devastating toll of conflict on humanity's shared cultural and spiritual heritage.

The *New York Times* reported the destruction as not merely an architectural loss but a "cultural and religious tragedy," underlining the mosque's significant historical and religious value to the Islamic community and the global heritage.[594] The 845–year-old minaret, affectionately known as the "Hunchback" (al-Hadba), had leaned over the city for centuries and was featured on Iraq's 10,000–dinar banknote. Its demise severed a vital link to Iraq's historical and cultural identity, echoing the grief and loss permeating the nation's modern narrative.

The obliteration of such sites strikes a grievous blow to the collective historical consciousness, erasing irreplaceable fragments of shared human heritage and spiritual legacy. It underlines the imperative to safeguard the sanctity and integrity of sacred spaces across the globe, preserving their profound significance for future generations amidst the tempests of contemporary conflicts.

Amidst the din of warfare and the shadows of destruction, humanity's resilient spirit perseveres, embarking on the arduous journey of rebuilding and restoration. As reported by Al Jazeera, initiatives to restore the Great Mosque of al-Nuri and its iconic leaning minaret have been launched, a beacon of hope and renewal amidst the ruins, reflecting our unwavering quest for healing, reconciliation, and the preservation of our shared spiritual and historical legacy.[595]

The destruction of such edifices has far-reaching ramifications. As George Santayana stated, "Those who cannot remember the past are condemned to

---

[594] Ben Hubbard and Leila Fadel, "Mosul's Renowned Religious Complex Will Rise From the Rubble," *New York Times*, April 27, 2018, https://www.nytimes.com/2018/04/27/world/middleeast/mosul-mosque-iraq.html.
[595] Iraq's Al-Nuri Mosque to be Rebuilt by Egyptian Engineers," Al Jazeera, April 15, 2021, https://www.aljazeera.com/news/2021/4/15/iraqs-al-nuri-mosque-to-be-rebuilt-by-egyptian-engineers.

repeat it."[596] By obliterating these historic markers, the collective memory of entire communities gets disrupted, creating a void that is often filled with revised or skewed narratives.

For the Yazidis, an ethno-religious group indigenous to regions in Iraq, the destruction of their shrines by extremist factions is not just an assault on their faith but an existential threat to their identity.[597] Similarly, the Christian communities, tracing their lineage back to the apostolic age, have seen their ancient churches reduced to rubble. The Church of Saint Ahoadamah in Syria, one of the oldest surviving churches, was razed during the Syrian Civil War.[598]

Such incidents are poignant reminders of the volatile mix of religion and politics. As philosopher Alain de Botton suggests, while religion can be a source of unity and solace, its misinterpretation or manipulation can lead to some of the grimmest chapters in human history.[599] The Middle East's sacred sites, with their profound religious significance, are more than just structures; they encapsulate diverse communities' aspirations, struggles, and shared histories. Thus, their preservation is paramount for the followers of the faiths they represent and humanity at large.

Conclusion: Why Temples Resonate Across Cultures

In our ever-evolving world, where technology and secularism often seem to supersede traditional beliefs and practices, the importance of sacred spaces remains a compelling and enduring testament to our spiritual longings. In the face of increasing secularism, these natural and human-made spaces

---

[596] George Santayana, *The Life of Reason* (New York: Dover Publications, 1980).
[597] Khanna Omarkhali Rashow, *The Yezidi Religious Textual Tradition: From Oral to Written* (Wiesbaden: Harrassowitz Verlag, 2017).
[598] Daniella Talmon-Heller, *Islamic Piety in Medieval Syria: Mosques, Cemeteries, and Sermons Under the Zangids and Ayyūbids* (Leiden: Brill, 2007).
[599] Alain de Botton, *Religion for Atheists: A Non-believer's Guide to the Uses of Religion* (London: Hamish Hamilton, 2012).

stand as sanctuaries of solace, reminders of our transcendent aspirations and the quest for meaning.[600]

Given our advancements and the increasing shift toward a secular worldview, one might wonder why sacred spaces resonate so profoundly with humanity. Psalm 122:1 reads, "I was glad when they said unto me, Let us go into the house of the Lord." This ancient yearning, a calling toward a space where one can connect with the Divine, is as relevant today as it was millennia ago. In times of joy and sorrow, these places offer solace and a deep sense of belonging.[601]

From the soaring cathedrals of Europe to the tranquil Zen gardens of Japan, from the vastness of a mountain's peak to the cozy corner of a home dedicated to personal reflection, sacred spaces serve as touchpoints. They ground us, reminding us of the broader cosmic narrative of which we are but a small part.[602] These spaces stand as a testament not only to our faith traditions but also to our shared human journey. They whisper tales of our ancestors, cultural epochs, and spiritual revelations.

For believers, such places can be transformative. In the LDS faith, temples are not just buildings but houses of the Lord, spaces where heaven feels a bit closer, sacred covenants are made, and families are bound together for eternity.[603] One need not be religious to sense the gravitas and reverence of such places either. The tranquility of sacred spaces, their architectural marvels, and their spiritual energy can resonate with even the most secular among us.

In a world saturated with turmoil and unpredictability, a fleeting excursion to these sanctuaries may offer the tranquil reprieve our spirits ardently crave. As the world around us becomes increasingly noisy, the silence and serenity of sacred spaces beckon us to pause and reflect. In the words of Thomas

---

[600] Charles Taylor, *A Secular Age* (Cambridge, MA: Harvard University Press, 2007).
[601] Eliade, *The Sacred and the Profane: The Nature of Religion.*
[602] Rudolf Otto, *The Idea of the Holy* (Oxford: Oxford University Press, 1923).
[603] Russell M. Nelson, "Blessings of the Temple," *Ensign*, April 2010.

Merton, a Christian mystic, "The true purpose of Christian solitude is not escape but engagement."[604]

Engaging with these spaces, whether through pilgrimage, quiet reflection, or merely appreciating their cultural and historical significance, can be enlightening. It fosters understanding and respect for the diversity of human experience and the myriad ways humanity seeks the Divine.[605]

---

[604] Thomas Merton, *Thoughts in Solitude* (New York: Farrar, Straus and Giroux, 1999).
[605] Smith, *The World's Religions: Our Great Wisdom Traditions.*

Chapter 11: Life Beyond Death: Heaven, Hell, and the Afterlife

The concept of the afterlife, a realm beyond the veil of mortality, has intrigued the human psyche for millennia. From the earliest cave paintings to the grandest cathedrals, countless civilizations have sought to grasp, define, and articulate this ethereal realm, where the essence of the person, often termed as the "soul," transcends after death.[606] This universal query about the hereafter isn't merely a philosophical or religious concern; it also encapsulates our deepest hopes, fears, and yearnings as a species.

As I reflect on this pervasive fascination, I'm reminded of the vast number of tales that form the tapestry of human history—tales of valiant warriors journeying to the halls of their ancestors, of pharaohs entombed with treasures to accompany them in the afterlife, and of saints and mystics describing paradisiacal realms filled with divine light.[607] The Epic of Gilgamesh, often regarded as one of the earliest works of literature, sheds light on the Mesopotamian perspective of the afterlife, while the Egyptian Book of the Dead provides a guide for souls navigating the trials of the underworld.[608]

Central to Christian theology is the promise of a life beyond death. In 1 Corinthians 15:20, the Apostle Paul affirms this hope: "But now is Christ risen from the dead, and become the firstfruits of them that slept." This assurance of resurrection and the potential of eternal life shape our conduct, choices, and aspirations in the present.

Christianity doesn't hold a monopoly on these beliefs. Cultures across epochs—the ancient Greeks with their Elysian Fields, the Vikings with Valhalla, or the indigenous tribes with their ancestral spirits—have

---

[606] Mircea, *The Sacred and the Profane: The Nature of Religion.*
[607] Karen Armstrong, *A History of God: The 4,000-Year Quest of Judaism, Christianity and Islam* (New York: Ballantine Books, 1994).
[608] N. K. Sanders, *The Epic of Gilgamesh* (London: Penguin, 1960).

perceived an existence beyond death.[609] Each culture's unique tapestry of rituals, narratives, and practices contributes to a more extensive mosaic of understanding, giving insights into how societies process grief, honor the departed, and seek solace in the promise of reunion.

From a moral standpoint, the afterlife serves as an incentive and a deterrent. The promise of heavenly rewards or the threat of infernal punishments has guided the moral compasses of countless souls.[610] While critics argue that moral behavior should arise from intrinsic values rather than extrinsic rewards or threats, there's no denying the profound impact that beliefs about the afterlife have had in shaping ethical codes across cultures.[611] In the Christian tradition, the Beatitudes elucidate a path of righteousness, humility, and compassion, offering solace that those who mourn "shall be comforted," and "Blessed are the meek, for they shall inherit the earth" (Mt 5:4–5). Similarly, within the LDS faith, the promise of eternal families and progression provides a tangible framework that enriches our moral choices in the here and now.[612]

In sum, the afterlife isn't just a matter of theological debate or spiritual contemplation. It intertwines with our daily lives, influencing our decisions, strengthening our resolve in trials, and offering hope in our moments of deepest despair. As we embark on this exploration of life beyond death, we are not merely traversing theological tenets but also delving into a realm that echoes with the collective human spirit's hopes and aspirations, understanding that every heartbeat, every whispered prayer, and every tear shed carries the weight of eternity.

---

[609] John R. Hinnells, *The Penguin Dictionary of Religions* (London: Penguin, 1997).
[610] Lewis, *Mere Christianity*.
[611] Jonathan Haidt, *The Righteous Mind: Why Good People Are Divided by Politics and Religion* (New York: Vintage, 2013).
[612] Doctrine and Covenants.

Historical Overview of Mainstream Christian Beliefs

The question of what awaits us beyond the veil of death has persisted as one of Christianity's most profound theological inquiries. It intertwines with foundational tenets regarding salvation, redemption, and God's nature and character. As I venture into this exploration, it remains essential to acknowledge the myriad of ways in which Christianity, in its diverse forms, has approached the subject over millennia.[613]

Rooted in the teachings of Jesus Christ, Christianity began its journey against the backdrop of Greco-Roman philosophical discourses that influenced early Jewish beliefs. The early Christians, drawing heavily from Jewish eschatology, upheld a belief in the resurrection of the dead, tied to Christ's triumphant victory over death.[614] Paul's letters are among the earliest Christian writings, and he proclaims, "For as in Adam all die, even so in Christ shall all be made alive" (1 Cor 15:22). Such references underscore the hope of an afterlife, where death is not an end but a passage to the next phase of existence.

In Christian belief, heaven is often depicted as a realm of eternal peace and communion with God, a place where souls are enveloped in unending light and divine love. The conception of heaven as a place of eternal bliss and connection with the divine is expressed in numerous religious texts. One example is the Book of Revelation, where the Apostle John envisions a new heaven and a new earth, a place where God will dwell with his people and "wipe every tear from their eyes" (Rev 21:1–4).

Conversely, hell emerges as a contrasting realm of eternal separation from God, described as a place of anguish and despair. The story of the rich man and Lazarus in the Gospel of Luke provides a stark biblical depiction of the chasm between the abodes of the blessed and the damned. In his place of

---

[613] Justo L. Gonzalez, *The Story of Christianity, Vol. 1: The Early Church to the Dawn of the Reformation* (New York: HarperOne, 2010).

[614] N. T. Wright, *The Resurrection of the Son of God* (Minneapolis: Fortress Press, 2003).

torment, the rich man yearns for a drop of water to cool his tongue while Lazarus rests in Abraham's bosom (Lk 16:19–31).

As illustrated in Christian teachings, the dichotomy between heaven and hell reflects broader human questions and beliefs regarding the nature of the afterlife, divine justice, and the moral implications of earthly actions. This bifurcation of the afterlife has profoundly influenced Western religious thought and has parallels in other religious traditions as well.

In Islamic tradition, similar visions of the afterlife exist. Heaven (Jannah) is depicted as a place of unimaginable bliss and beauty, where the faithful enjoy spiritual and physical pleasures, while Hell (Jahannam) is a place of intense suffering and despair.

While the modern discourse around the afterlife remains varied, with divergent beliefs even within religious traditions, the themes of reward, punishment, and divine justice persist as central elements in discussions of life beyond death.

The doctrine of resurrection holds a paramount place in Christian theology. Jesus's resurrection serves as a cornerstone, a tangible promise of what awaits the faithful. "Jesus said unto her, I am the resurrection, and the life: he that believeth in me, though he were dead, yet shall he live" (Jn 11:25). This assurance imbued early Christians with hope and fortified them in the face of persecution.

As Christianity evolved and branched into various denominations over the centuries, it contributed a diverse and multifaceted spectrum through which the afterlife is perceived and understood. Each tradition within the Christian fold adds layers of complexity and nuance to conceptions of life beyond death.

The Roman Catholic Church, grounded in centuries of theological exploration, built upon the works of revered theologians like Augustine of Hippo and Thomas Aquinas. This tradition introduced and solidified the doctrine of purgatory—a state of existence where souls believed to be destined for heaven undergo a process of purification. This belief holds that purgatory is a transitional state where souls atone for their sins before achieving the beatific vision, the direct visual perception of God.[615] The idea of purgatory is interwoven into the theological and eschatological framework of the Catholic Church.

However, this belief has encountered significant contention, notably during the Protestant Reformation in the sixteenth century. Among others, figures like Martin Luther and John Calvin emerged as vociferous challengers of this doctrine. Luther criticized the Church's practice of selling indulgences, which were believed to reduce the punishment one had to undergo for sins in purgatory.[616] He asserted that the Bible did not provide a clear and unequivocal basis for the existence of purgatory, thus igniting a theological debate that rippled through Christianity, leading to the emergence of Protestant denominations that rejected the doctrine.

The Protestant Reformation marked a pivotal moment in Christian history, leading to a profound and enduring schism that reshaped the religious landscape of Europe and beyond. In the ensuing divisions, varying perspectives on the afterlife, heaven, hell, and intermediate states like purgatory further diversified. In Eastern Orthodoxy, for instance, there isn't an exact equivalent to purgatory prayers for the dead, but a belief in an intermediate state reflects related concerns with the soul's fate after death.[617]

In the modern era, discussions and debates about the afterlife continue to evolve within and outside Christian traditions. The diversity of beliefs underscores the enduring human quest to understand the mysteries of life,

---

[615] Jerry L. Walls, *Purgatory: The Logic of Total Transformation* (Oxford: Oxford University Press, 2012), 25–27.

[616] Martin Luther, "Disputation of Doctor Martin Luther on the Power and Efficacy of Indulgences," Project Gutenberg, https://www.gutenberg.org/ebooks/274.

[617] Paul Gavrilyuk, "The Eastern Orthodox Doctrine of the Afterlife," in *The Oxford Handbook of Eschatology*, ed. Jerry L. Walls (Oxford: Oxford University Press, 2008), 286–287.

death, and what may lie beyond, each practice, offering distinctive insights and perspectives on these profound existential questions.

While the afterlife remains a central theme across Christian denominations, the emphasis isn't merely on the hereafter. The core message is about nurturing a relationship with Christ in the present, allowing his teachings to shape our lives and leading us to that promised eternal communion.

In delving deep into the annals of Christian thought, I've come to appreciate the rich tapestry of beliefs that have evolved over time. The afterlife, in its myriad interpretations, serves as a mirror, reflecting humanity's hopes, aspirations, and innate yearning for the Divine. As Christians, whether Catholic, Protestant, Orthodox, or LDS, our shared belief in Christ's redemptive power binds us, reminding us of the eternal promise that lies beyond the temporal realm.

LDS Perspective on the Afterlife

In my journey of faith as a member of the Church of Jesus Christ of Latter-day Saints, the intricacies of our beliefs regarding the afterlife have been a beacon, providing solace and direction. The LDS perspective on the afterlife, characterized by profound depth and optimism, paints a picture of God's expansive love and the eternal potential of his children.[618]

Foundational Beliefs

The vast tapestry of LDS theology is defined by a continuum of existence that stretches infinitely in both directions beyond the narrow confines of our earthly life. This broad, panoramic view of existence serves as a guidepost for Latter-Day Saints in understanding their purpose and place within the divine scheme.

---

[618] M. Russell Ballard, *Our Search for Happiness* (Salt Lake City: Deseret Book Co., 1993).

Central to LDS teachings is the notion that our spirits do not begin to exist at birth, nor do they cease to exist at death.[619] We hail from a premortal existence where we lived in the divine presence of our Heavenly Father as his spirit children.[620] This state was a passive existence and an active educational experience. It was a classroom of eternal proportions where the foundational plan of salvation was unveiled. Here, we learned of our divine potential, the need for agency, and the role of a Savior in our journey. Lucifer rebelled against God's plan in this premortal realm, leading to his expulsion.[621] It was also where we, armed with the gift of agency, made the significant choice to follow the Savior and enter mortality, knowing the challenges and growth opportunities it would provide.

Following our premortal existence, we embarked on the next phase: mortal life. The LDS perspective views our time on Earth as more than a mere accident of biology; it's a crucial, divinely appointed phase of our eternal progression.[622] This mortal experience, with its blend of joy, sorrow, trials, and triumphs, is often described as a probationary period. It's a refiner's fire, a period that hones our spirits, tests our faith, and allows us to develop Christlike attributes.[623] Here, we are granted agency, the ability to make choices, and draw closer to Jesus Christ through those choices.

In LDS theology, the postmortem spirit world is a realm of vibrant growth and learning. It's not a dormant, static existence but a dynamic one filled with opportunities for continuous advancement and enlightenment. This world is visualized as a paradise and a prison, where spirits await the resurrection in their diverse states.[624] In this interim period, spirits continue to learn, evolve, and make choices that impact their eternal progression.

---

[619] Russell M. Nelson, *The Gateway We Call Death* (Salt Lake City: Deseret Book Co., 1995).

[620] Bruce R. McConkie, *Mormon Doctrine* (Salt Lake City: Bookcraft, 1966).

[621] Smith, *Teachings of the Prophet Joseph Smith*.

[622] David A. Bednar, *Power to Become* (Salt Lake City: Deseret Book Co., 2014).

[623] Henry B. Eyring, *To Draw Closer to God* (Salt Lake City: Deseret Book Co., 1997).

[624] "Death and Afterlife in LDS Theology," in *Life After Death: A Study of the Afterlife in World Religions*, ed. Farnáz Ma'súmián (Oxford: Oneworld Publications, 1995), 123–124.

Beyond the event of resurrection lies the profound moment of judgment. Here, individuals are assessed for their actions, intents, desires, and the context of their life's journey. Following this, the realization of our eternal potential unfolds. Individuals are seen as literal children of God, with the potential to inherit and partake in the divine glory prepared by God for his children.[625] This perspective imbues death with a sense of hope, continuity, and purpose, transforming it from an end to a significant milestone in the soul's eternal progression.

LDS doctrine on death and the afterlife paints a picture of unbroken continuity, where every soul matters, and every journey is sacred and significant in the vast expanse of eternity.

This grand narrative of existence, a story of learning, choosing, growing, and becoming, underscores the profound optimism inherent in LDS theology. It suggests that our lives, both before and after mortality, have divine purpose and potential, and it serves as a powerful reminder of our eternal value in the eyes of our Heavenly Father.

The Plan of Salvation

The "plan of salvation"—poetically also known as the "plan of happiness"—stands as the heart of Latter-Day Saint doctrine, offering a panoramic overview of God's grand design for his children.[626] It is not merely a theological concept but a divine roadmap, charting our journey from a premortal existence through the challenges of mortal life and into eternity.[627]

---

[625] The Church of Jesus Christ of Latter-day Saints, "The Family: A Proclamation to the World," Salt Lake City, 1995.

[626] Dallin H. Oaks, *Life's Lessons Learned: Personal Reflections* (Salt Lake City: Deseret Book Co., 2011).

[627] M. Russell Ballard, *Our Search for Happiness* (Salt Lake City: Deseret Book Co., 1993).

At the foundation of this plan lies an eternal truth: God's love and his unquenchable desire for his offspring's eternal happiness and progress.[628] Moses 1:39 beautifully articulates this purpose when God declares, "For behold, this is my work and my glory—to bring to pass the immortality and eternal life of man." Here, two aspects of salvation are highlighted: *immortality*, the promise of resurrection and eternal life made available to all through the atonement of Jesus Christ, and *eternal life*, the opportunity to live in God's presence and continue progressing.

Central to this plan is the Savior, Jesus Christ. His atonement—comprising his suffering in the Garden of Gethsemane, his crucifixion, and his subsequent resurrection—serves as the keystone.[629] Through Christ, the bonds of physical death are broken, and resurrection becomes a universal gift.[630] Moreover, his atonement provides the means by which we can be cleansed from sin, overcome personal weaknesses, and be sanctified, making a return to God's presence possible for those who believe, repent, and remain faithful to his commandments.[631]

Stages of Existence: As noted in a previous section, this plan provides clarity and context to our journey through the different stages of existence:

1. *Premortal Life:* As spiritual offspring of our Heavenly Father, we lived with him, developing our nascent personalities and making the pivotal choice to follow God's plan, knowing it would involve challenges and opportunities for growth.[632]
2. *Mortal Life:* Upon coming to Earth, we entered a state where we could grow through experiences, learn from mistakes, make

---

[628] Gordon B. Hinckley, *Standing for Something: 10 Neglected Virtues That Will Heal Our Hearts and Homes* (New York: Three Rivers Press, 2000).

[629] Jeffrey R. Holland, *Christ and the New Covenant* (Salt Lake City: Deseret Book Co., 1997).

[630] Russell M. Nelson, *Jesus the Christ: A Study of the Messiah and his Mission* (Salt Lake City: Deseret Book Co., 1999).

[631] Dieter F. Uchtdorf, *The Infinite Atonement* (Salt Lake City: Deseret Book Co., 2001).

[632] Bruce R. McConkie, *The Promised Messiah: The First Coming of Christ* (Salt Lake City: Deseret Book Co., 1978).

covenants with God, and use our agency to draw closer to Christ.[633]

3. *Postmortem Life:* After death, our spirits move to the spirit world, a place of learning and preparation for the resurrection. The ultimate promise of the plan is the resurrection, where our spirits and bodies reunite in a perfected state. Following a final judgment based on our desires, actions, and the grace of Christ, we inherit a degree of glory.[634]

This divine plan, rich in its details and profound in its implications, offers knowledge and comfort. It paints a picture of a loving God, a redeeming Savior, and a purpose-driven existence. Through it, Latter-Day Saints find direction and hope for the future.[635]

The Three Kingdoms of Glory: The doctrine of the three kingdoms of glory is a remarkable and uniquely LDS understanding of the eternal destinies that await God's children. It underscores the breadth of God's mercy, the depth of his love, and his unwavering commitment to honor every individual's agency and personal choices.[636]

- *Celestial Kingdom:* This is the pinnacle of God's kingdoms of glory. It is a place where the pure in heart, those who have embraced the fullness of the gospel of Jesus Christ, received the necessary saving ordinances, and remained steadfast in their covenants, will dwell.[637] The glory of the celestial kingdom is likened to the brightness of the sun, and it's in this kingdom that familial relationships can continue eternally. Inhabitants of this kingdom are privileged to be in the presence of God the Father and his Son, Jesus Christ. As the apostle Paul says, "Eye hath not

[633] David A. Bednar, *Act in Doctrine* (Salt Lake City: Deseret Book Co., 2012).

[634] Joseph Smith, *Doctrines of Salvation* (Salt Lake City: Bookcraft, 1954–56).

[635] Henry B. Eyring, *Because He First Loved Us* (Salt Lake City: Deseret Book Co., 2002).

[636] James E. Talmage, *The Articles of Faith* (Salt Lake City: Deseret Book Co., 1899).

[637] Russell M. Nelson, *The Power of the Covenant* (Salt Lake City: Deseret Book Co., 2011).

seen, nor ear heard, neither have entered into the heart of man, the things which God hath prepared for them that love him" (1 Cor 2:9).

- *Terrestrial Kingdom*: Often compared to the shining of the moon, this kingdom is designated for those who, in the words of Joseph Smith in Doctrine and Covenants, "were honorable men of the earth, who were blinded by the craftiness of men" (76:75). These individuals may have led honorable lives, upheld moral standards, and even believed in Christ, but they did not fully embrace or accept the gospel or receive the requisite ordinances during their time on Earth.[638] However, during their life in the spirit world, they accept the gospel and its ordinances performed on their behalf by the living.

- *Telestial Kingdom*: Even the telestial kingdom's glory surpasses all mortal comprehension, likened to the glory of the stars in the firmament. This realm is reserved for those who did not accept the redemptive power of Jesus Christ in life and continued in their rejection even after death.[639] While they will be visited by the Holy Ghost and be served by Jesus Christ, they will be excluded from the presence of God the Father and the Son.[640] It's a testament to God's mercy that even those who made a myriad of wrong choices are still embraced in a kingdom of glory.

This doctrine of varying kingdoms of glory emphasizes the individualized and just nature of God's judgments. Rather than a simplistic binary of heaven or hell, the three kingdoms of glory provide a nuanced understanding of the afterlife, reflecting God's perfect balance of justice and mercy.[641]

---

[638] Bruce R. McConkie, *Mormon Doctrine* (Salt Lake City: Bookcraft, 1966).

[639] Jeffrey R. Holland, *The Grandeur of God* (Salt Lake City: Deseret Book Co., 2003).

[640] David A. Bednar, *Come and See* (Salt Lake City: Deseret Book Co., 2014).

[641] Dallin H. Oaks, *The Challenge to Become* (Salt Lake City: Deseret Book Co., 2000).

Outer Darkness: When delving into the depths of LDS eschatology, one encounters a realm that starkly contrasts the three kingdoms of glory, known as the outer darkness.[642] The outer darkness differs profoundly from the kingdoms of glory. While even the telestial kingdom is bathed in a measure of divine light, the outer darkness is complete spiritual desolation, an abyss of eternal separation from God's presence.[643]

The term "sons of perdition" often arises when discussing those consigned to the outer darkness.[644] Unlike ordinary sinners or those who reject the gospel without a complete understanding of it, sons of perdition are unique in their spiritual journey. They have reached the pinnacle of enlightenment, gaining a perfect knowledge of God's existence and his redeeming love. As the scriptures articulate, they have been "made partakers" of the heavenly gift and have tasted the world's powers to come (Heb 6:4–6).

However, after having been exposed to this fullness of truth, they turn against it. Their rebellion is not borne out of ignorance or misunderstanding but is a willful and defiant act against the very God they know to be true.[645] In this they deny the Holy Ghost after having received it, and the Christ's atonement ceases to have efficacy for them. It's a state of spiritual self-destruction, wherein they reject the very means by which they could have been redeemed.[646]

The outer darkness isn't akin to the traditional Christian concept of hell, where the wicked suffer eternally.[647] The majority of God's children, regardless of the mistakes they make during their mortal life, are not

---

[642] McConkie, *Mormon Doctrine*, 550.

[643] Russell M. Nelson, "The Atonement," *Ensign*, Nov. 1996.

[644] Doctrine and Covenants, 76:31–38.

[645] Jeffrey R. Holland, "The Justice and Mercy of God," *Ensign*, May 1999.

[646] Neal A. Maxwell, "All Hell Is Moved," Brigham Young University Devotional, Nov. 8, 1977.

[647] Robert L. Millet, *The Vision of Mormonism: Pressing the Boundaries of Christianity* (New York: Paragon House, 2007), 131.

destined for the outer darkness.[648] Instead, it's reserved for a select group who commit what's often referred to as the "unpardonable sin."[649]

In fact, Church leaders have often emphasized the limited number who will ever meet such a fate. Christ's love and mercy ensure that the vast majority of God's children will inherit a kingdom of glory.[650]

First, Satan and his followers, the rebellious spirits who opposed God's plan in the premortal existence, are destined for the outer darkness. They never gained mortal bodies, having been cast out of heaven due to their rebellion (Rev 12:7–9). As Doctrine and Covenants reveals, they are "the devil and his angels, who rebelled against me" (76:28). Their fate was sealed because they chose to oppose God's plan, even in the face of complete knowledge.[651]

For mortals, the criteria are similarly stringent. It's not merely a matter of committing grave sins or even opposing God's work during one's life. The sons of perdition, as mentioned, have received an absolute knowledge of God's existence, his divine love, and his grand plan of salvation. These individuals have been blessed with profound spiritual experiences that they cannot deny.[652] However, after receiving this fullness of truth, they turn against it, denying the Holy Ghost.[653]

Mere disbelief or opposition to Church teachings or even grievous sins do not qualify someone as a son of perdition. Instead, it is a knowledgeable and purposeful rebellion against the essence of divine truth.[654] Only a tiny fraction of humanity will ever reach such a state.[655]

---

[648] Gordon B. Hinckley, "The Loneliness of Leadership," *Ensign*, Nov. 1969.

[649] Doctrine and Covenants, 76:30–37.

[650] Spencer W. Kimball, *The Miracle of Forgiveness* (Salt Lake City: Bookcraft, 1969).

[651] McConkie, *Mormon Doctrine*, 216.

[652] Joseph Smith, *Doctrines of Salvation Vol. 1* (Salt Lake City: Bookcraft, 1954–56), 45.

[653] Doctrine and Covenants, 76:31.

[654] Russell M. Nelson, "The Atonement," *Ensign*, Nov. 1996.

[655] David A. Bednar, *Come and See* (Salt Lake City: Deseret Book Co., 2014), 105.

Even some of history's most notorious figures wouldn't necessarily meet the criteria set for the sons of perdition.[656] This presented me with a profound question, one that has perplexed many people before me: I understand how God's love is boundless and forgiving, but how can individuals responsible for the most heinous of crimes—like Joseph Stalin or Adolf Hitler, who, between them, are implicated in the deaths of nearly 20 million souls—possibly be considered for eternal salvation?[657]

Church leaders have often emphasized the rarity of those who will be consigned to the outer darkness. Elder Dallin H. Oaks, for instance, says, "It is . . . likely that the number of sons of perdition is very small."[658]

This dilemma was presented to LDS missionaries, whose insight, while rooted in personal belief rather than official church doctrine, was illuminating. They highlighted a fundamental aspect of the LDS belief system: tracing back to their premortal existence, these malevolent figures, despite their grievous actions on Earth, had once chosen to align with God and embark on their earthly journey. They didn't reject God in the manner of Satan and his disciples.[659] In this light, comprehending the LDS perspective requires an understanding that goes beyond earthly actions, no matter how grievous, and delves into a realm of premortal choices and eternal possibilities.

The outer darkness is a sobering testament to the immense value that God places on agency. He honors our choices even when they lead to self-imposed separation from him. However, it also underscores the vastness of Christ's redemptive power, that only those who knowingly and willingly reject it after fully embracing it are beyond its reach.[660]

---

[656] Jeffrey R. Holland, "The Justice and Mercy of God," *Ensign*, May 1999.

[657] Neal A. Maxwell, "The Atonement of Jesus Christ," *Ensign*, July 1996.

[658] Dallin H. Oaks, "The Great Plan of Happiness," *Ensign*, Nov. 1993.

[659] Elder Moon and Elder Perry, *Conversations*, Sept. 15, 2023.

[660] Bednar, *Come and See*, 98.

Temple Work and Proxy Baptisms: In LDS theology, temples stand as a beacon of hope, love, and eternal connectivity. They aren't just places of worship but are venues where heaven meets Earth, linking generations past, present, and future.[661] This is especially evident in the practice of proxy baptisms, a poignant manifestation of the Church's commitment to ensuring every child of God has access to the blessings of the atonement.

Central to this belief is the understanding that God's love is impartial. He does not consign souls to eternal separation simply because they lived in a time or place where the fullness of the gospel was inaccessible.[662] This perspective resonates with the core Christian principle that God "will have all men to be saved, and to come unto the knowledge of the truth" (1 Tim 2:4).

As covered previously, temples serve as hallowed grounds where these vicarious ordinances occur. They are edifices of purpose, driven by the objective to bind humanity in a divine, eternal family.[663] After performing extensive genealogical research, members come to these temples and undergo baptisms, endowments, and sealings on behalf of their ancestors.[664]

The act of proxy baptism is deeply symbolic. It signifies an unbroken chain of love and commitment, transcending the veil of death.[665] When a living member is immersed in the baptismal waters on behalf of someone who has passed on, it's not just a ritual; it's an offering—a hand extended across the corridors of time.[666]

Some might question or misconstrue the intent behind proxy baptisms, perceiving them as an attempt to convert individuals to Mormonism posthumously. However, this isn't the case. LDS doctrine clarifies that the

---

[661] M. Russell Ballard, "The Importance of the Temple," *Ensign*, Feb. 1995.

[662] James E. Talmage, *The House of the Lord* (Salt Lake City: Deseret Book Co., 1968), 83.

[663] Russell M. Nelson, "Prepare for the Blessings of the Temple," *Ensign*, Oct. 2010.

[664] Dale G. Renlund, "Family History and Temple Work: Sealing and Healing," *Ensign*, May 2018.

[665] David A. Bednar, "The Hearts of the Children Shall Turn," *Ensign*, Nov. 2011.

[666] Steven E. Snow, "Ask of God: Our Solitary Personal Quest," *Ensign*, Nov. 2019.

deceased retain their agency in the afterlife.[667] The act of vicarious baptism doesn't enroll them as Latter-Day Saints. Instead, it merely extends an invitation, leaving the choice to accept or decline entirely with the individual in the spirit world.[668]

Paul's enigmatic reference to baptism for the dead in 1 Corinthians is a testament to this practice's ancient roots (1 Cor 15:29). While the exact nature and context of proxy baptisms during Paul's time remain subjects of debate among biblical scholars, the very mention indicates that the concept was neither alien nor controversial to early Christian communities.[669]

In the grand mosaic of LDS belief, temple work and proxy baptisms epitomize the faith's encompassing vision of redemption—a vision where no soul, no matter how distant or disconnected, is left behind in the eternal scheme of things.[670]

Final Thoughts: In delving deeper into the LDS perspective on the afterlife, it becomes increasingly evident how boundless and all-encompassing God's love is. This theology isn't merely a series of doctrines or practices; it's a heartfelt testament to a divine love that refuses to be constrained by time, death, or spatial dimensions.[671]

Central to this perspective is the inherent divinity and potential within each of God's children. As we traverse through the different phases of existence—be it the premortal life, our mortal journey, or the vast expanses of eternity—a divine blueprint is etched into the fabric of our souls, reminding us of who we are and who we have the potential to become.[672]

The doctrine of the afterlife in the LDS faith is not just about destinations or end states. It is dynamic, focusing on progression, learning, and the

---

[667] Dallin H. Oaks, "Baptism for the Dead: The Covenants," *Ensign*, Aug. 1995.
[668] Doctrine and Covenants, 137:7–9.
[669] Wright, *The Resurrection of the Son of God*, 143–145.
[670] Jeffrey R. Holland, "Missionary Work and the Atonement," *Ensign*, March 2001.
[671] Dieter F. Uchtdorf, "The Love of God," *Ensign*, Nov. 2009.
[672] Boyd K. Packer, "The Pattern of Our Parentage," *Ensign*, Nov. 1984.

relentless journey of becoming more like our Heavenly Father.[673]It emphasizes that our choices—whether in this life, our premortal existence, or in the life to come—aren't just fleeting moments; they are pivotal crossroads that can shape our eternal trajectory.[674]

Beyond doctrines and principles, what truly stands out is the message of hope and assurance these beliefs offer. For those who have weathered the heartbreak of losing loved ones, the teachings provide a comforting balm, assuring them that death is not an end but a mere transition.[675] It's a promise that families can be together forever, that bonds forged in this life can transcend the mortal plane and perpetuate in eternity.[676]

Moreover, the LDS perspective on the afterlife is not just about looking forward; it's also about informing our present. It acts as a compass, guiding our actions, refining our character, and helping us forge meaningful relationships. It reminds us that our time on Earth is preparatory—a sacred period of learning, growth, and decision-making, setting the stage for the grand cosmic narrative that will continue to unfold.[677]

In sum, the LDS teachings on the afterlife paint a picture of an omnibenevolent God, a deity intimately involved in his children's lives and destinies. A God who has prepared a plan so intricate and encompassing that it accounts for every soul, ensuring that everyone has a chance at salvation and eternal joy irrespective of their circumstances.[678] It's a narrative that doesn't just provide solace—it inspires, motivates, and beckons us toward a greater understanding of our purpose in this vast cosmic tapestry.

---

[673] Russell M. Nelson, "Choices," *Ensign*, Nov. 1990.

[674] Dallin H. Oaks, "The Challenge to Become." *Ensign*, Nov. 2000.

[675] Henry B. Eyring, "Our Perfect Example," *Ensign*, Nov. 2009.

[676] Gordon B. Hinckley, "The Family: A Proclamation to the World," *Ensign*, Nov. 1995.

[677] David A. Bednar, "Therefore They Hushed Their Fears," *Ensign*, May 2015.

[678] Jeffrey R. Holland, "The Grandeur of God," *Ensign*, Nov. 2003.

The Soul: Its Origin, Journey, and Destiny

Few subjects have fascinated humankind as persistently as the concept of the soul. It's a term that conjures feelings of mystery, reverence, and introspection. Throughout history, various religious and philosophical traditions have attempted to understand the soul's elusive nature. The soul's seemingly ephemeral quality, juxtaposed with its eternal significance, makes it a focal point of many theological discourses. I find the narrative surrounding the soul to be not only illuminating but also profoundly reassuring.

Traditional Christian Understanding of the Soul

Historically, many Christian theologians have conceptualized the soul as an individual's immortal and invisible essence, which grants them consciousness, emotion, will, and moral agency.[679] It is this intangible essence that continues its existence beyond physical death. Many Christians believe the body is transient; it is the vessel that houses the soul during our earthly journey, but the soul's true nature transcends the physical. This belief finds resonance in the Apostle Paul's writings. By invoking the terms "spirit," "soul," and "body" in his epistle to the Thessalonians, Paul acknowledges the multi-faceted nature of human existence (1 Thess 5:23). While the "body" is clearly our physical form, "spirit" and "soul" are often seen as closely related yet distinct entities: the spirit is often perceived as the divine breath or spark that gives life while the soul embodies our personality, character, and individuality.

LDS Perspective on the Soul

While harmonizing with many Christian beliefs, the Church of Jesus Christ of Latter-day Saints brings additional insights into this discourse. Latter-Day Saints view the body and spirit not as conflicting entities but as two

---

[679] Augustine of Hippo, *Confessions,* trans. Henry Chadwick (Oxford: Oxford University Press, 2009).

halves of a sacred whole. This union forms the soul.[680] Far from seeing the body as a mere temporary vessel, LDS theology uplifts the body's sanctity, viewing it as an essential component of our eternal identity. This belief underscores the importance of the resurrection when the spirit and the body will be inseparably united in a perfected form.[681]

This holistic understanding of the soul, where the physical and the spiritual are intertwined, elevates the significance of our mortal experiences. Every joy, sorrow, trial, and triumph we experience in our bodies is not just a temporal event but a soul-shaping experience. In this light, our mortal journey becomes even more profound. The choices we make, the lessons we learn, and the relationships we form are etched in our memories and the fabric of our souls. It accentuates the idea that our existence here is not just preparatory but essential to our eternal progression and joy.

The Premortal Existence

Diving deeper into the LDS view of the soul, we encounter a doctrine distinct from many other Christian traditions: the belief in a premortal existence.[682] Before our birth into mortality, we lived as spirit children of our Heavenly Father, in what Latter-Day Saints refer to as the premortal life. This doctrine offers a panoramic view of our existence, painting a vast timeline that extends before and after our brief time on Earth.[683] It speaks to our Heavenly Father's infinite love and meticulous planning for his children. Knowing we lived before we were born lends a sense of purpose and direction to our lives, grounding us in the awareness that we are on a purposeful journey that we chose to embark upon.[684]

In the premortal realm, we had relationships, identities, and a level of agency. As revealed to the Prophet Joseph Smith, Scripture records a grand

---

[680] James E. Talmage, *Articles of Faith* (Salt Lake City: The Church of Jesus Christ of Latter-day Saints, 1984).
[681] Doctrine and Covenants, 88:15.
[682] Russell M. Nelson, "The Creation," *Ensign,* May 2000.
[683] Russell M. Nelson, "The Magnificence of Man," *Ensign,* Jan. 1988.
[684] Henry B. Eyring, "Our Perfect Example," *Ensign*, Nov. 2009.

council where God's children were presented with the Father's plan. Central to this plan was the role of a Savior, and it was Jesus Christ, known then as Jehovah, who stepped forward to fulfill this role.[685] Our decision to accept this plan and come to Earth was not made in ignorance. We understood the challenges and the opposition we would face but chose mortality for its divine potential.[686]

This unique LDS perspective sheds light on questions of identity and self-worth. If we once lived with God and were known by him, it reaffirms the intrinsic value and potential within each of us.[687] This doctrine also offers comfort and perspective when grappling with life's challenges. The adversities we face aren't arbitrary but are part and parcel of a refining process we once understood and accepted.[688]

It also brings clarity to our relationships with others. If we are, in essence, spiritual siblings, having shared that premortal existence together, it underscores the need for love, kindness, and unity in our mortal relationships. Understanding that we once rejoiced together in our Heavenly Father's presence can inspire greater empathy and patience in our interactions.[689]

Furthermore, the doctrine of a premortal life deepens the Christian narrative of redemption. The atonement of Jesus Christ is not just about redeeming us from our mortal sins but is also about fulfilling promises and potentials first kindled in that premortal existence.[690]

This belief is a cornerstone of LDS theology that profoundly influences the Latter-Day Saint worldview. It adds depth and dimension to our understanding of life, purpose, relationships, and the nature of God. With

---

[685] Abraham 3:22–28.

[686] M. Russell Ballard, "Our Search for Happiness," *Ensign*, Oct. 1993.

[687] Dieter F. Uchtdorf, "Remembering Who You Are," *New Era*, Jan. 2010.

[688] Jeffrey R. Holland, "However Long and Hard the Road," *BYU Devotional*, 1983, Brigham Young University.

[689] Quentin L. Cook, "Roots and Branches," *Ensign*, May 2014.

[690] Jeffrey R. Holland, "The Atonement of Jesus Christ," *Ensign*, March 2008.

this perspective, life is not a random sequence of events but a purposeful journey that began long before our mortal birth and will continue into eternity.

The Journey of the Soul

One of the fundamental Christian beliefs is the resurrection of the dead, with Christ being the "firstfruits" of them that slept (1 Cor 15:20). In LDS theology, the resurrection is not just a return to life but a glorious reunion of the spirit and body in perfect form.[691] This doctrine underscores the sacredness of the body and its role in our eternal progression.

The spirit world, as described in LDS teachings, is a bustling realm of activity, reflection, and redemption. Just as mortality offers opportunities to grow closer to God, the spirit world presents its own set of unique opportunities. Paradise is often depicted as a haven of rest where righteous souls find solace and fellowship, rejoicing in the truths they embraced in mortality.[692] They engage in holy work, reaching out to those in spirit prison with the light of the gospel.

Conversely, spirit prison is not necessarily a place of punishment but rather a state of waiting and potential enlightenment. Many who reside here are individuals who, for a myriad of reasons, did not have the opportunity to hear or accept the gospel in their mortal lives.[693]

God's vast mercy ensures that they, too, are allowed to learn and choose. The interplay between paradise and spirit prison speaks volumes about the collaborative nature of salvation, emphasizing the idea that we are our brother's keeper, even in the afterlife.

---

[691] Russell M. Nelson, "Resurrection," *Ensign,* May 1987.

[692] Joseph Smith, *Answers to Gospel Questions Vol. 2* (Deseret Book Co., 1957), 55–56.

[693] Bruce R. McConkie, "The Seven Deadly Heresies," in *BYU Devotional* (Provo, UT: Brigham Young University, 1980).

The temple work done by the living on behalf of the deceased is a poignant symbol of interconnectedness and the eternal family. Baptisms for the dead, endowments, and sealing ordinances bridge the gap between the living and the deceased, further entwining our souls in a network of love and shared purpose.[694] It's a profound testament to the belief that God will leave none of his children behind, provided they walk the path he has laid out.

In piecing together the overarching journey of the soul, a compelling narrative of hope, purpose, and eternal progression emerges. It challenges the nihilistic view that life is a mere coincidence or that our existence is purposeless. Instead, it proposes a perspective where every soul matters, every choice has eternal implications, and every individual is a participant in a grand divine plan.[695]

When seen through this lens, mortality challenges take on new meaning. While real and often overwhelming, our sufferings become refining fires, molding us into beings capable of celestial glory. The joys and love we experience are but a foretaste of the eternal happiness promised to the faithful.[696] Our journey from the premortal existence to the vast eternities ahead is a poignant reminder of our worth in the eyes of our Creator. As the Apostle Paul beautifully articulates, "For I am persuaded, that neither death, nor life, nor angels, nor principalities, nor powers, nor things present, nor things to come, Nor height, nor depth, nor any other creature, shall be able to separate us from the love of God, which is in Christ Jesus our Lord" (Rom 8:38–39).

Resurrection and Eternal Life

Within Christian teachings, the doctrines of resurrection and eternal life stand out as pillars of hope and divine love. Central to these principles is the foundational scriptural evidence found throughout the Old and New

---

[694] Henry B. Eyring, "Hearts Bound Together," *Ensign*, May 2005.
[695] Dieter F. Uchtdorf, "Of Things That Matter Most," *Ensign*, Nov. 2010.
[696] Thomas S. Monson, "Finding Joy in the Journey," *Ensign*, Nov. 2008.

Testaments. The resurrection, by definition, alludes to the reunion of our spirits with our bodies, immortal and inseparable.[697] In the midst of his anguish, Job professed, "For I know that my redeemer liveth, and that he shall stand at the latter day upon the earth: And though after my skin worms destroy this body, yet in my flesh shall I see God" (Job 19:25–26).

This resurrection, a rebirth into an immortal state, is only possible because of the central figure in Christian theology: Jesus Christ.[698] His personal triumph over death provides a template and a promise for the rest of humanity, indicating that his rise from the grave was the inaugural event in a broader universal promise (1 Cor 15:20). In essence, through his unparalleled sacrifice, Jesus displayed his divinity and forged a path from mortality to eternity for all of God's children.[699]

While many Christian denominations celebrate the concept of life after death and a glorious resurrection, the LDS faith unfolds a grander tapestry of what lies beyond the grave. Central to this expansive view is the concept of exaltation, an elevation beyond mere resurrection. This isn't just about living again but about ascending spiritually, continuing to learn, grow, and evolve throughout eternity. Within this framework, it's believed that individuals don't just return to God's presence but have the potential to inherit some of his divine qualities and, in a sense, become more like him.[700]

Eternal progression, as taught by the LDS Church, suggests a continuum of growth that doesn't just start or stop with mortal life or even the afterlife in the traditional sense. It's an eternal journey where souls constantly evolve, gain knowledge, and achieve higher levels of understanding and godliness.[701]

[697] "Resurrection," *Bible Dictionary* (Salt Lake City: Church of Jesus Christ of Latter-day Saints, 1979).

[698] James E. Talmage, *Jesus the Christ* (Salt Lake City: Deseret Book Co., 1915).

[699] Jeffrey R. Holland, *Christ and the New Covenant* (Salt Lake City: Deseret Book Co., 1997)

[700] McConkie, *Mormon Doctrine*.

[701] Russell M. Nelson, "The Salvation and Exaltation of Our Dead," *Ensign*, May 1988.

An aspect of this teaching that often captures attention is the idea that individuals can become like God. This isn't about usurping his role or becoming independent deities but rather achieving a state where they can share in God's glory, knowledge, power, and joy.[702] Such thoughts might seem audacious to some, but they find scriptural support in the LDS canon. Doctrine and Covenants, a collection of modern-day revelations to LDS prophets, elaborates on this theme: "Then shall they be gods, because they have no end; therefore shall they be from everlasting to everlasting" (132:20). This passage suggests a future where the faithful aren't just passive recipients of God's glory but active participants in eternal kingdoms of creation and progression.[703]

This nuanced understanding of post-mortal existence adds depth and dimension to the LDS worldview. It illustrates a God who is not content with merely saving his children but who also desires to elevate them, sharing with them everything he has and all that he knows.[704]

The concept of family holds a paramount position in LDS theology, often depicted as central to God's eternal plan for his children. Families aren't fleeting constructs that dissolve with the veil of death; they are foundational, intended to endure beyond the confines of mortality into eternity.

One of the unique doctrines of the LDS church is the potential for families to be "sealed" together for all time and eternity, a sacred ritual performed in temples. Such sealings bind parents to children and spouses to each other and link generations together in an unbroken chain.[705] When families are sealed in the temple, they're believed to be joined in a way that death cannot sever. This celestial commitment starkly contrasts the traditional marital

---

[702] "Becoming Like God," The Church of Jesus Christ of Latter-day Saints, https://www.churchofjesuschrist.org/study/manual/gospel-topics-essays/becoming-like-god?lang=eng.

[703] Bruce C. Hafen, *Spiritually Anchored in Unsettled Times* (Salt Lake City: Deseret Book Co., 2009).

[704] Neal A. Maxwell, "Enduring Well," *Ensign*, April 1997.

[705] M. Russell Ballard, "The Eternal Blessings of Marriage," *Ensign*, April 2011.

vow of "till death do us part," suggesting a bond that extends far beyond our mortal existence.

As stated in Doctrine and Covenants 132:19, "ye shall come forth in the first resurrection . . . and shall inherit thrones, kingdoms, principalities, and powers, dominions." This paints a majestic picture of the glorious future promised to the faithful. But it's not just a promise of individual glory and progression. Embedded within this passage is the understanding that these blessings will be enjoyed in the company of our beloved family members.

The doctrine of eternal families in LDS belief provides solace and hope, especially for those mourning the loss of dear ones. It assures the grieving heart of a reunion, untainted by the anguish of death, wherein earthly relationships continue to thrive beyond the mortal realm. This belief transforms the perspective on life and relationships, affirming the seamless connection between ancestors and descendants, forming a grand, eternal lineage that transcends the boundaries of time.

This doctrine's impact permeates the lives of many Latter-Day Saints, guiding their actions and decisions with a view toward eternity. It elevates the importance of family bonds, positioning them as divine gifts that enhance the intricacy and beauty of life. This emphasis further amplifies the boundless love and potential imprinted within each individual by divine design, affirming a narrative of enduring hope and celestial continuity beyond the earthly sojourn, as echoed in various sacred scriptures.

Challenging Questions and Contemporary Views

For many people, the journey of faith is interspersed with moments of doubt, introspection, and challenging questions. In our modern era, where empirical evidence reigns supreme, concepts like the afterlife, a loving God, and the existence of hell are often met with skepticism. General Christianity and the teachings of the Church of Jesus Christ of Latter-day Saints provide answers, albeit through different lenses.

Contemplating the afterlife is a task that many people grapple with. What does the afterlife look like? Is it an expansive void or a realm of endless possibilities? The essence of these questions can be traced back to our innate desire for continuity and understanding. The Bible reassures us of God's promise: "In my Father's house are many mansions: if it were not so, I would have told you. I go to prepare a place for you" (Jn 14:2). This scripture offers comfort and a sense of certainty, suggesting a place has indeed been prepared for us in the hereafter.

And yet, doubts persist. The question of suffering has perplexed theologians, philosophers, and truth seekers for centuries. The contradiction between a God of infinite love and a world teeming with pain, injustice, and calamity often prompts deep introspection. This issue, known in theological circles as theodicy, wrestles with vindicating divine goodness in the face of earthly suffering.[706]

From the early days of Christianity, believers found solace in the narrative of Adam and Eve. Their choice, as captured in the Bible, introduced knowledge and suffering into the world. But rather than viewing this merely as a punishment, the LDS Church views it as an inevitable outcome of agency.[707] If humanity is to be genuinely free, they must also be free to err, to choose paths that lead to pain for themselves and others. The ripple effects of these choices, combined with the natural processes of the physical world, produce much of the suffering we see.

But this explanation only goes so far. What about the innocent who suffer, those who bear the weight of others' choices, or the inexplicable tragedies that befall without reason? Here, Christian thought offers another layer of understanding: suffering, while undeniably painful, can also be transformative.[708] In the crucible of adversity, souls are refined, virtues like patience and empathy are cultivated, and individuals often turn more

---

[706] John Hick, *Evil and the God of Love.*
[707] Ibid.
[708] Lewis, *The Problem of Pain.*

wholeheartedly to the Divine, seeking solace and understanding. Despite his own trials, the Apostle Paul proclaimed, "And not only so, but we glory in tribulations also: knowing that tribulation worketh patience; And patience, experience; and experience, hope" (Rom 5:3–4).

Remember, God's perspective is eternal. While your current suffering might seem overwhelming and insurmountable, from an eternal vantage, it's a brief moment in the soul's journey. Christianity does not promise a life devoid of pain; it promises the hope of redemption through a loving God who can turn even the most profound sorrows into avenues of growth and, ultimately, joy.[709]

It's a perspective that doesn't diminish the reality of suffering but instead offers a broader context to understand it. God's grace isn't just a Band-Aid for the wounds of the moment; it's the promise of a future where every tear will be wiped away, and today's trials will give way to the triumphs of eternity.

The concept of eternal punishment and damnation has been a matter of deep theological contemplation and debate throughout the ages. At its core, the question revolves around the nature of God's justice and mercy. If God is love, as Christian teachings profess, how does the existence of hell square with his infinite compassion? (1 Jn 4:8).

In broad strokes, Christianity often sees hell not as an act of God's willful punishment but rather as the outcome of personal choice. Just as individuals have agency in mortal life, they also possess it in matters of salvation. In this context, hell is less about fire and brimstone and more about the absence of God's presence. It's akin to a spiritual distance one places between themselves and the Divine. When one deliberately rejects God's love, grace, and teachings, one positions themselves in a state of separation.

---

[709] Ibid.

For Latter-Day Saints, hell is more instructive than punitive. It serves as a place of learning and repentance. The ultimate purpose isn't to condemn but to refine, teach, and provide every possible chance for progression. The atonement of Jesus Christ plays a central role in this theology. Through his sacrifice, Christ extends his love and redemption even to those in spirit prison, offering them an opportunity to accept the gospel, repent, and progress to higher realms of glory. This framework presents a God whose primary attributes are endless compassion, patience, and a genuine desire for all his children to return to him.

Additionally, the LDS perspective underscores the depth of Christ's atonement. Rather than a one-size-fits-all salvation, it acknowledges the vast spectrum of human experience, choice, and potential. Every soul, regardless of their choices on Earth, is precious in God's eyes and deserves as many chances as needed to draw nearer to him.

This intricate tapestry of beliefs emphasizes a divine balance between justice and mercy. While personal choices bear consequences, the ever-present promise of redemption and the boundless scope of the Savior's atonement ensure that no soul is beyond the reach of God's encompassing love.

As presented in LDS teachings, this detailed view of the afterlife provides a roadmap for those seeking clarity. The visions and revelations reported by prophets like Joseph Smith give detailed accounts of the afterlife's realms, emphasizing God's unwavering love and the eternal potential of every soul.[710]

While doubts and questions are inevitable in the spiritual journey, Christianity and LDS teachings offer profound insights. They invite individuals to believe and seek, ponder, and gain personal testimonies of these eternal truths. In a world teeming with questions, these doctrines

---

[710] Smith, Doctrine and Covenants, 137–138.

provide answers that resonate with the soul's eternal yearning for understanding and connection.

Conclusion

The quest to grasp what lies beyond the veil of mortality is a universal endeavor.[711] As I have navigated the intricate tapestry of beliefs, particularly within the Christian and LDS framework, I've realized that our understandings and beliefs about the hereafter profoundly influence our mortal journey.

Jesus once remarked, "I am come that they might have life, and that they might have it more abundantly" (Jn 10:10). While undoubtedly addressing spiritual rebirth and salvation, this pronouncement underscores the principle that the quality of our current lives can be elevated by our comprehension of eternity. Our beliefs about the afterlife aren't mere esoteric or theological musings. They shape our values, guide our decisions, and offer a lens through which we perceive suffering, joy, and the essence of existence.[712]

For if we genuinely internalize the promise of a glorious resurrection, the transient nature of our current trials becomes clearer. The sufferings of the present time are not worth comparing with the glory that will be revealed in us (Rom 8:18). Such a perspective doesn't diminish our mortal challenges; instead, it places them within a grander narrative of eternal progression and divine purpose.

When one contemplates the LDS doctrines of eternal progression and families bound for eternity, the idea of an afterlife becomes a continuation and a sublime expanse where our souls, unfettered by mortal limitations, continue their journey of growth, discovery, and joy.[713] If we genuinely believe in such a future, it instills the present with a sense of sacred purpose.

---

[711] Mircea, *The Sacred and the Profane: The Nature of Religion.*
[712] Lewis, *Mere Christianity.*
[713] Smith, Doctrine and Covenants, 132.

Each relationship becomes more treasured, every choice more significant, and every experience an opportunity for growth reverberating into eternity.

Exploring afterlife beliefs also beckons us to plumb the depths of God's love. Within Christianity, the sacrifice of Jesus on the cross is a testament to God's incomprehensible love. However, as LDS teachings further illuminate, this love isn't just about redeeming us from fallibility but exalting us to divine potential.[714] It's a love that desires not just to save but also to empower, uplift, and glorify. The Apostle Paul encapsulates this sentiment when he says, "Eye hath not seen, nor ear heard, neither have entered into the heart of man, the things which God hath prepared for them that love him" (1 Cor 2:9).

While faith traditions offer insights, revelations, and testimonies about the hereafter, the spectrum of beliefs and philosophies outside these frameworks is vast. Some find comfort in the cyclical patterns of nature, believing in rebirth and reincarnation.[715] Others, drawing from existential or secular worldviews, see this life as a singular, unique, and thus profoundly precious existence.[716] Regardless of our beliefs or doubts, contemplating the afterlife is fundamentally a contemplation of existence itself, of meaning, purpose, and the deepest yearnings of the human soul.

In this pursuit, I invite readers to pause and reflect on the vastness of God's love. Even if some details about the afterlife remain enigmatic, the foundational promise remains: a love that transcends mortality, a plan that cherishes each soul, and a future brimming with potential and glory. By anchoring our lives in this understanding, we can navigate the intricacies of mortality with hope, purpose, and the assurance that our story, underpinned by divine love, is eternal.

---

[714] Jeffrey R. Holland, "The Grandeur of God," LDS General Conference, Oct. 2003.

[715] Smith, *The World's Religions: Our Great Wisdom Traditions*.

[716] Jean-Paul Sartre, *Being and Nothingness* (New York: Philosophical Library, 1956).

Chapter 12: Faith Under Fire

When I reflect upon history and the relentless march of time, I am often struck by the resilience and tenacity of faith. From the whispered prayers of a solitary shepherd in ancient pastures to the soaring cathedrals that punctuate our city skylines, faith has been an enduring testament to humanity's quest for the Divine.[717] As with all quests, this one has also been marked by periods of profound certainty and moments of intense doubt. It is fitting that in our contemporary age—an age replete with its own set of unique challenges—this dance between faith and doubt continues with renewed enthusiasm.

". . . for we walk by faith, not by sight," the Apostle Paul says in his second letter to the Corinthians (2 Cor 5:7). But what happens when the path we tread becomes obscured by the thick fog of sociopolitical shifts, cultural upheavals, and rapidly changing norms? The landscape of postmodernity presents an array of challenges to believers. In this changing terrain, the lines between faith, doubt, and the broader societal currents intertwine in complex ways.[718]

One cannot survey the current religious milieu without acknowledging the elephant in the room: *doubt.* In many ways, doubt is an old companion to faith, pushing believers to question, reflect, and, ultimately, to solidify their convictions. Indeed, some of the most profound spiritual epiphanies have been birthed from the crucible of doubt.[719] But in today's world, where information is at our fingertips and diverse viewpoints coalesce and clash globally, doubt has taken on new dimensions. Now more than ever, believers are reconciling deeply held convictions with a barrage of new

---

[717] Jonathan Z. Smith, *Imagining Religion: From Babylon to Jonestown* (Chicago: University of Chicago Press, 1982).

[718] Taylor, *A Secular Age.*

[719] Elisabeth Kübler-Ross and David Kessler, *On Grief and Grieving: Finding the Meaning of Grief Through the Five Stages of Loss* (New York: Scribner, 2005).

perspectives, scientific findings, and the ever-present "woke" culture that seeks to redefine traditional norms.[720]

Amidst this apparent tumult lies an opportunity to refine and deepen one's faith. As metals are purified through fire, so too can faith emerge more radiant and unyielding through the challenges of contemporary life.[721] For all their complexity, sociopolitical shifts also offer believers a platform to engage, discuss, and bear testament to their beliefs in innovative ways.

The political divide in America and the broader Western world is palpable. One cannot peruse a newspaper or scroll through a news app without encountering stories that highlight this chasm. For many, this divide is seen, rightly or wrongly, as an assault on religious values. The secular seems to be encroaching upon the sacred, pushing religion to the peripheries of public discourse.[722] How should believers navigate this intricate maze? How can they bear witness to timeless truths in an age that often seems at odds with them?

It's crucial to remember that the essence of faith lies in its ability to transcend the temporal. While societies evolve, cultures shift, and political landscapes undergo transformation, the eternal truths espoused by faith remain constant. The challenge, then, is not in the truths themselves but in how believers articulate, embody, and live them daily.

In the subsequent sections, we will delve deeper into these challenges and explore the myriad ways that faith is tested and strengthened in the crucible of modernity. Through this journey, my hope is that readers, whether believers or not, will gain a nuanced appreciation for the vast tapestry of

---

[720] Helen Pluckrose and James A. Lindsay *Cynical Theories: How Activist Scholarship Made Everything about Race, Gender, and Identity* (Durham: Pitchstone Publishing, 2020).

[721] Alister E. McGrath, *Doubting: Growing Through the Uncertainties of Faith* (Downers Grove, IL: InterVarsity Press, 2006).

[722] Robert D. Putnam and David E. Campbell, *American Grace: How Religion Divides and Unites Us* (New York: Simon & Schuster, 2010).

belief, doubt, and the undying human spirit that seeks connection with the divine in an ever-changing and turbulent world.

Today, we live in the latter days.

Doubt: The Unexpected Stepping Stone of Faith

To many people, faith and doubt might appear like polar opposites, a dichotomy where the presence of one negates the other. However, an examination of history, scripture, and personal experience reveals a more intricate dance between the two. Doubting, questioning, and wrestling with one's beliefs can carve a path to a more profound, resilient faith.[723]

"O ye of little faith," Jesus once remarked to his disciples when they were seized by fear during a storm at sea (Mt 8:26). This was not a repudiation of their faith but rather a call to delve deeper, strengthen their trust, and confront the uncertainties that lurked in their hearts. Throughout the Bible, we encounter figures who grappled with doubt, only to emerge with a faith that was refined and unshakeable.

Take, for instance, the tale of Thomas, one of the twelve apostles. Often dubbed "Doubting Thomas," he refused to believe in Jesus's resurrection until he saw and touched the wounds of Christ himself (Jn 20:25). While some might view his skepticism as a shortcoming, I perceive it as a manifestation of a profoundly human yearning for understanding and certainty. And when he did encounter the risen Christ, his exclamation, "My Lord and my God!", is a testament to a faith reborn, resilient and unwavering (Jn 20:28).

Or consider Job in the Old Testament. Despite his unparalleled suffering, his journey from questioning God's purpose to submitting to God's divine

---

[723] Søren Kierkegaard, *Fear and Trembling*, trans. Alastair Hannay (London: Penguin Books, 2003).

wisdom exemplifies the transformative power of doubt. Job's faith was not diminished through his trials but elevated to new heights.

Turning our gaze to more recent history, the phenomenon of doubt is not confined solely to the annals of ancient scriptures. The Church of Jesus Christ of Latter-day Saints offers rich insights into the continuing saga of humanity's dance with doubt. Within the corridors of its recent history are stories of early LDS pioneers and leaders who grappled with uncertainties, questions, and moments of spiritual crisis.

A prime example is the Church's founder, Joseph Smith. As a fourteen-year-old boy, he faced a crisis of faith, confronted by many religious sects and a cacophony of competing truths.[724] In this crucible of doubt and confusion, he sought solitude in a grove of trees and offered a fervent prayer for clarity. This act of seeking, born from doubt, led to what Latter-Day Saints recognize as the First Vision, where God the Father and Jesus Christ appeared to him, offering divine guidance and setting the restoration of the gospel in motion.[725]

Another illustrative figure is Parley P. Pratt, an early church apostle. Before his conversion, Pratt wrestled with theological questions that seemed irreconcilable with the religious teachings of his day. His spiritual questing eventually led him to the Book of Mormon, which provided clarity and answers to his most profound spiritual concerns.[726]

Beyond these iconic figures, countless Latter-Day Saints, both past and present, have encountered moments where they've wrestled with theological complexities, historical controversies, or personal tragedies. Much like their biblical counterparts, these periods of doubt become the impetus for profound spiritual growth. They drive individuals to their knees in prayer,

---

[724] Richard L. Bushman, *Joseph Smith and the Beginnings of Mormonism* (Urbana: University of Illinois Press, 1988).
[725] Pearl of Great Price, 1:14–20.
[726] Parley P. Pratt, *Autobiography of Parley P. Pratt* (Salt Lake City: Deseret Book Co., 1985).

push them to delve deeper into the scriptures, and inspire them to seek spiritual reaffirmations.

Indeed, the Church acknowledges the vital role of questioning in the faith journey. Church leaders have consistently emphasized the importance of gaining a personal testimony, an individual and deeply personal conviction of the truthfulness of the gospel, often cultivated in the crucible of doubt and sincere questioning.[727] This ethos is encapsulated in a statement from the Book of Mormon, which encourages individuals to "ask, and ye shall receive; knock, and it shall be opened unto you."[728]

This process of introspection, questioning, and seeking divine affirmation underscores the LDS view that doubt can be a conduit for spiritual growth.

Such examples serve as powerful reminders that doubt is not an endpoint but often a beginning. It is a catalyst that propels us into a deeper engagement with our beliefs, urging us to seek answers, to pray more fervently, and to immerse ourselves in scripture and reflection. In this process we don't just find answers to our questions; we often discover a deeper, more intimate relationship with God.[729]

To the skeptics among us, I offer this perspective: doubt is not a sign of weakness but an invitation to strength. It is an opportunity to shed superficial understandings and to forge a faith built on bedrock. As we grapple with uncertainty, we are beckoned to turn to the scriptures, engage in sincere prayer, and seek spiritual mentors' counsel. Through these avenues, we don't just find solace; we find a resilient, tested, and true faith.

---

[727] Dallin H. Oaks, "Testimony," *Ensign*, May 2008.
[728] 3 Nephi 14:7.
[729] Lewis, *Mere Christianity*.

This is not to say that doubt is easy. It can be deeply unsettling, even painful. But like gold purified in the crucible, a faith that has wrestled with doubt emerges more refined and precious.[730]

The "Woke" Era and Its Impact on Religious Views

As the dawn of a new era unfurls its influence on our social fabric, grappling with the transformation and ideological shifts accompanying it is increasingly vital. The rise of the "woke" movement is a testament to these changing tides.[731] This movement, born out of a commitment to social justice and an awareness of systemic oppression, has become twisted and perverted, dramatically corrupting discourse in our contemporary society. But what is "wokeness," and how does it intersect with traditional religious views, especially within the Christian and LDS paradigms?

Wokeness Within A Historical and Cultural Lens

As the term "woke" transformed from a simple adjective into a socio-political force, its impact on modern dialogue intensified, leaving an indelible mark on public conversation. The values underpinning wokeness—inclusivity, equity, intersectionality—while noble in their origins, have been co-opted and weaponized. A movement initially heralded for amplifying marginalized voices has become a tool of oppression. While the primary intention was to create spaces where everyone felt seen, heard, and validated, it has transformed into a space where dissent or deviation from a particular narrative isn't just discouraged but actively silenced.[732]

The framework of wokeness began by promoting critical thinking, challenging individuals to deconstruct internal biases, and advocating for

---

[730] Dietrich Bonhoeffer, *The Cost of Discipleship*, trans. R. H. Fuller (New York: Macmillan, 1963).

[731] Anderson, Carol. *White Rage: The Unspoken Truth of Our Racial Divide* (New York: Bloomsbury Publishing, 2016).

[732] Greg Lukianoff and Jonathan Haidt, *The Coddling of the American Mind: How Good Intentions and Bad Ideas Are Setting Up a Generation for Failure* (New York: Penguin Books, 2019).

societal overhaul where needed. Over time, however, certain segments have become more rigid and dogmatic. For some people, the ethos of open dialogue and mutual respect has been replaced by a myopic view of what constitutes "correct" or "acceptable" beliefs.

To complicate matters further, wokeness has also been commercialized and commodified. Brands and corporations, attempting to appear progressive and align with younger, socially conscious demographics, have co-opted the movement's language and imagery. This commercialization risks diluting the genuine calls for systemic change and paints wokeness as just another trend rather than a legitimate call for justice.[733]

Where Political Correctness and Traditional Religious Views Intersect

While navigating the confluence of wokeness and religious belief, we find ourselves in turbulent waters. Among the chief points of turbulence is the emphasis the woke movement places on political correctness. Ostensibly, political correctness arose as a way to encourage respectful and inclusive discourse. However, in its modern embodiment, political correctness appears to many people, including me, as an instrument of constriction rather than one of understanding and connection. While political correctness claims to promote respectful, inclusive language, critics argue that when abused, it limits freedom of speech and religious expression.[734]

In numerous instances, the concepts of political correctness and wokeness have transcended their roles as social movements and solidified into a form of stringent dogma that supporters hold to with a religious fervor. This new-age ideology often replaces traditional religious beliefs, substituting the Divine with a rigid adherence to the principles of equity, inclusion, and diversity. The exchange of religious tenets for woke ideology signals a profound shift in societal values and priorities, presenting challenges and

---

[733] Ahmed, Sara, "A Phenomenology of Whiteness." *Feminist Theory* 8, no. 2 (2007): 149–168.
[734] Lukianoff and Haidt. *The Coddling of the American Mind: How Good Intentions and Bad Ideas Are Setting Up a Generation for Failure.*

questions for individuals navigating the intersections of faith, societal norms, and personal beliefs. People often find themselves at a crossroads with the modern woke ethos within the ever-evolving tapestry of social and cultural values. Delving deeper into the crux of this dissonance reveals a complex interplay of traditions, interpretations, and changing societal paradigms.

Traditional Christian and LDS doctrine, grounded in scripture, perceives heterosexual marriage as the divinely sanctioned standard. Such positions, rooted in millennia-old scriptures and teachings, aren't mere opinions but deeply held convictions for believers. Passages like Genesis 2:24, "Therefore shall a man leave his father and his mother, and shall cleave unto his wife: and they shall be one flesh," form the basis for these convictions.

Given this backdrop, believers often find themselves labeled as regressive or bigoted when they adhere to their traditional views. These hurtful labels are being used to target non-conformers who do not support the ever-changing social narrative. This characterization can be deeply painful, especially when many Christians and LDS members ardently believe that the core of their faith, despite certain doctrinal positions, is grounded in principles of love, compassion, and respect. For them, doctrinal disagreements don't equate to personal animosity. As iterated in Matthew 22:39, the call is to "love thy neighbour as thyself." This encapsulates the essence of Christian conduct—a principle of unconditional love, even in the face of disagreements.

But a challenge remains: how do we stay true to our religious convictions in a world that is rapidly shifting its norms and expectations? Many believers grapple with this problem daily. They seek to find a balance between upholding their faith, which provides them with purpose, solace, and a moral compass, while navigating a society that often misconstrues their convictions as mere prejudice.

While doctrinal tenets might remain unchanging, believers are called upon to express their faith in ways that reflect Christ's love and understanding. They're challenged to distinguish between holding a belief and imposing it.

Furthermore, society at large also has a role to play. It's crucial to differentiate between individuals who use religion as a cover for bigotry and genuine believers whose convictions, though differing from contemporary norms, are rooted in love and a profound spiritual journey.

Spotlight on Current Events: Religion in the Crosshairs

Amid a rapidly changing sociopolitical landscape, several significant events have underscored a perception of religion within the United States as being under assault. I've observed with increasing concern the tensions between long-held religious beliefs and the evolving fabric of modern society. As powerful shapers of public opinion, the media often play a pivotal role in this narrative, sometimes accentuating divides and framing religious adherents in a less-than-flattering light. This has implications for the perception of believers and raises concerns about the fundamental tenets of religious freedom and expression.

A Chronicle of Contemporary Events

To grapple with the threats to religious beliefs in contemporary society, one must delve into the critical news stories and events that have brought faith under scrutiny. Consider, for example, the widely reported case involving a Colorado baker. This baker, standing firm on his Christian convictions, declined to create a custom wedding cake for a same-sex couple. This act incited significant controversy across the nation.[735]

Mainstream media outlets covered the story extensively, frequently framing it as a struggle between gay rights and the right to religious freedom.[736] The vast array of headlines, interviews, and editorials offered a window into the

---

[735] Masterpiece Cakeshop, Ltd. v. Colorado Civil Rights Commission, 584 U.S. ___ (2018).
[736] Sheryl Gay Stolberg, "Justices Sharply Divided in Gay Rights Case," *New York Times*, Dec. 5, 2017.

national psyche, revealing deep divisions in how Americans interpreted the case.[737]

When the Supreme Court ultimately ruled in favor of the baker, reactions were deeply divided. Many within religious communities saw the decision as an affirmation of First Amendment rights.[738] On the other hand, advocates for gay rights saw it as a tacit endorsement of discrimination.[739]

From my vantage point during the unfolding of this case, and as someone who identified as an atheist then, my lens was slightly different. I found myself wrestling with the idea of the government compelling a private establishment to produce a product against its will. Such an imposition seemed to border on an excessive exercise of authority.

The heart of this debate revolves around a complex question: how does society balance religious convictions with the rights of individuals in a pluralistic nation? This case and others like it highlight the challenge of interpreting and upholding religious freedoms in an evolving societal landscape.[740]

Furthermore, in recent years, America's political landscape has witnessed a surge in legislative endeavors across multiple states seeking to increase access to abortion.[741] The media often paints efforts to oppose abortion as emblematic of Christian dogma encroaching upon legal and healthcare decisions. This perspective postulates that the core motivation behind such

---

[737] Adam Liptak, "Baker Who Refused to Serve Gay Couple Wins Supreme Court Case," *New York Times*, June 4, 2018.

[738] Douglas Laycock and Thomas C. Berg, "Religious Freedom and the Nondiscrimination Principle," *Virginia Law Review Online* 106 (2020): 94.

[739] Cass R. Sunstein, "Sex, Lies, and Religious Freedom," *Duke Law Journal* 69.2 (2019): 487–514.

[740] Michael W. McConnell, "The Supreme Court, 2017 Term—Comment: Free Exercise in a Hostile World? Two New Supreme Court Decisions, and the Open Questions They Leave," *Harvard Law Review* 133 (2019): 221–240.

[741] Sabrina Tavernise, "With Abortion Bans, States Embark on a Legal Game of Chicken," *New York Times*, May 18, 2019.

laws stems predominantly from religious convictions, particularly evangelical Christian tenets that uphold the sanctity of life from conception.

Critics argue that these legislative measures challenge the bedrock principle of the separation of church and state, a misinterpretation of the First Amendment of the United States Constitution. They contend that policy decisions about reproductive rights should be informed by scientific, medical, and ethical considerations rather than religious beliefs. They worry that allowing religious perspectives to shape laws could set a precedent, potentially blurring the lines between religious teachings and state governance.

Conversely, many proponents of restrictions or bans on abortion believe that religious beliefs do not solely dictate their stance. They often point to scientific arguments about when life begins or the rights of the unborn. However, it's undeniable that religious sentiments play a significant role, with many viewing their advocacy against abortion as a moral imperative grounded in faith and reason.

This ongoing debate underscores the complex interplay between religion, morality, and governance in a nation founded on the principles of religious freedom and secular governance. As America continues to grapple with these issues, the tension between upholding individual rights and accommodating religious beliefs remains a focal point of contention.

The Media's Pivotal Role

The role of the media in shaping perspectives on religion is undeniable. While the Fourth Estate is tasked with presenting unbiased, factual information, the news is a product shaped by human hands, biases, and economic imperatives. In many cases, the portrayal of religious issues tends to skew toward sensationalism, emphasizing divides, controversies, and extremes.

For example, the aforementioned Colorado baker case coverage was replete with polarizing headlines and soundbites Rarely did we see deep, nuanced discussions about the intricate balance between religious freedom and civil rights. Instead, it was often framed as a battle, pitting one group against another, which only fanned the flames of division.[742]

This, of course, is not to dismiss the media en masse. Numerous outlets and journalists are dedicated to impartial and comprehensive coverage. However, it's a reminder that, as consumers of news, discernment is crucial.

Religious Freedom and Expression: A Precarious Balance

The First Amendment of the United States Constitution ensures that "Congress shall make no law respecting an establishment of religion, or prohibiting the free exercise thereof."[743] For centuries, this foundation has been a beacon of hope for many, ensuring that they can live according to their beliefs without fear of government interference.

However, recent events and the media's portrayal of believers have left many people feeling cornered and concerned about the future of religious freedom in the country. When beliefs are framed as bigotry or when adhering to one's faith might lead to legal repercussions or public shaming, it creates an environment of trepidation.

From a Christian and LDS standpoint, there's an inherent call to "let your light so shine before men, that they may see your good works, and glorify your Father which is in heaven" (Mt. 5:16). However, in a society where these good works are sometimes perceived as regressive or harmful, the challenge of living authentically to one's faith becomes all the more pronounced.

---

[742] Michael M. Grynbaum, "In Cake Case, Media Take Sides," *New York Times*, Dec. 8, 2017.
[743] U.S. Constitution, amend. I.

The intersection of contemporary events, media portrayals, and religious beliefs presents believers with complex challenges and concerns. While the path forward might seem fraught with challenges, believers need to remember the core tenets of their faith: love, understanding, and compassion. It's equally crucial for society to ensure that the line between protecting civil rights and preserving religious freedom remains clear.

American Society in Flux: A Closer Look at Structural Changes

As societies have evolved throughout history, so have their ideologies, values, and concerns. America's transformation over the years has also been stark, with the decline of the traditional two-parent family structure—a foundation once rooted deep in the nation's fabric.

Diving into Data: The Waning Two-Parent Household

Over the last several decades, the prototypical American family has morphed dramatically from the time-honored norm, prompting various scholars and institutions to delve deeper into this transformation. The Pew Research Center has highlighted the diminishing number of children growing up in two-parent households since the 1960s.[744] This decline in the conventional family model has given way to diverse family structures. Single-parent homes are more prevalent, and cohabitation without the legal bonds of matrimony is increasingly common.

To unpack the reasons behind these shifts, one must first understand America's socio-cultural and economic environment over the past half-century.

The Sexual Revolution's Ripple Effects: The late 1960s and 1970s witnessed a seismic shift in societal attitudes toward sexuality and relationships. The sexual revolution championed greater freedoms and led to more liberal

---

[744] Pew Research Center, "The Modern American Family," Sept. 14, 2023, https://www.pewresearch.org/social-trends/2023/09/14/the-modern-american-family/.

attitudes toward premarital sex, contraception, and living arrangements.[745] The newfound freedom altered the traditional progression of relationships, with marriage often getting postponed or even eschewed by some.

The Ubiquity of Pornography and its Societal Implications: The dawn of the digital age brought unprecedented access to explicit content. The easy availability of pornography, particularly to impressionable youth, has had insidious ramifications. Not only does it often present distorted representations of female worth, it also imprints skewed stereotypes of female sexuality onto young men. Such portrayals undermine genuine emotional intimacy and warp perceptions of healthy sexual dynamics. This pervasive exposure can impact relationship expectations and might contribute to the reluctance or inability of some to forge the deep, meaningful connections that are essential for the foundation of stable family units.[746]

Economic Strains and Transitions: As the industrial economy paved the way for a more service-oriented one, job stability became more tenuous, leading to financial stresses and impacting family decisions.[747] In some situations, financial strain acted as a deterrent to marriage; in others, it led to the dissolution of existing marital bonds.

Legislative Changes in Divorce: The advent of "no-fault" divorce laws in many states during the late twentieth century made the dissolution of marriage more straightforward, reducing the social and legal obstacles

---

[745] John D'Emilio and Estelle B. Freedman, *Intimate Matters: A History of Sexuality in America* 3rd ed. (Chicago: University of Chicago Press, 2012).

[746] Gail Dines, *Pornland: How Porn Has Hijacked Our Sexuality* (Boston: Beacon Press, 2010).

[747] David H. Autor, David Dorn, and Gordon H. Hanson, "When work disappears: Manufacturing decline and the falling marriage-market value of men," *The American Economic Review: Insights* 1, no. 2 (2019): 161–178.

previously associated with divorce.[748] As a result, those in unhappy marriages found it easier to separate, leading to a rise in divorce rates.

Evolving Societal Attitudes: Beyond economic or legal changes, a broader societal metamorphosis was at play. Over time, the societal consensus on marriage, procreation, and familial responsibilities became less stringent. Living together before marriage, having children out of wedlock, or opting for alternative family structures began gaining broader acceptance.[749]

Social Welfare Dependency in Inner Cities: Another significant aspect influencing family structures, especially in inner cities, is the dependency on social welfare programs. Critics argue that certain welfare policies inadvertently incentivize out-of-wedlock births, given that benefits may be more readily accessible to single mothers as opposed to nuclear families.[750] This diminished the perceived necessity of a two-parent household. Such policies, even if well-intended, contributed to fracturing the conventional family structure.

Connecting Societal Shifts to Crime and Mental Health: A Multifaceted View

Many people of faith believe that robust traditional family units are the defenders against societal decay. From this standpoint, the visible decline in such family structures is a harbinger of societal issues. Indeed, numerous studies have established a connection between single-parent households and certain challenges that children raised in such households may encounter. Statistically, compared to their counterparts from two-parent homes, these children exhibit a heightened propensity toward economic hardships and academic struggles, which culminate in increased dropout rates,

---

[748] Betsey Stevenson and Justin Wolfers, "Bargaining in the shadow of the law: Divorce laws and family distress," *The Quarterly Journal of Economics* 121, no. 1 (2006): 267–288.
[749] Andrew J. Cherlin, *The Marriage-Go-Round: The State of Marriage and the Family in America Today* (New York: Alfred A. Knopf, 2009).
[750] Charles A. Murray, *Losing Ground: American Social Policy, 1950–1980* (New York: Basic Books, 1984).

entanglement with the criminal justice system, and grappling with mental health concerns.[751]

However, the landscape of these societal challenges is vast and intricate. The family structure is undoubtedly influential, but it's a single cog among many socio-cultural determinants that shape individual trajectories. For instance, socio-economic factors play a pivotal role. Economic disenfranchisement can create an environment conducive to crime, especially in communities that lack sufficient educational and job opportunities.[752] The quality of schooling available to children, often linked to the socio-economic status of their residential area, can dramatically affect their life outcomes. Likewise, community environments encompass neighborhood safety, availability of community resources, and peer influences, significantly swaying young minds. Moreover, an individual's intrinsic qualities, resilience, and coping mechanisms, honed by their experiences and innate temperament, are indispensable factors to consider.

A holistic understanding demands an acknowledgment that various societal changes have converged to impact crime rates and mental health trends. For example, the narcotics epidemic, rapid urbanization, technological advancements, and shifting economic landscapes have profoundly influenced societal metrics.[753]

It would be an oversimplification, perhaps even a misrepresentation, to attribute the shifts in societal health solely to the changes in family structure. While it's integral to the discussion, it's equally crucial to consider the multifaceted nature of our society's challenges. Through a Christian and LDS lens, the solution involves reinforcing traditional family values and

---

[751] Sara McLanahan and Gary Sandefur, *Growing Up With a Single Parent: What Hurts, What Helps* (Cambridge: Harvard University Press, 1994).

[752] Robert J. Sampson and William Julius Wilson, "Toward a theory of race, crime, and urban inequality" in *Crime and Inequality*, ed. John Hagan and Ruth D. Peterson (Stanford, CA: Stanford University Press, 1995), 37–54.

[753] James Q. Wilson, "The Crux of Broken Windows Policing," *National Institute of Justice Journal* 270 (2011): 23–25.

while also addressing these myriad factors to foster a more harmonious and resilient society.

Evaluating the Correlation: Does Dwindling Faith Fuel Societal Unrest?

As we gaze upon the transformation of American society, a pronounced shift away from traditional religious adherence is evident. Recent surveys show that the younger generations, particularly Millennials and Generation Z, are more likely to identify as religious "nones"—those who classify their religious affiliation as either atheist, agnostic or "nothing in particular."[754] Such statistics have ignited fervent debates. Is it possible the fabric of our society is unraveling due to this decline in faith? Or is it something entirely different?

Scripture has long warned believers about potential moral decay in society. In Matthew 24:12, a prophecy rings clear: "And because iniquity shall abound, the love of many shall wax cold." Does this verse mirror the current state of our society? Have we drifted into a cold indifference where moral anchors are increasingly scarce?

As with many societal phenomena, there's a nuanced tapestry of causative and correlative factors. It's an oversimplification to blame the decline in religious adherence as the sole cause of society's challenges. Moving away from stringent religious dogmas is perceived as a liberating evolution for a population segment—a shift toward a more open, inclusive, and diverse society where individuals are free from orthodox constraints.[755]

Faith has always been more than mere dogma. It embodies a moral compass directing individuals toward compassion, love, service, and community values. Churches serve as communal havens, fostering connections and

---

[754] Pew Research Center, "In U.S., Decline of Christianity Continues at Rapid Pace," Oct. 17, 2019, https://www.pewresearch.org/religion/2019/10/17/in-u-s-decline-of-christianity-continues-at-rapid-pace/.

[755] Robert D. Putnam and David E. Campbell, *American Grace: How Religion Divides and Unites Us* (New York: Simon & Schuster, 2010).

shared values. They instill a sense of purpose, grounding individuals in adversity and prosperity.

It is imperative to understand the multifaceted nature of America's societal transformation. While it's tempting to pinpoint a singular catalyst, the reality is much more intricate. The fading prominence of time-honored family constructs and religious convictions unquestionably influence our societal fabric. However, these shifts merge with many other determinants— technological advancements, economic transitions, or global influences. As intelligent, vigilant witnesses to this dynamic era, our task isn't merely to mourn the changes or reminisce about bygone days. Instead, our calling is to discern these shifts with wisdom and adapt where indispensable while maintaining the integrity of our faith. In an ever-fluctuating world, let faith be our compass, guiding us toward love, understanding, and the unchanging truth amidst the tide of change.

Religion's Role in Social Cohesion

Throughout history, religion has consistently acted as a pivotal force, knitting together the fabric of societies and offering a sense of purpose and direction. It has built communities, framed moral codes, and provided solace during distress. As I delve into the significance of faith, it's essential to recognize its profound impact on social cohesion, both historically and contemporarily.

Exploring Historical Patterns: Religion as Societal Glue

Religion's foundational role in the annals of human history cannot be overemphasized. Its influence permeates far beyond mere ritualistic practices or spiritual doctrines. Historically, religious principles were embedded within the rhythms of daily life, establishing moral codes, shaping societal laws, and providing a sense of collective belonging.

In ancient civilizations, from the Mesopotamian plains to the banks of the Nile, religious rituals and festivals were not just ceremonial events. They acted as significant occasions for community bonding. These gatherings, often centered around seasonal cycles, life events, or celestial phenomena, served numerous purposes. While they were spiritual expressions, they also fortified communal bonds, passed down cultural heritage, and solidified a shared identity.[756]

For instance, in ancient Egypt, the annual flooding of the Nile—linked with the god Osiris—was marked by ceremonies and festivals. These events were occasions of giving thanks and crucial moments that brought disparate communities together in a shared experience of reverence and joy.[757]

As we transition to America's formative years, religion's role in shaping societal norms remains paramount. One must discuss the Puritans' influence to narrate the story of early America. These devout settlers, who braved the vast Atlantic to establish colonies in New England, were driven by a vision steeped in their Christian convictions. Their communities were built around churches, and their daily routines, from schooling to governance, reflected their profound faith. In these nascent settlements, the church was more than a place of worship—it was the community's heart, around which everything else revolved.[758]

The Bible, central to the Puritans and foundational for many today, underscores unity and collective strength. The eloquence of Psalms 133:1 resonates across the ages: "Behold, how good and how pleasant it is for brethren to dwell together in unity!" This sentiment isn't just a call for spiritual unity, but an acknowledgment of the strength derived from communal bonds, a truth recognized since time immemorial.

The Decline of Religious Observance and Its Implications for Societal Stability

---

[756] Armstrong, *A History of God: The 4,000–Year Quest of Judaism, Christianity, and Islam*.
[757] Toby Wilkinson, *The Rise and Fall of Ancient Egypt* (New York: Random House, 2010).
[758] Francis J. Bremer, *The Puritan Experiment: New England Society from Bradford to Edwards* (Hanover, NH: University Press of New England, 1995).

The modern era has ushered in profound changes in how societies perceive and interact with religion. Religious institutions' once-unwavering sanctity and influence have begun to recede, overshadowed by rapid scientific discoveries, burgeoning philosophical skepticism, and a society in flux, marked by unprecedented technological advancements and evolving socio-cultural paradigms.[759]

Historically, religious establishments were not confined to their spiritual mandates. They were cornerstones of community vitality, offering many social services, ranging from care for the impoverished to educational initiatives.[760] Churches, synagogues, and mosques were more than mere worship venues; they were epicenters of community cohesion, platforms for forging interpersonal bonds, and sanctuaries for those seeking solace or assistance.

As religious institutions lose their once-central role in community life, the ripple effects can be discerned in multiple dimensions of society. Communities, absent these cohesive forces, risk becoming more fragmented. The fallout is a weakened community spirit and a rise in feelings of isolation[761] and detachment among individuals, especially in an era where digital connections often overshadow face-to-face interactions.[762]

Furthermore, at the heart of many religious doctrines, particularly within the Christian and LDS traditions, are tenets that underscore virtues like love, charity, forgiveness, and compassion. For centuries these teachings have acted as moral compasses, guiding believers in their interpersonal interactions and broader societal engagements. The diminishing adherence

---

[759] Taylor, *A Secular Age.*

[760] Robert D. Putnam, *Bowling Alone: The Collapse and Revival of American Community* (New York: Simon & Schuster, 2000).

[761] "COVID-19 Pandemic Triggers 25% Increase in Prevalence of Anxiety and Depression Worldwide," World Health Organization, accessed November 16, 2023, https://www.who.int/news/item/02-03-2022-covid-19-pandemic-triggers-25-increase-in-prevalence-of-anxiety-and-depression-worldwide.

[762] Sherry Turkle, *Alone Together: Why We Expect More from Technology and Less from Each Other* (New York: Basic Books, 2011).

to these religious values might portend a society where such virtues are less emphasized, potentially leading to increased discord, diminished empathy, and a weakening of the collective moral fabric.

While it's important to acknowledge that morality is not the sole preserve of the religious and that many non-believers lead lives anchored in strong ethical principles, the broad societal shift away from organized religion does raise pressing questions about the sources of moral guidance in contemporary society and the frameworks that might replace religious doctrines as foundational guides.

Addressing Critiques: Is It Fair to Attribute Societal Issues to Diminished Religiosity?

The nexus between religiosity and societal stability has always been the focus of vigorous discussion and debate. In contemporary discourse, this topic has gained even more traction with the backdrop of waning religious adherence. Critics often express skepticism over claims that pin societal challenges predominantly on diminishing religiosity. They contend that societal issues are multifactorial, and attributing them to a single cause, like the decline in religious adherence, oversimplifies the nuanced dynamics at play.[763]

One salient critique is that religious institutions have not been immune to controversy. Scandals, ranging from financial improprieties to sexual abuse allegations, have tarnished the image of some religious establishments. Additionally, certain religious doctrines have sometimes propagated exclusivist or discriminatory views, challenging the assertion that religion invariably promotes inclusivity and societal cohesion.[764]

---

[763] Grace Davie, *Religion in Modern Europe: A Memory Mutates* (Oxford: Oxford University Press, 2000).
[764] Phil Zuckerman, *Society Without God: What the Least Religious Nations Can Tell Us About Contentment* (New York: NYU Press, 2008).

These critiques, while valid, must be dissected carefully. It's crucial to differentiate between the actions or failings of specific religious institutions and the broader ethos of faith and spirituality. Every institution, religious or otherwise, is composed of individuals, and human fallibility can manifest regardless of the domain. However, the potential missteps of individuals within these institutions should withstand the profound societal benefits of a faith-based, community-centric ethos.

From my perspective, the discourse shouldn't be about portraying religion as the ultimate antidote to societal challenges. Instead, it's about acknowledging and understanding the diverse ways in which faith and religious communities have contributed to societal cohesion, moral guidance, and individual solace.[765]

While the decline in religious adherence is an irrefutable trend in contemporary American society, its effect on societal cohesion, both positive and negative, need to be examined from a balanced perspective. A holistic understanding mandates that we recognize the historical significance of religion in promoting societal bonds while simultaneously being attentive to the critiques and acknowledging the limitations and challenges posed by religious institutions.

Challenges and Opportunities: Faith in the Modern Age

A significant strategy for believers lies in embracing technology to bolster faith. Digital platforms, from online Bible study groups to podcasts and live-streamed church services, offer avenues to bridge the physical and spiritual distances that might emerge in our technologically driven era.[766] This digital engagement, combined with a commitment to cultural

---

[765] David Myers, *The American Paradox: Spiritual Hunger in an Age of Plenty* (New Haven: Yale University Press, 2000).

[766] Heidi A. Campbell, *Digital Religion: Understanding Religious Practice in New Media Worlds* (London: Routledge, 2012).

sensitivity and inclusivity, can forge deeper connections. The Apostle Paul's assertion, "I am made all things to all men, that I might by all means save some" (1 Cor 9:22) resonates profoundly in this context. By understanding and engaging with diverse cultural perspectives, believers can make faith messages relatable and inclusive.[767]

As believers navigate this intricate web of modern influences, continuous growth remains paramount. Lifelong learning, steeped in religious tenets and secular knowledge, equips believers to discern through the myriad viewpoints that permeate society.[768]

Amid this evolving landscape, faith communities have golden opportunities to be vanguards of dialogue and understanding. Interfaith initiatives, for instance, serve as platforms to foster mutual respect among diverse religious groups, dispelling myths and emphasizing shared human values.[769] Furthermore, by creating platforms for the youth, churches can address generational shifts, ensuring that their teachings resonate with the challenges and aspirations of younger members.[770] It's vital to remember that despite theological differences, all religions underscore values like love and compassion. Faith communities can act as bridges in a fragmented world by foregrounding these universal principles.[771]

Beyond internal community engagement, religious institutions can enact positive societal change on a broader scale. Many churches, for instance, have been at the forefront of charitable initiatives, embodying the Christian call to "bear one another's burdens" (Gal 6:12). Their efforts span disaster relief, community services, and support for society's marginalized people.

---

[767] Paul Knitter, *Introducing Theologies of Religions* (Maryknoll: Orbis Books, 2002).

[768] Thomas H. Groome, *Will There Be Faith? A New Vision for Educating and Growing Disciples* (New York: HarperOne, 2011).

[769] Alan Race, *Christians and Religious Pluralism: Patterns in the Christian Theology of Religions* (London: SCM Press, 1983).

[770] Kenda Creasy Dean, *Almost Christian: What the Faith of Our Teenagers is Telling the American Church* (New York: Oxford University Press, 2010).

[771] Hans Küng, *Christianity and the World Religions: Paths to Dialogue with Islam, Hinduism, and Buddhism* (New York: Doubleday, 1986).

Additionally, in response to our era's rising mental health challenges, religious institutions are uniquely positioned to provide solace through counseling and support groups.[772] Beyond spiritual nourishment, they can also offer a holistic education that melds moral values, life skills, and intercultural understanding.[773]

Faith's Resilience – Charting the Course Amidst Societal Flux

In quiet moments of introspection, we often find ourselves contemplating the intricate tapestry of existence, shaped as much by temporal ebbs and flows as by enduring constants. One such constant as we've navigated through this exploration is the profound influence of faith. Amidst the kaleidoscope of societal transformations, the anchor of spiritual belief remains an unwavering anchor.

To say that we live in transformative times would be an understatement. Technological advancements, ideological shifts, and cultural evolutions create an ever-shifting landscape. Yet, as the sands of time reshape our societal terrains, the bedrock of faith remains unyielding. As stated in Hebrews 13:8, "Jesus Christ is the same yesterday, and today, and forever." This unchanging nature of faith serves as a reminder that while cultures evolve, spiritual truths are timeless. These truths connect us to divine wisdom and tether us to generations past, offering a reservoir of strength, guidance, and perspective.

In our journey through the annals of history, faith has consistently emerged as a beacon during tumultuous times.[774] Its influence permeates the arts,

---

[772] Harold Koenig, *Religion and Mental Health: Research and Clinical Applications* (San Diego: Academic Press, 2018).

[773] Jack Seymour, *Mapping Christian Education: Approaches to Congregational Learning* (Nashville: Abingdon Press, 1997).

[774] Rodney Stark, *The Rise of Christianity: How the Obscure, Marginal Jesus Movement Became the Dominant Religious Force in the Western World in a Few Centuries* (San Francisco: HarperSanFrancisco, 1997).

shapes political and social narratives, and underpins foundational ethical principles. Through the ages, religious teachings have continually guided communities during crises, providing solace and direction.[775]

While it's undeniable that we're experiencing shifts in family structures and societal dynamics, one cannot overlook the profound interconnections between societal health, family, and faith. A society's well-being is inextricably linked to its foundational units—families. As discussed earlier, families are often bound together and guided by shared faith values.[776] When the threads of belief run strong, they weave families into close-knit cohesions, forming the rich fabric of society. This is not to say that non-faith structures don't offer societal stability, but rather, for many, faith emerges as a core adhesive.

A symbiotic relationship exists here. Just as faith nourishes the family's soul, families sustain and perpetuate faith. The teachings passed from generation to generation, shared rituals, and collective aspirations all feed into a cycle of spiritual reinforcement. When one ponders upon "And these words, which I command thee this day, shall be in thine heart: And thou shalt teach them diligently unto thy children," the enduring bond between familial teachings and faith becomes clear. It's a dynamic continuum, with each element bolstering the other.

But let's also acknowledge the critiques and challenges of our time. Faith and its institutions aren't immune to scrutiny or reform, as with any other societal element. It's essential, however, to differentiate between human fallibility and the innate value of spiritual teachings. To discard the entire edifice of faith based on the actions of a few would be akin to missing the forest for the trees.[777] Our task is to continually seek the essence of faith,

---

[775] Philip Jenkins, *The Next Christendom: The Coming of Global Christianity* (New York: Oxford University Press, 2011).

[776] Christopher Lasch, *Haven in a Heartless World: The Family Besieged* (New York: W. W. Norton & Company, 1977).

[777] *The Oxford Dictionary of World Religions,* ed. John Bowker (New York: Oxford University Press, 1997).

refining our understanding and ensuring that its core values are upheld and propagated.

In concluding our odyssey, the interplay of faith, family, and society in this modern age underscores a profound realization. Despite the torrents of change, a resilient core remains—a spiritual epicenter that continually guides, nourishes, and unites. And while future pathways may yet be uncharted, when armed with the compass of faith, our journey promises purpose and fulfillment. With a spirit of hope, understanding, and commitment, we stride forth, bearing the torch of faith in a world that is ever in flux.

Final Thoughts and Conclusion

Having reflected on the six transformative months that reshaped my spiritual compass, I recognize that my transition from atheism's concrete bastions to the spiritual realms of the Church of Jesus Christ of Latter-day Saints was not just a leap of faith but a harmonious blend of reason, evidence, and revelation. With its foundations built around Jesus Christ and our Heavenly Father, the beliefs of the LDS Church wove seamlessly into my empirical worldview, creating a tapestry that enriched my scientific and my spiritual outlook. For every question answered, it seemed a myriad more sprouted, echoing the vastness of our universe and the complexity of our faith. Some mysteries may forever elude our grasp, yet our relentless pursuit of scientific and spiritual understanding is a testament to our indomitable spirit.

Part 1 of this book marked the beginning of my voyage, navigating the intricate crossroads where science intertwines with faith. My unyielding conviction dictated that the realms of God, religious lore, and empirical science should harmoniously coexist. Journeying back through epochs, we revisited the tales of Adam and Eve, peeling back layers of literal interpretations to uncover rich allegorical meanings. The awe-inducing revelations from science, spanning the age of our planet to the evolutionary dance of Homo sapiens, seamlessly melded with religious teachings. A pivotal realization was the LDS Church's progressive embrace of scientific revelations, particularly evolution.

Part 2 led us deeper into the rich tapestry of global religions, an enlightening journey that underscored the vastness and diversity of spiritual paths. Our expedition unveiled unique beliefs and practices and striking similarities in myths and legends, suggesting a shared, universal thread of divine wisdom. This mosaic of tales gave rise to a captivating thought: perhaps God, in his infinite wisdom, communicated in a myriad of tongues, offering eternal truths tailored to the unique cultural, historical, and linguistic fabrics of his diverse children.

Finally, Part 3, envisioned as a comprehensive discourse on God, Jesus, and Satan, took an unexpected detour. These subjects' profound depths and multifaceted dimensions soon revealed that condensing them into a single book would be a disservice. Recognizing their immense significance, I've charted a course to dissect these topics further, dedicating individual books to each topic and ensuring they're examined with the diligence they rightly deserve. The first of which, "The Jesus Dilemma: Faith, History, and Mythology," should be completed and in bookstores Spring 2024.

Thank you for embarking on this spiritual exploration with me. I invite you to join my continuing journey and stay updated on my upcoming books by signing up for announcements on my website: www.SMCarlson.com

Made in the USA
Columbia, SC
02 December 2023

26972698R00183